Jean Prouvé   Highlights: 1917–1944

In memoriam:

Our dear son Friedrich Sulzer, designer
(1962–2000)

Peter Sulzer

Jean Prouvé
Highlights: 1917–1944

Recent photographs
Erika Sulzer-Kleinemeier

Birkhäuser – Publishers for Architecture
Basel · Boston · Berlin

Translation from French into English:
Gerald B. Binding, London
Photographs of the plans: Optiplan, Stuttgart

A CIP catalogue record for this book is available from the Library of Congress,
Washington D.C., USA

Deutsche Bibliothek Cataloging-in-Publication Data
Prouvé, Jean:
Jean Prouvé, highlights: 1917 - 1944 / Peter Sulzer. Recent photogr. Erika Sulzer-
Kleinemeier. [Transl. from French into Engl.: Gerald B. Binding].
- Basel ; Boston ; Berlin : Birkhäuser, 2002
ISBN 3-7643-6695-8

© 2002 Birkhäuser – Publishers for Architecture,
P.O. Box 133, CH-4010 Basel, Switzerland
A member of the BertelsmannSpringer Publishing Group

© 2002 SCE Jean Prouvé, Paris, for the work of Jean Prouvé

On the cover:
Large-scale sketch by Jean Prouvé for an adjustable armchair, about 1930 (see no. 117a)

Printed on acid-free paper produced from chlorine-free pulp. TCF ∞
Printed in Germany
ISBN 3-7643-6695-8

9 8 7 6 5 4 3 2 1   www.birkhauser.ch

Contents

1

Preface

In 2001, the year of the 100th anniversary of Jean Prouvé's birth, the publishers and the author agreed on the publication of a paperback devoted to Jean Prouvé. We decided to publish in this English paperback edition a selection of "Highlights" of the work of Jean Prouvé from 1917–1944, the period covered by volumes 1 and 2 of my Complete Works catalogue.

The advantage of this decision is that it makes available to the many people interested in Jean Prouvé a book that is affordable. However, to consider only the "highlights", the peaks of thirty years of Prouvé's great work, might give the wrong impression. This book concentrates on what could be called the main works of Jean Prouvé, whereas my other catalogue documents his complete works. I would therefore recommend the reader to look at the Complete Works catalogue. You will also find there the commentary (with the Jean Prouvé Collection reference numbers), a bibliography, an index of names, and one of locations. For easy cross-reference we have retained the numbering of the Complete Works catalogue in this paperback. I should very much like this paperback to be published in French as well.

It is intended that this volume shall be followed by a second, covering the periods of the future volumes 3 and 4 of the Complete Works. I am often asked about the publication date of Volume 3 of the Complete Works catalogue (covering the years 1944–54). We still hope to find the necessary financial support and to continue our work on Jean Prouvé, who is so highly and widely admired.

I must especially thank:
the Société Civile SCE Jean Prouvé, Paris, which holds the rights; the publisher Birkhäuser – Publishers for Architecture, especially Werner Handschin and Karoline Mueller-Stahl; the former colleagues of Jean Prouvé, the other researchers, the personnel of the Departmental Archives of Meurthe-et-Moselle; and all persons and institutions who have supported the Complete Works catalogue – without this help this Highlight-edition would not have been feasible.

Gleisweiler, October 2001
Peter Sulzer

Introduction

It was in 1959 that I met Jean Prouvé for the first time. As a young architecture graduate, full of the ideas about industrialised methods of building that I had picked up from the seminars of Konrad Wachsmann, I had gone to Paris on a French government scholarship. I enrolled at the Ecole des Beaux-Arts, but the teaching there made me feel I was still in the nineteenth century, and I soon gave up attending. I preferred to visit the masterpieces of modern architecture in which Paris is so rich, and, indeed, its building sites; and that is how I first came across Jean Prouvé's work: the Maison du Peuple at Clichy, the houses at Meudon, the façade of the apartment building on the Square Mozart, the experimental school building of Villejuif, the large window-walls of CNIT at la Défense. A friend of mine gave me Prouvé's address Rue Picpus, a factory that looked like a garage; while I was searching for someone to direct me, I came across a man in working clothes ... the great builder himself, Jean Prouvé. He showed me what they were making (at the Goumy et Cie. factory): aluminium sandwich panels, produced with quite simple machinery, and, young as I was, Jean Prouvé made the time to explain everything to me in detail. I would have liked to work with him, but he could not afford to pay me – I now know that he had, in fact, only one collaborator, Jean Boutemain. He sent me to the engineer Vladimir Bodiansky, who had no work for me, and Bodiansky passed me on to Camus – which is how I became an expert on prefabricated concrete.

I thought I understood what Jean Prouvé meant when he used to say that young architects should go and work in factories. I had the good luck to develop, with a team, a framework system that was manufactured in ten factories and used in hundreds of buildings. I became part of this world of industrial enterprise, with its hierarchical structure and division of labour ... It was only much later that I understood how Jean Prouvé had fought against all this and created a quite different working environment in his workshops. Today I know that the ambience of the J. Prouvé Workshops was one of the conditions necessary for the high quality of the work they produced. I admired, and wished to emulate, the system put forward by the winning team of Candilis, Josic, Woods, Schiedhelm and Prouvé, for

the Free University of Berlin: the "tabouret" or "stool" system, that made possible a large variety of building arrangements. On another occasion, I found Jean Prouvé at Aubervilliers. Now associated with CIMT, he had modern machinery at his disposal; by the side of the aluminium building in which he worked were models and prototypes ... he explained to us the façade of stamped metal panels for Pierrelatte, a panel with a frameless window of safety glass, all of which we found fascinating. In 1976, my university made Jean Prouvé an Honorary Doctor of Engineering. This gave me the opportunity to study his work in greater depth, and led to visits to Nancy, and conversations in the Prouvé living room, sitting amid a unique collection of furniture arranged in a Jean Prouvé space – a place where I spent many happy hours in subsequent years.

In the Commendatory Address I gave on this occasion in 1976[1], I find: "His guidelines: in realising a project, the techniques to be used will be determined by scientific assessment ... it is necessary to study in great detail materials and the ways in which they can be worked ... and to seek inspiration and make decisions by practising the most up-to-date techniques ... it is important that the designer should execute his ideas immediately ... the importance of dialogue with the workman, and of his opinion ... Jean Prouvé's work is influenced above all by the example of his father, and the environment created by the avant-garde artists of the Ecole de Nancy in which he spent his childhood; by the fact that he can himself execute what he designs – he is thoroughly acquainted with his trade; by his enthusiasm for mechanical engineering, especially aeronautical and automotive; by the progressive ideas on industrial management that brought about an atmosphere of harmony and cooperation in his factory.

Jean Prouvé is a pioneer of the industrialisation of building construction. When he started work, industrialisation had already begun to transform building methods: the new materials, steel, cast iron and aluminium, had been invented, semi-finished products, such as sections and sheet metal, were already being produced ... machines for working it, the presses, were already available ...

The situation prompted in Jean Prouvé the desire to use these machines to work the new materials.[2] The finished building elements that left his factory had only to be put in position ... and he was always ahead of others. The most advanced solutions were created by an 'homme-artiste', by an architect of our time ... Jean Prouvé is in the avant-garde tradition of Telford, Paxton, Bogardus, Eiffel, Freyssinet, Nervi ... all of them entrepreneurs, engineers and builders ... Jean Prouvé has pupils and friends throughout the world (I am not referring to those who have copied the results of his work), who understand his principles and methods ... who study and make use of the available resources of our time, and who build for modern man. They are the School of Jean Prouvé!"

It was in this spirit that our team began to work in factories with our students and to construct experimental selfbuild buildings with the young people. At the beginning of the 1980s, we at the University of Stuttgart began to set up an archive of Jean Prouvé's work. Prouvé made available all the documents he had at his home in Nancy, so that we could copy them, and many conversations with him and his former colleagues were recorded. We

2

3

4

1. Maison du Peuple at Clichy.
2. Houses at Meudon.
3. Façade of the apartment building on the Square Mozart in Paris.
4. Experimental school building of Villejuif.

searched out, visited and photographed the projects that had been realised. I spent many weeks in the Archives Départementales de Meurthe-et-Moselle in Nancy, studying the thousands of documents that make up the J. Prouvé Collection there; and the work on Jean Prouvé continues.

Works in danger

Some of the works presented in this volume have been listed as historic monuments, including the Maison du Peuple of Clichy (see no. 704), which is in the course of restoration after being listed on 30 December 1983. Jean Prouvé died three months later, on 23 March 1984. Two days later, the newspaper Le Monde published a telegram sent by Jack Lang, the Minister for Cultural Affairs, to his family: "I learn with deep sorrow of the death of Jean Prouvé. By his death we have lost a great engineer who left his mark on all contemporary French and foreign architecture. With a determination that surprised all those dealt with him, this astonishing creative artist overturned the building industry between 1925 and 1952, as well as housing and furniture. The Ministry for Cultural Affairs has lost great creative force and a friend." (Hervé Baptiste, 1993) Jean Prouvé's house, built in 1954 and now inhabited again, has also, with some other works, been listed.[3] The Aluminium Centenary Pavilion (1954), re-erected at Lille and taken down again, is now, thanks to the association "Les amis de Jean Prouvé", is now re-erected in Villepinte. After the demolition of many works such as the Palais des Expositions of Lille, there is now finally some hope … Although admired by architects the world over, the works of Jean Prouvé are in danger. It is the early wrought iron works, admired by their owners, and the lamp stands and furniture, valued by the galleries and museums, that are best protected. It is quite ironic, because although Jean Prouvé always improved the quality of his furniture, the last model in a series being the best, it is the early pieces, the prototypes and the special orders (see no. 963) that command the highest prices. It is the houses and facades of the 50s that are in danger. Happily, operations to save them are beginning to develop. This catalogue will perhaps encourage them…

A lesson to be learnt

Was not Jean Prouvé a man of the nineteenth century? At once artist, designer, craftsman, "natural engineer" (Peter Rice), industrialist, modernist, pioneer of worker participation? An engineer who was not frightened of creating new forms? A lesson for us who live in an era of automated industrial production, a period when robots are beginning to replace the workman in the installation of prefabricated elements on building sites?

We can certainly learn from him that the tool and the materials, if you know them well, can have an important effect on the form of the product. During the period covered in this volume Jean Prouvé gives an example: knowledge of the possibilities of a tool such as the folding press and harmonious teamwork made possible the creation from a simple sheet of metal the magnificent curtain wall of the Maison du Peuple of Clichy, functional, economical and new in its three dimensional form (see ill. 704,23 and 704,24).

It is up to us to study the possibilities of our time and make use of them. Others have used the industrial methods of their time. They have manufactured metal houses without daring to move away from the traditional image of the "house", or modern factories encased in the most banal envelopes, produced by the most modern machines.

Another lesson to be learnt from Jean Prouvé concerns the team spirit. In 1982 Jean Prouvé said, in connection with the Maison du Peuple: "…nevertheless, they will have a certain line of action in mind, and I have to say that at the time I worked on Clichy there was in my workshop a spirit I have never come across elsewhere. The colleagues who built it and the designers who prepared things held nothing back. For them it was a competition. They were proud of what they were doing…"[4]

Jean-Claude Bignon and Catherine Coley, who in their researches (1990) deal in detail with the social aspects of the J. Prouvé Workshops, remark: "… Moreover, everyone was ready to work harder and without pay, voluntarily giving up their Sundays to finish off an urgent job – a thing that apparently happened quite often. Well before the employment legislation of 1936, the social organisation of the Prouvé Workshops foreshadowed the improvements it made. The national strike of June 36 did not affect the Workshops, the symbolic occupation of which was not a sign of a local dispute, but a gesture of solidarity with the Building Union. Work continued, without incident but at a slower pace, during the eleven days of the "strike" in an atmosphere of co-operation. Since paid holidays had for several years been the norm in the Workshops, the only change was an increase in wages of 17.5%. In 1939 supplementary insurance, paid by the company, was introduced for foremen, employees and technicians who had been with the company for at least 6 months…"

During the war these arrangements were again improved, and we read in a document entitled "Pay arrangements" and published in 1944:

"We want to do away with wage-earning. We have not yet reached that point. At the present time:
1. We guarantee all our personnel, wage-earning or salaried, a minimum we think essential, based on the collective agreements interpreted as widely as possible. This minimum determines professional status.
2. First of all we give our employees a share in their team profit.
3. All personnel, employees and workers share in the saving of general costs arising from time-saving in the manufacturing process, the general costs being limited to manufacture, that is, to the factory level. We are anxious that these savings and benefits shall arise as a direct result of the influence and control of those who will share them. After a year and a half of operation, we have undoubtedly created an atmosphere of both moral and physical community. We believe that the most important social question to be settled is fair pay for work. All the others are side issues.
The results for 1943 were as follows: …production increased by 30%. That means that our budgetary forecasts on the one hand, and our manufacturing schedule, which was for 12 months, have been achieved in 8 months. We have gained 4 months in a year in which no one has wasted his time.

How this is applied:
We are anxious to say, first of all, that it seems to us impossible to make any method of payment uniform and general. It has to be reconsidered and

adapted for each job. We make a variety of products: we move from a large building to a series of furniture or to individual pieces…

Conclusions:
We are, then, at the first stage. We are considering the possibility of everyone sharing in the saving of raw materials and equipment. There is still much individualism to battle against. On the other hand, the sense of responsibility and organisation is developing considerably. Supervision is no longer necessary; it has disappeared. Everyone is beginning to 'live the job' and really collaborate. Another happy consequence is the necessity for an in-depth and very detailed study of prices, which generally means they relate more closely to the actual cost. We really do know the direction in which we are heading."

One of his former colleagues told me that Jean Prouvé was "a boss who was not a capitalist". He was an extremely unpretentious man, and I had the opportunity to note this unpretentiousness, this simplicity, during the days I was lucky enough to spend at the home of Jean and Madeleine Prouvé. Founder of the J. Prouvé Workshops and managing director – with his brother-in-law André Schott – of the limited company incorporated in 1932, Jean Prouvé drew 3,000 francs a month (as "foreman"), which remained unchanged until 1943, with a 10% share of the profits, only paid to him once, in 1932 (Jean-Claude Bignon and Catherine Coley 1990, p. 45). He was a boss who remained a fellow worker. Perhaps this unpretentiousness lay at the root of the thrift that was apparent in his thinking about building: a thin sheet of shaped sheet, the use of off-cuts from sheets, the module of a metre of curtain wall based on 1.20 m with edges folded back, etc. A "2-CV" way of thinking, as he used to say, in contrast with most metal building firms, who sold "by the kilo".
In 1982 Jean Prouvé told us: "choosing this technique from the industrial point of view: you know when you build in commercially produced sections, workshops have to stock, or send out orders for very varied sections – beams of various sections, T iron, channel iron – which makes ordering and stocking very complicated. The advantage of sheet metal construction for buildings is that you need only a supply of sheet. We got in sheet from 40/10 to 10/10 thick, which was simple to stock and easy to find. And obviously we had to think of the off-cuts, and put sheets together taking account of the commercial sizes they came in, so as to avoid excessive loss and consignment to the smelter of sheets we had paid a lot of money for. But in the end, that's the art of the designers and those who install the building…"

This economy, together with the team spirit and his ingenuity in building, explains, no doubt, why Jean Prouvé has "survived", whereas the ideology of his time, "Fordian industrialisation of the structure", advocated by, among others, Walter Gropius and Le Corbusier, is seen to be a mistake. We now know well enough that the application of car and aircraft-building technologies cannot resolve the world-wide housing problem, nor our ecological problems.[5] But what interests us today is Jean Prouvé the "forerunner" (Jean-Claude Bignon and Catherine Coley 1990, p. 11): "…Prouvé did not anticipate what he believed to be the future of building, that is, serial mechanical production of the structure. From this point of view, like many modern architects, he re-

mained a prisoner of the ideological limitations of a period and, as we shall see, his practice met with a number of setbacks. …Prouvé anticipated what is only gradually becoming apparent, post-Fordian industry that some have called industry of the third type. …In his practical experiments Prouvé anticipated an industry based on the intelligence of the worker and the enterprise culture, not on the de-skilling of the work force. An industry of the work collective, no longer piece-meal work. An industry of tailor-made production, not simple serial repro-

duction. The industry that today seeks through computerised design and manufacture, through manufacturing automata that can be programmed, through quality circles, to produce using the workers' skills, and all the other ideas that are for ever changing, this industry that is still in sketch form at the end of the 20th century, has a curious similarity to the craft empiricism mixed with industrial illusions that fired J. Prouvé."
So let us learn our lesson: let us seek out the housing and the architecture of the present day!

7

8

5

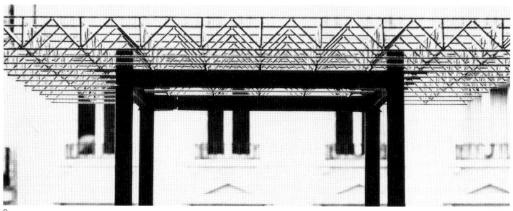

6

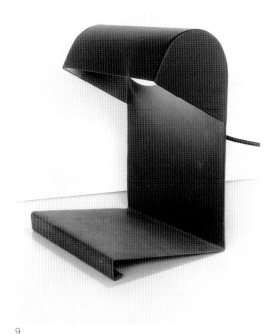

9

ATELIERS
JEAN
PROUVÉ
CONSTRUCTIONS
MÉTALLIQUES
● NANCY ●

PRÉFABRICATION DÈS 1936
AÉRO-CLUB DE BUC
Beaudoin et Lods, architectes

10

5. Large window-walls of CNIT in Paris-La Défense.
6. "Stool" system of the winning team (Candilis, Josic, Woods, Schiedhelm and Prouvé) for the Independant University of Berlin.
7. Jean Prouvé's office at Aubervilliers.
8. Living-room at Jean Prouvé's house in Nancy at the end of the 70s.
9. Desk lamp for the Cité Universitaire of Nancy.
10. J. Prouvé workshops advertising, issued about 1937.

Some comments on the Complete Works of Jean Prouvé

The first catalogue of Jean Prouvé's works was made by his wife, Madeleine Prouvé, typed until 1968, and hand-written thereafter until 1981. Prouvé's last work is the radar tower at Ouessant. During a conversation at Prouvé's home, in 1982, she said, "To think that it was me who got all that information together! It was difficult, because he (Prouvé) didn't help me; at that time he didn't like looking back into the past." This catalogue served as our starting point when, in 1982, we began to set up a small Franco-German group at the University of Stuttgart (Gottfried Bondzio, Jean-Marie Helwig, Peter Sulzer). We began to organise an archive of Jean Prouvé's works, classified chronologically by project. Jean Prouvé lent us, for copying, all the documents he had in his house at Nancy, and some of those that were in his Paris office. I remember especially a box of glass photographic plates, some of which were broken, that I spent many long evenings printing in my wife's dark-room. We collected a large amount of published material on Prouvé. We recorded most of the conversations with him and his wife that took place in his Nancy home while we were showing him the photographs. During these conversations he made sketches to explain to us what he was talking about. The sketches, and some quotations from these conversations, are included in this book. We had already been helped by Jean Boutemain, who had worked with Prouvé for over thirty years. Then we set about locating, visiting and photographing those of his works still in existence – having as yet little idea of the extent of the achievements of this tireless worker and his teams. The research project, financed by the Deutsche Forschungsgemeinschaft, produced a preliminary catalogue, a bibliography and the archive.

Since 1983 my wife and I have undertaken several journeys in search of Jean Prouvé's work. It was during one of these journeys that we heard the sad news of his death on 23 March 1984.

About 1988, I began to work at the Archives Départementales de Meurthe-et-Moselle, where the J. Prouvé Collection is kept. I looked at every plan, and I hope I saw all the plans and sketches of the period covered by this book, with the exception of a few not yet discovered ...

The work has not been without its problems. There are, for example, in the J. Prouvé Collection, unnamed photographs of a circular lift cage in polished stainless steel that I have not been able to identify (see no. 220, Complete Works). The plans and sketches of the earlier years usually have no designation or date, nor are they numbered; though they can be dated approximately on the basis of the paper used. About 1930, plans began to be numbered, the same number being given to all plans relating to the same project; but how can one tell how many plans there were? The research unit at the rue des Jardiniers workshop installed a drawing cabinet, numbered the plans systematically and registered them in a note-book, giving the number, identification, initials of the designer and the date; unfortunately the note-books that have been found and are in the J. Prouvé Collection only begin on 8 February 1935. In many of the folders there are sketches in Jean Prouvé's hand, without any identification, date or number. Prouvé did not draw them to be preserved and put in archives!

In dating projects and works, we have, nevertheless, some indicators: the designers dated some plans; the exactly dated patents have proved invaluable; the Jean Prouvé leaflets and catalogues, and some of the publications of the early years, carry no date, but they can be dated fairly accurately; some buildings, such as the Villa Reifenberg (see no. 101), can be dated from inscriptions that appear on them.

Conversations with Prouvé's former collaborators have been an important source of information, but have raised problems as well. If, for example, one of them said, "I've never seen that" or even, "That's not by Prouvé", it was important to know when he had been absent from the workshop owing to military service. Another problem was subcontracting. (Prouvé worked as a subcontractor for other firms and subcontracted some of his own work as well.) Unfortunately, there are dating errors, which I have tried to correct, in most of the publications. Two examples: the project of a small house on piles is often dated 1930 (Huber, Steinegger, Jean Prouvé, une architecture par l'industrie, p.180), but the sketch for it is numbered 8257 and was drawn on 17 May 1939 with the title "vacation house of 4 x 6.75" (inventory of plans p. 42, initialed J.P., ADMM 230 J). The sketches for furniture designed by Jean Prouvé for Intérieur no. 2, 1965 are another source of incorrect dating; Prouvé gave the date of the early chairs as 1924, whereas it should be, in fact, about 1930 (see no.118, Complete Works).

During our work we have had some pleasant surprises: an initial suspicion that the banisters at the Brasserie Excelsior (see no. 133) might be by Prouvé was confirmed by Pierre Missey, who had made them; or the discovery of the cloak room in polished stainless steel (see no. 205), which the former owner, Monsieur France, remembered Prouvé had made.

My work is based, to start with, on the catalogue of works prepared by Madeleine Prouvé; the drawings of the J. Prouvé Workshops design office and the sketches of Jean Prouvé (untitled and undated) that are in the J. Prouvé Collection of the Departmental Archives of Meurthe-et-Moselle (unfortunately I have not been able to research the archives of the architects with whom Jean Prouvé worked). These documents are supplemented by conversations with Jean Prouvé, recorded by my former colleague Jean-Marie Helwig; conversations with former colleagues of Jean Prouvé; on-site research; our archive of copies, begun fifteen years ago; the research of Jean-Claude Bignon and Catherine Coley of the Nancy School of Architecture, and other publications. Happily, I have been able to work with a copy of the design office "plans book" (ill. 24), begun on 8 February 1935, which contains the plan numbers, their titles, the initials of the designer and the date; the document is entirely in manuscript and sometimes illegible.

It has not always been possible to decide from these documents whether we are dealing with a design, a bid, or a work actually carried out. The reports of the Board of Directors and J. Prouvé Workshop advertising (ill. 10) have helped me, but there are still documents, sketches and notes that are difficult to interpret.

One problem arises from the large number of projects and the limited number of pages of a book. This is why I have had to make choices: in the Complete Works catalogue I have devoted a considerable number of pages to projects I consider essential, such as the Maison du Peuple of Clichy (see no. 704); less important projects have been assigned only a few lines of text. There are designs and works, such as small pieces supplied to other companies, that do not figure in the Catalogue at all. With regard to the furniture, in order to enable the reader to reconstruct the development of a piece, I have tried to give as complete a documentation as possible, despite the difficulty caused by a large number of variants. The Catalogue order is chronological, following the number of the first J. Prouvé Workshops drawing. For the "Cité" beds, for example, you can follow the development by referring to number 258.1, 515, 516, 534.1, 537, 545, and 759 in the Complete Works, and the variants of the 50s in the third volume of the Catalogue. For the desks you can refer to numbers 256, 396, 482, 545.28, 624, 799, 838, 847, 848, 892, 897, 899, 924 to 926 and the post-1944 variants in the third volume of the Catalogue. I have already described the development of the "Prouvé chair" (Peter Sulzer 1990, pp. 127 to 129). The reader can reconstruct its evolution by referring to numbers 402, 403, 404, 405, 445, 879, 915,1 to 915,5, and the post-1944 variants in the third volume of the Catalogue. The "design idea": a chair that does not break when you lean backwards in it; the solution: back legs of uniform strength, slim, light front legs. Designed in folded sheet, the chair was produced in wood during the war, was later demountable, and was even made with cast aluminium legs: adaptation of a principle to new conditions.

However, the furniture is not always in chronological order, because I have preferred to group together furniture designed for the same building, even if several years separate the first and last drawings (see, for example, the works carried out for the lycée of Metz, 1935/36, no. 534). As much of the furniture designed between 1934 and 1944 is no longer in existence, or has not yet been discovered, I have concentrated on the drawings. From time to time new pieces will doubtless come to light. Thus, I discovered in a private collection an example of the desk lamp for the Cité Universitaire of Nancy (ill. 9), the drawing of which I published in volume 1 (see no. 76).

I am sure that there will be readers who discover objects made by the J. Prouvé Workshops or documents relating to the work of Jean Prouvé. If so, I should be very grateful if they could send me information about them.

Nancy le 10.11.81

JEAN PROUVÉ

Université de Stuttgart
Institut de la Construction

A l'Attention du Professeur Sulzer

Cher ami,
Votre lettre m'est bien parvenue, et votre récente visite à Nancy m'a confirmé vos intentions.
Je suis très sensible à votre initiative de constituer des archives concernant mes activités s'étalant sur 60 ans - Je vous en remercie vivement.
Pour le moment, il ne m'est pas possible de vous donner des documents avant qu'ils aient été centralisés à Paris ou à Nancy.
En effet les plus importants sont éparpillés - à Beaubourg, en Hollande, chez Binoud et à Nancy.
Je pense que ce rassemblement pourrait être effectif en janvier ou février prochain.
Je vous serais reconnaissant de me faire savoir si vous connaissez l'existence de documents originaux ?

37, RUE DES BLANCS-MANTEAUX, PARIS IV° - TEL. ARC. 53-30

Les Hollandais ont prélevé des dessins aux archives municipales de Nancy. Je ne sais combien - Ils en sont pour le moment responsables.
Peut être pourriez vous prendre contact avec le Directeur du Musée Boymans à Rotterdam d'une part et avec les élèves et professeurs architectes de Delft puis avec Monsieur Kees Stoop qui a été un fervent animateur de l'exposition de Rotterdam, d'autre part -
Ce dernier vous dira qu'il a amorcé quelque chose avec le ministère des affaires culturelles à Paris.
Il faudrait clarifier tout cela pour éviter les doubles emplois -
A Beaubourg il doit y avoir aussi des embryons d'archives (Madame Marie Claire Meyer CCI)
Bien entendu, personnellement dans la mesure du possible je vous apporterai ma collaboration.

Je vous propose de reprendre contact au début de l'année prochaine pour déterminer une méthode de travail -
Soyez assuré cher ami de mes sentiments amicaux

Adress : Monsieur Kees - Stoop
Leeuweriklaan 4
Jaffaye - Télé 90.65.03.71
Museum Boymans - Van Beuningen
Mathenesser Laan 18-20
Rotterdam
Télé - 10-360500
Gr. W. A L BEEREN.

1924	NANCY, Hôtel Thiers, portes entrée, cages ascenseurs, rampes, M. Charbonnier, architecte.
	BACCARAT, Hôtel de Ville, appareils éclairage, grilles, fermeture, porte, M. Deville architecte
1924 à 1930	Construction de la plupart des meubles
1925	PARIS, Exposition des Arts Décoratifs, Pavillon de Nancy, 2 grandes portes, MM. Le Bourgeois et Bourgon arch.
	PARIS, Exposition des Arts Décoratifs, portes en tôle pliée pour un pavillon, M. Herbé arch.
	PARIS, Grille Reifenberg, M. Mallet-Stevens arch.
	NANCY, Cristalleries de Nancy, travaux de ferronnerie

11. Extract from a letter of Jean Prouvé to the author, written 10 Novembre 1981.
12. Detail from the catalogue of Jean Prouvé's works made by his wife, Madeleine Prouvé.

13

14

13. Jean Prouvé in the 30s.
14. Jean Prouvé in his office at Maxéville in the 50s.

The importance of Jean Prouvé

Renzo Piano, on Jean Prouvé: "For many architects Jean Prouvé has been, and will remain, an exemplary figure, an inescapable point of reference. He has certainly been such for me; but he came to mean even more to me, and I can say that, in different guises, and with degrees of closeness and familiarity that have developed over the years, he has remained a constant presence, as model, master, and friend, from my first days as a man and architect until the moment of his death ... I have, myself, always kept in mind the fundamental truth that one must not separate the head and the hand, the idea and the means of realising it, that architecture is a matter of building, not drawing, and that it must be a deep understanding of materials that gives rise to its forms ..." [6]

Sir Norman Foster, on Jean Prouvé: "... it is very difficult to categorise him ... technocrat/visionary... pioneer/teamworker... innovator/constructor ... all the titles are applicable, even though such words are in contradiction with each other. I am particularly interested in the relationship between his creative process, what I perceive as the quest for quality ... and the resulting potential for a new aesthetic of the age. Perhaps the ingredient of 'loving care' is the true bond with the past."
Foster quotes Pirsig: " '... we have artists with no scientific knowledge and scientists with no artistic knowledge, and both with no sense of spiritual gravity at all, and the result is not just bad, it is ghastly.' ... On this last point Jean Prouvé is a shining exception and for me the inspiration that shows how art and technology can be reunified ..." [7]

Joseph Belmont, on Jean Prouvé: "My early meetings with his work were full of surprises. I expected to find a technologist; in fact, I found a painter who was designing great aluminium panels by imagining the effects that light would create on the metal sheets. He was as much artist as engineer ... I also discovered the cohesion, the competence and the enthusiasm of the team that surrounded him. Everyone was playing his part in a joint undertaking and giving of his best ... He was one of the great pioneers of our time, the inventor of a new industrial architecture, a visionary little understood in France, but known everywhere abroad ..." [8]

Jean Prouvé was not the first to construct buildings entirely of metal (he was preceded by Eiffel, Gropius/Hirsch, Fillod ...); but he was perhaps one of the first (with Hausermann) to produce movable sheet metal partitioning, and one of the first (with Buckminster Fuller) to create sanitary units entirely manufactured in the factory. He certainly used the materials and machines of his time to create new products – for his time; a wellknown example is the first curtain wall made entirely of sheet metal for the Maison du Peuple at Clichy. But while the best architects, such as Ludwig Mies van der Rohe, used semi-finished products (pressed steel, flat sheeting ...) in their architecture, Jean Prouvé worked the semi-finished products himself, and was thus able to economise on metal and create plastic forms of a kind until then unknown to architecture. He was able to do this not only because he was thoroughly acquainted with metal and the skills required to work it, but because, unlike most engineers and industrialists, he was not frightened of new forms. For these reasons he was able to design and build furniture, such as the early chairs and the armchair for the Cité Universitaire at Nancy, of a different quality from that being made by other avantgarde designers of the period (Chareau, Breuer, Stam ...). "A piece of furniture is not created on a drawing-board«, Prouvé told us. »I believe you have to build a preliminary version the moment you think of it, test it out, make corrections, get opinions on it, and only then, if it is worthwhile, do you settle all the details in very precise drawings." [9]

There is no doubt that Jean Prouvé is important as a creator of avant-garde furniture; but the fact that he has opened our eyes to the importance of the processes by which product quality is achieved has completely changed our perceptions about the act of creation. Prouvé has also taught us that the quality of an object cannot be separated from the spirit and atmosphere in which the creative team works. He tried to introduce a system that was later to be called "worker participation"; it was organised in such a way that the worker could control it – and no manipulation by the management was possible. It seems that Prouvé negotiated with a group of workers their pay for executing a project before he provided the customer with an estimate; the money was then placed in a bank account, to which the workers had access, "because it belonged to them". As a result, interesting products were produced more quickly and benefited from the intelligence and commitment of workers "who were friends", and who were involved in what they were doing. [10]

Former collaborators of his told me: "I always thought very highly of Prouvé"; "Prouvé wanted every worker to hold at least one share in the business, and he gave one to a concierge who could not afford to buy one"; "Prouvé was granting eight days holiday ten years before the Blum law came in"; "Prouvé used to make a sketch and quote a price ... any difference was passed on to us." Whenever he received prizes or awards, Prouvé used to say "that belongs to you, you're a fine team ... I want to share the honour with all of you." [11]

The J. Prouvé Workshops had more in common with today's, or tomorrow's, industrial systems than with the Ford model: they were founded on team spirit and the participants' sense of responsibility, created intelligently conceived products in short runs with the very best tools the age could provide, were responsive to changing needs ... were they a Utopia?

Jean Prouvé, childhood and youth[12]

Jean Prouvé was born on 8 April 1901 in Paris, and died on 23 March 1984 in Nancy. He spent his childhood in Nancy. He learnt wrought-iron making in the workshop of Emile Robert at Enghien (1916–19), worked with the ironsmith Szabo in Paris (1919–21); did his military service in the cavalry (1921–23); and during this time he created his first works in wrought iron (1917 to 1923).

At the age of 23, with the financial help of a family friend, he opened his first workshop at 35, rue du General Custine in Nancy. On 28 January 1931, in association with his brother-in-law, André Schott, who was an engineer, he set up the Société Anonyme Les Ateliers Jean Prouvé. A short time afterwards the workshop was moved to 50, rue des Jardiniers in Nancy. How can one describe the man himself? Jean Prouvé was a tireless worker, always gave his backing to those around him, a creator; and such an unassuming person. He used to talk about his exemplary family life, his mother, his father, his six brothers and sisters, a happy childhood that stayed with him for the rest of his life. His mother, a beautiful woman much younger than his father, devoted herself entirely to looking after the children with a composure that he remembered with admiration. His father, Victor Prouvé, painter, sculptor, engraver and craftsman, was a friend of Emile Gallé, and with him founded the Ecole de Nancy, of which he became director after Gallé's death.

Jean Prouvé, in a conversation with Jean-Marie Helwig in 1982, on his relationship with the Ecole de Nancy and Gallé:

JP: "That he was my godfather was a mark of the close relationship that always existed between the Gallé family and ours; it was a relationship that flowed from the harmony of ideas about artistic creation. This led to such friendship that my brothers, my sisters and I used to visit their house, which adjoined ours, every day by climbing over the wall. The relationship between the two families was very close, very affectionate."

JMH: "So you grew up surrounded by this harmony of ideas …"

JP: "Yes!"

JMH: "And there was an exchange of views on art, on the period…"

JP: "On artistic creation!"

JMH: "…On artistic creation."

JP: "On artistic creation, of course. It is clear that my father and Gallé shared the same ideas. And I want to add here that I believe they had the same ideas about sociological and general human matters; on such things they agreed, in spite of their very different backgrounds. I think the Gallé family was quite bourgeois, a family of industrialists, whereas my father was of very humble origin. His father was a designer in the embroidery industry and a sculptor.

We know that some items produced by the Gallé factories at St. Clement – they had not then moved to Nancy – particularly the 'cats' (see, there's one there), were modelled by my grandfather; he made the models, and then they were sold all over the world. At the present time it's the Americans who are 'cat-hunting', because they think they're full of character and a good investment; as they were industrially produced, they find them all over France. But we must remember that Gallé was the Founding President of the Ecole de Nancy, and the Ecole de Nancy had statutes, and the statutes laid emphasis on wide-spread distribution, in effect, on the reform of industrial production; so it is not at all surprising that he presided over a group of people who had this as their life's aim – a group whose vice-president was my father, who became president when Gallé died.

They wanted to promote high-quality industrial production, and they borrowed their ideas from the work of the glass-makers, who, working competitively or to order, undertook projects that were then industrially exploited; so the aim was to produce in as large numbers as possible."

JMH: "This is, in fact, the common ground of all Art Nouveau, in whatever field…"

JP: "They had the same idea in Brussels, I believe. I think these men of the Ecole de Nancy were undoubtedly the first to cultivate socialist feelings; they thought about other people, they were generous, and when the great socialist orator Jaurès appeared on the scene, he was their man; for them Jaurès was an extraordinary character…"

JMH: "He expressed the feeling of the time."

JP: "Of the time, exactly. They were entirely agreed about the means to be used; I remember all my father's words and his ways of behaving – it was very avant-garde behaviour, that made him enemies as well as friends in Nancy; obviously it was considered rather dangerous; people made use of his talents, but the bourgeoisie of Nancy – I'm using the word in the bad sense – looked upon him as a man to be kept at a distance; Gallé less so, because of his position as an industrialist, which made it quite a different matter. Yet Gallé himself invited to his home in Nancy posts and artists of very advanced ideas. He had visits from Verlaine, Sarah Bernhardt. They were, certainly, people who were beginning to wake up. That does not mean that their milieu was always a sympathetic one, but at least there were ideas in the air…"

JMH: "In making use of the materials available, you were following in Gallé's footsteps, and I suppose the next question was, how can I produce this object in an industrialised, serial form?"

JP: "Yes, that's right."

JHM: "I wanted to know that that was how you saw it."

JP: "Yes, you're absolutely right; yes, that's it."

JMH: "I believe your father was different from Gallé, in the sense that he worked as an artist…"

JP: "Yes."

JMH: "Always exploring, without considering mass-production or reproduction."

JP: "Oh, no, he did think about it. Because he wasn't just an Artist with a capital A; he considered himself a craftsman."

JMH: "A craftsman."

JP: "That is to say, he worked a great deal with his own hands, not only as a painter; he did chasing work, engraving, he carved and sculpted wood, he could carve stone, as he showed by sculpting the huge pediment of the Maison du Peuple at Nancy all by himself; so he considered himself a craftsman, and I remember that his followers at the Ecole de Nancy were not at all keen to be called craftsmen, because they felt the word undervalued them; they wanted to be called artists, and the very well-known potter who lives near here used to get furious when people referred to him as artisan Mougin; he wanted to be an artist.

The artist is free, tries to distance himself from function. There's a lot to be said about that, because I think that when you make something, it's best if it works, if it serves some purpose; functionalism is the word they make play with these days…"

15

16

17

15. "Little Jean for his mother", pastel by Victor Prouvé, 1903.
16. Jean Prouvé with his father Victor in 1911.
17. Jean Prouvé apprenticed to Emile Robert, 1916-19.

18

19

18. Jean Prouvé forging, drawing in red chalk by Victor Prouvé, 1923.
19. First notepaper, copy of a letter of July 1924.

JMH: "Your working methods and practice are those of an artist who keeps the industrial aspect in mind."

JP: "The first stage of a prototype, I would say, is the spontaneous creation by hand of the idea as soon as it comes to you, as they do in pottery, without going through the drawing stage. It's just the same with glass making, because the contribution of the glass-blower is considerable, it's he who blows the glass into shape, who fashions the object, in fact..."

Jean Prouvé used to say of his father that he was one of those men whose mind and hands were closely linked, a complete artist who did not have to use any intermediary. Victor Prouvé was a very free spirit, with ideas in advance of his time; and he was in love with nature.

Jean Prouvé remembered that when he came out of school he used to run to his father's workshop. When Victor Prouvé was painting in the open air, during the two or three months of "holiday", the children were always with him. Pencils and paper were always available, and that is probably how Jean Prouvé learned to draw. In this way, too, he learned "the important principles" and imbibed the spirit of the Ecole de Nancy: "industrial production for the widest possible public" ... "every object must be of the highest quality and a product of its time" ... "a man is put on this earth to create, never to imitate others" ... The importance of drawing inspiration from the study of nature: his father taught him to notice how a rose-thorn grows out of the stem ... these observations were the source of his idea of "twisting" sheet metal into forms of uniform strength at all points.

The 1914–18 war completely changed the life of the Prouvé family. Victor found it difficult to support his family by painting. The young Jean, who was passionately interested in aircraft and cars, had to give up his ambition to study engineering.

When he was very young his father had taken him to see a friend, Emile Robert, and when they left it appears he had said, "I want to be an ironsmith!" Some four years later he was apprenticed to Emile Robert.

Jean Prouvé in a conversation with Jean-Marie Helwig in 1982:

JP: "During the 1914–18 war, it became clear to my family that I would have to earn my living, because, as I think you know, there were seven children, and in war-time things were not easy for an artist. My father was helped by people who gave him decorating and painting work, but that was not enough to feed a family.

So at 16 I had to give up my studies; and, as I always say, they were going well, I was a good student; at the back of my mind I had the idea of becoming an engineer, a builder of things, and at that time I thought of machines because I loved mechanics; I loved aircraft, and could see myself as an aircraft constructor. I had no thoughts at all about building. Then, while I was trying to get started, to find myself an apprenticeship, my father took me to Paris, and we went to see Robert at his workshop, which was then in Enghien, a suburb of Paris. It was a small workshop employing only young men, because Robert, who was a sort of mystic, had lost all his children except one through illness; so he devoted himself to young people and spent all his time training apprentices.

Emile Robert came from the Berry; it was a tradition, most ironsmiths in the Parisian workshops came from there. He was a true ironsmith, a man of the trade, a skilful fashioner of iron who used the simple implements of the time – a hammer and an anvil, that's all.

He made wrought ironwork for buildings. At the same time as he was making artistically imagined wrought-iron figures – animals they were, and very good too, full of character; he was owner of a large concern in Paris, Borderel and Robert, a big metal-construction firm. But he never gave up working iron himself. When I knew him he was about sixty, sturdy, strong and, remarkably, still capable of working at the forge all day long. How did it all come to pass? He made contact with my father, and I wonder whether it wasn't through the articles my father wrote for, among other magazines, Art et Industrie, to which Robert also contributed examples of his work. Robert must have read my father's articles, and obviously they got in touch. They soon became very good friends, and Robert even asked my father to design some grills. There is an example in the Musée de Nancy, designed entirely by my father and forged by Robert. I can confirm that Robert made them himself, with his own hands; though it was very difficult work, it is marvellously done.

I was so pleased to see that there were six, seven, eight young men of my own age in the workshop at Enghien, that the matter was settled on the spot. Robert welcomed me to Enghien, and I lived in a room belonging to some local people, friends of Robert. At Robert's I learned to forge iron, and soon became his best worker. I was working with him all the time. And that's how my career as a metal-worker started. Obviously, when Robert entrusted a piece of work to me, what counted most with me was to complete it as quickly as possible. I got much faster than the others, and my work was none the worse for it. Robert appreciated that very much, so he gave me a lot of attention and a grounding in the whole trade of ironworking. I was then capable of forging anything, large or small; I could use the power-hammer, I did the work myself, with my own muscles; in those days I had muscles, because working with iron develops them. At that time, the working-day at Robert's was long...

My apprenticeship came to an end when Robert said 'It's time for you to work in a factory, and I suggest you take a job in my company.' "

JMH: "That was not at the same workshop?"

JP: "No. It was a much larger firm in the rue Damrémont, in the 18th district of Paris, an area of industrial buildings and working-class dwellings. I could not see any objections myself, but I was worried about the director, Monsieur Subes, who was much talked about in the ironworking world: he would do anything to get orders, and I didn't at all like the ironwork he produced. I wondered what I should be doing there. But I didn't want to disappoint Robert, so I went – though I only stayed a week. I'll tell you what happened. I was still a very young man; I arrived and was met by Subes. He spoke to me very unpleasantly, letting it be understood that I had been Robert's favourite pupil ... I didn't like that at all. Then he said, 'Well, it's agreed that we'll take you on, I'll get the foreman.' When the foreman I was to be put under arrived, Subes made a monumental mistake: he asked me to go outside while he spoke to the foreman; but the door was not properly shut, and at that time my hearing was very good. 'We're going to make that boy sweat a bit,' he said. 'We must show Robert that the boy can't have it easy, just because he thinks so highly of him. We must test him out.' 'This looks as if it's going to be fun!' I said to myself. I went down to the workshop, and, sure enough, they gave me a piece of work that was well beyond my physical strength, too heavy and too difficult; it was a test all right. But I took up the gauntlet and finished the job. At the end of the week I showed my work to the foreman, who said 'I think we'd better let the boss see it,' because he was, himself, rather taken aback. We went up to see Subes. 'I congratulate you,' he said to me. 'I didn't think you'd be able to do it; we are going to make you part of the team.' For the first time in my life I acted quite pigheadedly. 'It's too late, Monsieur Subes,' I said, 'I'm getting out!' I went straight to the door and left, just like that. I don't know whether I even collected my wages.

I knew another ironsmith in Paris, called Szabo. He was of Hungarian origin. I crossed Paris on foot to knock at his door. He took me on at once. I worked two or three years for Szabo, who was also a quite exceptional ironworker. He had the physical strength of an animal, like today's bodybuilders. Muscles like balloons. We all worked with an ordinary hammer, but he used a sledge-hammer that weighed eight kilos. He was so astonishingly skilful that he could make needles with this eight-kilo hammer, which he held in his right hand. He did a lot of work for a number of architectural firms in Paris.

At this time I lived with the ironworkers, and I used to join them in a Paris bistro for a meal of fried fish. The only difference between them and me was that they drank at least three litres of red wine a day, whereas I didn't drink at all. This caused me problems, though, because an ironworker sweats so much that he has to replace the water-loss by drinking.

I got on very well with Szabo, whom I had to leave to do my military service. During this period I spent all day long with the workmen; and at that time the Parisian workman was really someone. I was a very serious young man, and lived my life according to the principles my father had instilled in me. I didn't run after the girls. I did my work and went back home. I lived alone in my father's studio in Paris, and I worked a twelve-hour day – twelve hours a day at the forge! It was a time when I lived the life of a workman during the day, and then, in the evening, mixed with important university people, friends of my father. There was this contrast between what we call the life of the people, and the other life of the intellectuals. But they were not ordinary intellectuals; they were people who were thinking about the future, almost all were socialists, making plans for human advancement, you can be sure.

This lasted until I set up my own workshop, when I returned from military service.

So I worked as a forger from 1917 until, probably, 1921, when I started military service. This includes the short period I spent in the Borderel and Robert factory, and the time, until I was 21, with Szabo… Then I went back to Nancy and, before I opened my workshop, I worked in the forge of the Ecole des Beaux-Arts. For a short while I looked after the young people studying there. This did not last long, because I very soon set up my workshop. For several years after opening it, I worked at the forge myself. I was not at all an office-type, nor a man for the drawing-board. I lived in the workshop, and I remember that ironsmiths and forge-workers used to wear a leather apron, to protect them from the sparks. For many years I wore the leather apron."

Jean Prouvé's first workshop[13]

On the first of January 1924, Jean Prouvé moved into a workshop, 250 square meters and on two floors, at 35, rue du General Custine in Nancy. His first collaborators were the Wolff brothers, who were ironsmiths, and Pierre Missey, a craftsman in wrought iron who had already worked with Prouvé at the Ecole des Beaux-Arts in Nancy. In conversation, Pierre Missey recalled[14] how "we both worked together" on the pieces produced at this early stage. He explained how forge-welding is done, how to forge an oak-leaf … and he was able to tell me where to find some of the works of this period, such as the grill of a tomb in the Cimetière du Sud in Nancy (see no. 11, Complete Works), which he forged with Jean Prouvé.

A little later, other collaborators were taken on, among them the ironsmith Lefèvre, who became workshop foreman. The equipment was traditional: two forges, plus the forging tools and a few electrical machines such as drills and grinding machines. On his writing paper, he calls his workshop an "Ornamental and Wrought-iron Works", and offers to undertake "grills, hand-rails, balconies, chandeliers, etc." From the start, moreover, he signed some of his work in wrought iron (see nos. 55 and 56, Complete Works). It is clear that Prouvé created some works, such as lamp stands and grills, according to his own ideas, but that others were made to the requirements of architects and clients (see nos. 17 and 26, Complete Works).

In 1982, Jean Prouvé spoke to Jean-Marie Helwig about this early period:
JMH: "… So the vocabulary, the tools and the techniques were all traditional. The same vocabulary, the same tools that Jean Lamour used, those of earlier centuries?"
JP: "Yes, indeed. It was Robert's wish to preserve the traditional skills of the ironsmith. In Robert's workshop, the oxy-acetylene welding-torch was unknown; we used forge-welding, which is a very difficult technique.
At Robert's, work meant knowing how to make a fire, knowing which lumps of coal to use for the furnace, and how to heat up the metal so that it was just right for soldering; not letting it become so overheated and liquid that it ran off into the furnace. I learned all about that. That was the knowledge Robert was preserving. But as soon as I went to Subes, who ran a workshop where all kinds of work was done – traditional pieces and, at the same time, metalwork that was Monsieur Subes' own speciality, a sort of lace-work entirely made with the welding-torch – there was no more forging of metal, just bending and torch-welding.
You could say that Subes used modern equipment. But he did not turn it to good account, because he used the welding-torch to make things in the old style.
Robert was against that, and so was I. That is why, during the considerable period in my own workshop, when I was making very different things from what they were making at Robert's – you've seen the photos, I believe; lamps, things like that – I think I can truly say that I was the only one forge-welding pieces in that way … you mention the pressure-hammer at Robert's; it was not a pressure-hammer of thousands of tonnes, but what is called a tilt-hammer, with a pressure of two tonnes and worked by pressing a pedal; it uses a system of springs, and instead of holding the hammer in your hand, it

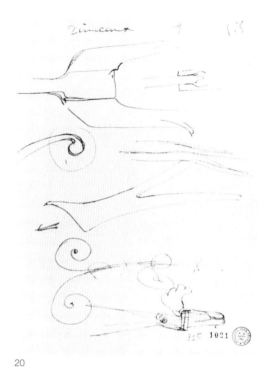

20

21

22

20. Sketches by Jean Prouvé for his course at the Conservatoire National des Art et Métiers.
21. Jean Prouvé's stamp about 1925.
22. 35, rue du Général Custine, Nancy, in 1984.
23. Collaborators in the Jean Prouvé Workshops about 1932.

23

is fixed to the pivot. It needs a light touch of the foot and some skill in turning the piece; and you have to learn to manage it very quickly, because it is very powerful – one blow too many, and the work is ruined. There was a tilthammer in Robert's workshop, but it was the one and only mechanical tool there. At Szabo's, it was the same, exactly."

JMH: "So it is a traditional piece of equipment in that it offers the same degree of manoeuvrability as the hammer and tongs."

JP: "Just so. Both Robert and Szabo refused to allow it to be modified in any way. It was the first piece of equipment I had at Nancy. The first equipment I bought consisted of a tilt-hammer, a forge and two anvils. My workshop was an ironsmith's workshop, with a complementary provision of vices, drilling machines, everything that allowed us to bring a mechanical element into our work. But the truth is that a real ironsmith pierces holes in the hot metal."

JMH: "With a punch?"

JP: "With a punch. It was used a lot. You get a different structure from rolled metal, more resistant. Obviously, whole grills were made, all the holes of which were forge-pierced.

Then one fine day, the light dawned on me. I said to myself, 'That's it. We must do something different. We've got to make use of modern methods of production.' So I moved over to construction, because that was essentially what I was interested in ...

And it came about very quickly. I took the view that craft production of small forged pieces was finished, and that it was necessary to move on to something else. If I thought like that, it was because I was living among people who thought like that; it was the ethos of the Ecole de Nancy.

So you see, a number of things came together at this point. Nothing is free, and one thing always depends on another. The important thing is to know how to make good use of the circumstances. I don't think I made a mistaken decision in com-

pletely changing the production of my workshop. That's why I installed what I believe was the first electric welding machine in Nancy. I discovered one day what could be achieved by electric welding and bought the equipment, which came from Switzerland ... I began to create works made possible by electric welding, that were only possible with electric welding, and I did more and more of this kind of work." [15]

This very considerable investment in autogenous and electric-arc welding was made in 1926. A little earlier, in 1925, Jean Prouvé had enlarged the workshop by making use of the upper floor. The J. Prouvé Collection contains drawings by himself and the designer, Mademoiselle Stieffel, a former pupil at the Ecole des Beaux-Arts. Hand-written on these early plans one finds, "Jean Prouvé, ironsmith," or "Jean Prouvé, metalwork contractor"; sometimes a stamp, "Jean Prouvé, ironsmith", is used; but we no longer find the words "ornamental ironwork".

Further machinery was installed: machines for punching, trimming and grinding, extra welding equipment, and welding and cutting torches (1928/29); Rosefelder was put in charge of a small metal-polishing section that consisted of a polishing machine and lathe – they were used for the Magasins Réunis (see no. 83).

Jean Prouvé told us in 1982/83: "I believe I was one of the first to use folded sheet-metal for building, and as I hadn't a platefolding machine in my small workshop, I had to go and find one in the boiler-makers' workshops; they had been folding metal for a long time, but for tanks and containers for chemical products, etc.

By chance, I met in Baccarat the engineer of a firm, the name of which I don't remember – I don't even remember the engineer's name. He was interested in what I was doing and helped me with the plate-folding; that is to say, I got him to do the work with his machines and finished it off in my own workshop. The moment I moved to a new workshop, in

1930, the first thing I did was to buy a plate-folding machine, to fit myself up with metal-folding machinery.

That's more or less how things developed. Up to 1925, I was making things in isolation, not influenced very much by other people. I was a provincial; Paris was where everything was happening. From time to time I came across an architectural journal; I was not especially interested, but, nevertheless, that's how I discovered that Le Corbusier existed, that Mallet-Stevens existed, that there was a painter called Fernand Léger, etc.

One day, I got together a small collection of photos, and very tentatively – because I was shy, never blew my own trumpet, was always very careful what I said – I said to myself, 'I'll go and see those people, and perhaps they'll give me some work.'

And the first person I went to see in Paris was Mallet-Stevens. I've already told you that story ..." (see no. 101).

It is probable that from 1925 onwards Jean Prouvé was aware of the work being done by the avant-garde. He showed two wrought-iron gates at the Exposition Internationale des Arts Décoratifs in Paris (see no. 23, Complete Works), and he certainly saw the Pavillon de l'Esprit Nouveau by Le Corbusier and Pierre Jeanneret, and Mallet-Stevens' Pavillon du Tourisme ... Jean Prouvé and his friends also exhibited with, and were active in, the Comite Nancy-Paris (Bignon/Coley, p. 28). His work was undoubtedly influenced by what the avant-garde was doing; we have only to look at the standard lamps and wall lighting (see nos. 45 to 70 in this Volume and in the Complete Works) – at the start they are wrought ironwork, but after two or three years become "lighting equipment" of the kind being produced by Chareau, Mallet-Stevens, Desny, Dufresne, Schenck ... Their designs, together with three centre lights by Prouvé, were published by G. Jeanneau. [16] This kind of production came to an end after 1931. About 1929, Prouvé published Le métal, which contained avant-garde works from outside France. We know that Prouvé became a member of the UAM in 1930, and that he exhibited at its first salon in Paris. On this occasion he saw the exhibition of the Werkbund and what the Bauhaus was making. He was a subscriber to Moderne Bauformen, as Jean-Marie Glatigny, who used to translate it for him from German, remembers.

About 1929 Jean Prouvé began to concentrate on the development of industrial products in folded sheet metal for the construction of buildings. He patented doors of curved plate, that exploited the elasticity of metal (see no. 170), movable partitioning (see no. 190), etc., products that, over the years, were the economic basis of the J. Prouvé Workshops – and are somewhat neglected in the literature. In the rue du General Custine workshop, he also began to research and construct lift cages in sheet metal (see nos. 146 to 156 in this volume and in the Complete Works).

This is the beginning of the period of folded metal; Prouvé has told us that he did not yet have a folding-machine and that he used one belonging to a firm in Baccarat. Emile Marchal remembers that metal sections, such as cover strips for partitioning, were drawn out in Paris ("we never drew them out ourselves").

In addition to the machinery that Prouvé bought in 1929 – a lever shearing-machine and a flexible-shafted sanding and grinding machine (Bignon/ Coley,

p. 29) – "we obtained presses for making shoes" (Pierre Missey), and machinery, such as a plate-clamping machine, was constructed in the workshop (see no. 170.9, Complete Works). Tubing was curved by filling it with lead and then reheating it (Pierre Missey). The early pieces of furniture were prototypes or were produced as craft work in short runs (see nos. 114 to 123 in this volume and in the Complete Works), and it needed highly skilled workers, such as Pierre Missey, to make them (which makes it difficult to reproduce them today). This furniture was made for Jean Prouvé's own home, for his sister and for friends of the family.

Jean Prouvé probably designed the furniture for the Cité Universitaire competition towards the end of the period of his first workshop; Pierre Missey remembers building the prototypes there (see no. 258).

Between 1927 and 1928, turnover doubled (Bignon/Coley, p. 35); for the large projects of 1928, Prouvé took on extra ironsmiths and metalworkers ... there was an office, run by Madame Huvé, a typewriter was bought, as well as a commercial vehicle. In 1928, the engineer André Schott (Prouvé's brother-in-law) became his partner, with a share in the business.

Jean Prouvé (1982):
"You can tell how rapidly my workshops developed, because very soon the premises in the rue du General Custine became too small. In 1930, machinery had to be bought, so a company was set up. One of my brothers-in-law who was an engineer became a partner, and essentially it was a company made up of friends. It grew considerably between 1930 and the end of the war. There was work all the time, all the time ..."

The beginning of Jean Prouvé's second workshop

J. Prouvé Workshops, registered on 28 January 1931, moved into its new premises, a factory building, with 1265 square metres on the ground floor and 412 on the first floor, at 50, rue des Jardiniers, Nancy. Bignon and Coley have published a study that gives a detailed account of the rue des Jardiniers workshop: they describe its production organisation, the tools used, its layout, personnel, materials, management, partners and backers, the Jean Prouvé articles of association, its financial management, the influence of the management ... its losses and deficits, the division of responsibilities ... its setting-up ... the premises, its markets and orders, the kind of work produced, the volume of business, research ... (Bignon/Coley, pp. 43–54). It was in this workshop that the work was done for large projects such as the Garage Citroen in Lyons (see no. 181), the Hôpital Grange Blanche in Lyons (see no. 204), and the Palais du Gouvernement General in Algiers (see no. 205). Jean Prouvé engaged highly qualified personnel (he was lucky, because the economic crisis had led to a shortage of work). He set up a research and design unit, headed by Jean-Marie Glatigny (an excellent technician with foundry experience), that included Robert Feck (a former pupil of the Ecole Supérieure of Nancy), and Jean Boutemain, a metal tracer. They were all excellent draughtsmen (Jean-Marie Glatigny: "It was Jean Prouvé who taught us to draw").
Mademoiselle Stieffel, the designer, and the foreman, Lefèvre, did not follow in the move to the rue

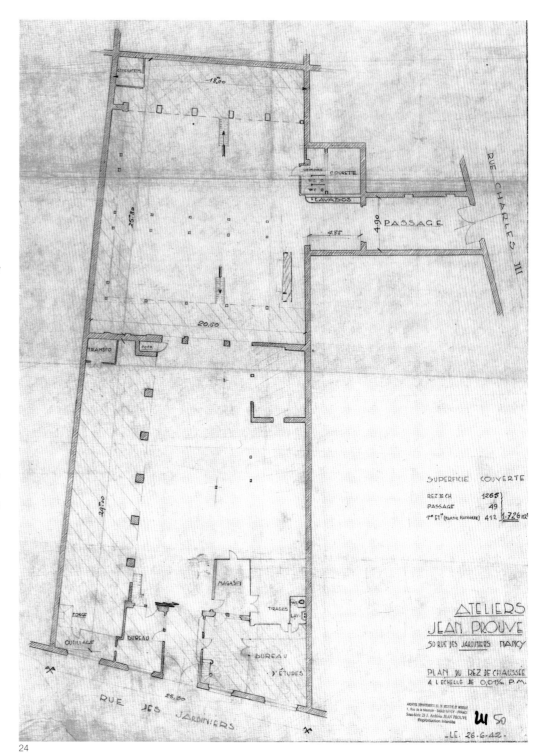

24

des Jardiniers; Barbier became foreman, and René Friot, who was engaged for the Grange Blanche project, stayed on in charge of the sheet metal operations. Emile Marchal (after studying as an aircraft mechanic) worked on the Paris projects, then in Algeria, and became head of machine tools. Soon about fourty people were being employed at the workshop. There is a photograph, taken on the Feast of St. Eligius (the patron saint of ironsmiths), that probably dates from 1932. Jean Boutemain, with the help of Pierre Missey, has named those of their colleagues who appear in it.

At the beginning a lifting-table press three metres wide was installed (using oil-pressure and prone to faults, it was replaced by several other folding-machines, and finally, in 1936, by a Peltz press). The workshops also had a small sheet-rolling mill, a machine for rolling bars, a bending-machine, and a

24. J. Prouvé Workshops, 50 rue des Jardiniers, Nancy. Plan of the ground floor, 26 June 1942. Total surface area 1,726 m².
25. Detail of the design office "plans book" of the Jean Prouvé Workshops.
26. Sketch by Jean Prouvé: a "2-CV".
27. Sketch by Jean Prouvé: "visitor" armchairs.

16

25

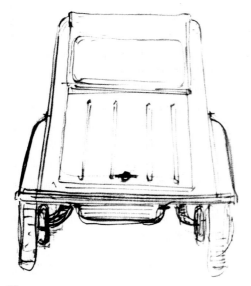

26

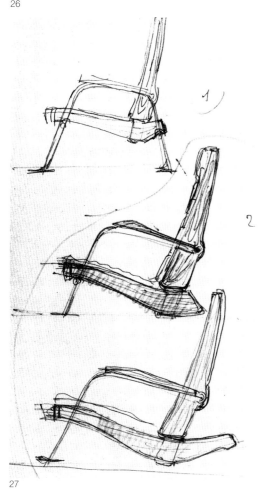

27

drawing-out machine and drawbench. Emile Marchal recalls that sections were not drawn out in the workshop; plan 1559 ter of 25 July 1932 contains the sections to be drawn out for metal frames. A polishing room was set up on the first floor, though a nearby polishing works was also used; welding became the preferred technique for assembly, so appropriate equipment was installed, and very soon spot welding was introduced. Pierre Missey, ironsmith since the start and specialist in prototypes, was put in charge of the assembly team, and René Friot of the manufacturing team (Bignon/Coley, p. 49, give a list of the members of the two teams). Iron-forging, which was less important to Prouvé in the 1930s, was done by other ironsmiths. It was, according to Jean-Marie Glatigny, "the real beginning of sheet metal construction".

Jean Prouvé (1982/83):
"That's the way things went; there was a constant need to renew the tooling. We needed the most up-to-date possible, because it gave us enormous advantages; all my collaborators appreciated that, because a modern tool made their work so much easier. They played the game; they were pleased to do so, and I was able to make things in a different way from others. It was difficult, because my board of directors did not completely agree with me. The fact that I made all the changes in one sweep was certainly the result of what I saw happening in engineering. Aircraft engineering was an important influence. Automobile engineering rather less so, because I was working thin plate before Citroën; before Citroën introduced its light 11 CV, I had invented, in my workshop, girders in thin plate, and was using electric spot welding; the spot welding machine I bought was one of the first in Nancy. I think I was naturally influenced by the passionate interest I had in aeronautical engineering, and it led me to ask myself why such techniques should not be used in building construction. I had the idea very suddenly! Why isn't building construction developing in the same direction as automobile and aircraft construction? Why do the building methods of the Middle Ages still persist? I had already realised that construction was no longer genuinely medieval, but faked, and that they were beginning to create a decoration and an architecture that I did not like. That was very clear to me."

Prototypes and large-scale models played an important role; Prouvé's working method – sketch, prototype, modifications, then construction plans – predominated. Jean-Marie Glatigny remembers that Prouvé often bypassed the research and design unit and brought sketches straight into the workshop. Prototypes were shown to architects and clients, and, since it was not then possible to make

calculations for sheet metal constructions, models were submitted to resistance and deformation tests. At a later date, joints were tested for water-tightness. I asked Jean Prouvé's former collaborators how he controlled product quality, and was told that he seldom went away on journeys, and that each day he made a point of speaking to every designer and workman. In his workshops there was an exceptional atmosphere that I have described elsewhere.

It was in the rue des Jardiniers workshop that, a little later, Jean Prouvé and his collaborators designed and manufactured the first buildings in folded sheet steel, such as the Club d'Aviation of Buc, the Maison du Peuple at Clichy, as well as furniture.

In 1933 the company "Les Ateliers J. Prouvé S.A." had approximately forty employees and workmen. The design for the coach station at La Villette (see no. 270), the first for buildings entirely in folded sheet, was of great importance to Jean Prouvé. On the list of "works in progress on 31 December 1933" (ill. 30), the works carried out for the Cité de la Muette at Drancy (see no. 353, Complete Works) are the largest. They were to remain on the list for several years. Jean Prouvé asked the Board of Directors for new machinery (folding press, shearing machine, etc…), but the company lost money on several projects (Jean-Claude Bignon and Catherine Coley 1990, pp. 46, 47); the order for the "Pels" folding press is cancelled.

A noticeable fall in turn-over on 1933 (1931: 2,363,000 francs; 1932: 3,293,000 francs; 1933: 2,952,000 francs; 1934: 2,233,676 francs). The largest activities are the Cité de la Muette and the Town Hall of Boulogne-Billancourt (see no. 340, 353, Complete Works), where Jean Prouvé made operable partitions 8 m high. One large design project resulted in the making of desks (see nos. 396 to 398, Complete Works and in this volume) and office chairs (see no. 403) for the Compagnie Parisienne de Distribution d' Electricité. The "semi-metal" chair designed in this year (see nos. 404 and 405) was to be made serially from 1935 onwards and – with variants – during the 40s and 50s. Among the other projects: seats for the lecture hall of the Ecole des sciences politiques (see no. 442) and a large study for furniture for the Open-air School of Suresnes, by Eugène Beaudouin and Marcel Lods (see no. 482). In 1934 and 1935 the introduction of new organisation to the workshop enabled profits to be increased (Jean-Claude Bignon and Catherine Coley 1990, p. 49).

In September/October 1935 the J. Prouvé Workshops received several large orders: the first order from the Ministry of Justice for an approved school (see no. 445, Complete Works) and that for the Flying Club at Buc (see no. 543). During the meeting of the Board of Directors on 10 May 1935, the chairman, Saint-Just Péquart, complained: "In spite of the comments and the advice already lavished on the subject, there is still an unjustified growth of the research and design department. Each enquiry seems to be an excuse for studies of new procedures, which may well be improvements, but which do not bring costs down, and which do not seem to be taken into account in setting the cost price. There must therefore be no further research that is not absolutely indispensable and the cost of which may not be covered by profitable price-setting" (Jean-Claude Bignon and Catherine Coley 1990, pp. 51 and 53). A machinery department was set up under the direction of Emile Marchal; it was an important element in the company (Jean-Claude Bignon and Catherine Coley 1990, p. 55).

In June 1936 the Board of Directors finally agreed to purchase the "Pels" folding machine (ill. 32). It went into service in December, as a result of the order for the Maison du Peuple of Clichy (see no. 704). According to Jean-Claude Bignon and Catherine Coley (1990, p. 75), the workshop had available the following equipment:

1 Pels folding press weighing 120 tonnes, length 4 m;
1 fly press with a Manez oil bath, length 3 m (all-purpose folding machine?) or Darrieux 40 tonnes;
1 swan-neck shearing machine, controlled by a lever;
1 Pels shearing machine, length 3 m, for 4 mm sheet (ill. 33);
4 arc-welding stations;
1 vertical spot-welding station (Languepin machine, single-phase 80 kW, welding 3 + 3 mm steel);
2 gas-welding stations;
1 bench pillar drilling machine;
1 Jost rapid drilling machine and several hand drilling machines;
3 lever punching machines;
1 all-purpose notcher for channel iron;
several hand lever shears for various thicknesses of sheet;
2 balance fly presses;
1 extrusion bench;
1 polishing bench.

Among the other projects: start of designs for the P.T.T. Ministry (see no. 572) and for the works in extruded bronze for the French Legation in Ottawa. A considerable amount of furniture was designed and made about 1936 (see nos. 534, 545, 599 and 612, Complete Works and in this volume).

In 1937 Pierre Prouvé, Jean's younger brother, was engaged as a tool maker. Jean Prouvé organised "internal training" and the spirit in the workshop was good (Jean-Claude Bignon and Catherine Coley 1990, p. 77). It was the year of intense research for the Maison du Peuple of Clichy (see no. 704); designs and works carried out, such as the staircase of the Union des Artistes Modernes pavilion (see no. 654) for the Exposition Universelle in Paris; the prototype of the B.L.P.S. holiday house (ill. 34) (see no. 715) and the classroom furniture (ill. 31) (see nos. 682 to 703, Complete Works). The very positive balance sheet for this year 1937 made it possible to think of buying larger industrial premises (Jean-Claude Bignon and Catherine Coley 1990, p. 73).

According to Jean-Claude Bignon and Catherine Coley (1990, p. 75), the personnel of the J. Prouvé Workshops in 1938/39 consisted of forty-seven workmen and fourteen salaried employees. There were several large work sites: the P.T.T. Ministry in Paris (see no. 572); the Maison du Peuple in Clichy (see no. 704), and the Fench Legation in Ottawa (see no. 716). The prototype of the B.L.P.S. holiday house (see no. 715) was exhibited at the Salon des Arts Ménagers. The J. Prouvé Workshops entered the competition for demountable barracks for the Ministry of Aviation (see no. 786), for which Jean Prouvé invented the principle of central portal frames, patented in 1939. A variant with an external frame as used at Onville (see no. 828). The profit for the year 1938 was only average because of the loss on the Maison du Peuple of Clichy.

28

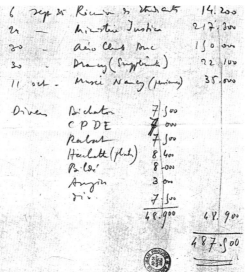

29

TRAVAUX EN COURS	
au 31 Décembre 1933	
(Annexe N° 3)	
DRANCY H.B.M.	490.874,--
REUNION FONCIERE	35.000,--
GRANGE-BLANCHE (Cache-radiat.)	17.112,--
METRO	173.400,--
ZOO (Vitrines)	63.148,--
SARREGUEMINES (Mobilier)	24.094,--
NEURO (Grange-Blanche)	48.141,--
BOULOGNE-BILLANCOURT	8.508,--
GERMAIN ALGER	23.227,--
CHARDOT (Rampe)	2.588,--
KRUGER ORAN	3.496,--
MEYER (1 porte)	391,--
	889.979,--

30

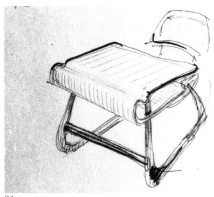

31

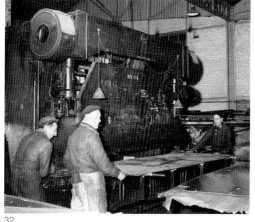

32

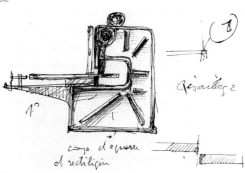

33

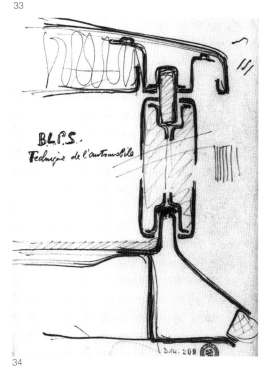

34

The directors Antonin Bergeret and Saint-Just Péquart announced their resignation. André Schott, co-founder and business director, opposed too ambitious programmes and "high risk" collaboration with architects such as Marcel Lods, Le Corbusier, Pierre Jeanneret (Jean-Claude Bignon and Catherine Coley 1990, p. 9). Several years earlier Jean Prouvé had introduced paid holidays. In 1939 he instituted supplementary insurance, paid by the company, for foremen, salaried employees and technicians who had been with the firm at least six months (Jean-Claude Bignon and Catherine Coley 1990, p. 77). The Maison du Peuple of Clichy was finished. There were other large projects: works for the World Exhibition in New York (see no. 788, Complete Works) and for the Vox cinema in Strasbourg (see no. 840, Complete Works), demountable barracks for the Génie (see no. 850), buildings for the Société Centrale des Alliages Légers (S.C.A.L.) at Issoire (see no. 854), in collaboration with Pierre Jeanneret and the Bureau Central de Construction (B.C.C.).

It was a war economy in 1940 with quotas on electricity and raw materials. Jean Prouvé avoided working for the Germans. The designs and works for the Bureau Central de Construction (B.C.C.) continued. The J. Prouvé workshops carried out boiler works (see 859, Complete Works) and began the manufacture of gas generators and carbonisation ovens (see nos. 868 and 869, Complete Works).

At the end of 1941 the J. Prouvé Workshops became a private limited company (Jean-Claude Bignon and Catherine Coley 1992, p. 27). They produced "Pyrobal" stoves (see no. 870), bicycle frames (see no. 871), continued to carry out works for approved schools (see no. 875, Complete Works), and made many designs for furniture in wood (see no. 883) (ill. 27).

In 1942 André Schott resigns. The J. Prouvé Workshops were commissioned to repair the railings of the Place Stanislas in Nancy (see no. 867, Complete Works). The production of ovens, furnaces, and wood furniture continued (see nos. 893 to 896, 912, 915, 928, Complete Works).

In the year 1943 four colleagues of the J. Prouvé Workshops were conscripted by the Compulsory Work Department (S.T.O.). The production of ovens (1,957,554 francs), furniture (504,831 francs) and "various works" (1,628,520 francs) continued. The J. Prouvé Workshops made a full-scale prototype of the metal house for Eugène Beaudouin and Marcel Lods (see no. 790) and did finishing work. The arrangements for paying personnel were changed.

In April 1944 the Germans wanted to requisition the "Pels" press, but were unable to get it out. Jean Prouvé proposed "blowing it up". The J. Prouvé Workshops bought some land in Maxéville on which the future factory was to be built. At the Liberation, Jean Prouvé, who had been active in the Resistance, became mayor of Nancy.

28. The building site of the Maison du Peuple of Clichy (1938). Jean Prouvé retouching the stairway of the offices, damaged in transport.
29. Orders received in September/Oktober 1935.
30. List of works in progress on 30 September 1942.
31 Sketch by Jean Prouvé: classroom furniture
32. The "Pels" folding machine, still in service in the Maxéville factory.
33. Sketch by Jean Prouvé: shearing machine.
34. Sketch by Jean Prouvé: the B.L.P.S. holiday house.

1 Complete manuscript, 1976, archive of the author.
2 On the shaping of metal in Prouvé's work: Sulzer 1991.
3 Works by Jean Prouvé listed as historic monuments. (List drawn up by the Archives modernes de l'architecture Lorraine, A.M.A.L.)
4 For the American sources of Jean Prouvé's ideas on human relations in industry, see Philippe Potié 1998.
5 If we analyse the history of the prefabricated metal house, we find that it goes in waves, generally before and after wars (for example the military barracks of Jean Prouvé), and above all after wars, when the arms industry is subsidised: "Airoh-house", by the Aircraft Industries Research Organisation (54,500 houses between 1946 and 1948), and "Lustronhouse", produced in the United States in the Curtis-Wright military aircraft factory (Gustav Kistenmacher 1950).
6 Paper by Renzo Piano, written for the Association of the Friends of Jean Prouvé, no date, archive of the author.
7 Norman Foster in: Jean Prouvé, cours du CNAM 1962 to 1962, J.-P. Levasseur, Paris 1984.
8 Joseph Belmont in: Jean Prouvé, meubles 1924-53, exhib. cat. 1989.
9 Jean Prouvé, une architecture par l'industrie, 1971, p. 142.
10 Conversations with Prouvé: Helwig 1982/83, archive of the author.
11 Conversations with Jean-Marie Glatigny, René Friot and Pierre Missey.
12 Conversation with Prouvé: Helwig, 9 November 1982, archive of the author; Madeleine Prouvé: Victor Prouvé, 1958; Henri Claude: "Jean fils de Victor: l'Ecole de Nancy", in: Jean Prouvé, constructeur, monograph by the Centre Georges Pompidou, 1990, pp. 93–99.
13 Bignon and Coley, Jean Prouvé entre artisanat et industrie, 1923–1939, Nancy, 1990, pp. 25–41.
14 Conversation with Pierre Missey, 1989.
15 Conversation with Prouvé: Helwig, 9 November 1982, archive of the author.
16 G. Jeanneau: Le Luminaire, Editions d'Art Ch. Moreau, about 1930.

Catalogue

The item numbers are those used in the Complete Works, Volumes 1 and 2.

4. Stand for a vase by Emile Gallé. Before 1923. Wrought iron. The Gallé vase of 1896 (in the form of a two-handled drinking-cup) belonged to Prouvé's parents. The young Prouvé made the stand in the spirit of Emile Gallé, who was his godfather. Photograph (ill. 4,2)

4,2

22

22. Two Gates in the Pavillon de Nancy at the Exposition Internationale des Arts Décoratifs, Paris. 1925. Pierre Le Bourgeois and Jean Bourgon, architects. Wrought iron. Prouvé was awarded a Diploma of Honour for these interior gates. Jean Prouvé (1983): "...They were interior gates ... entirely forged ... Yes, that diagonal was important, because it supported everything else ... I superimposed two iron plates and welded them in the forge, or, rather, when they were taken out of the forge."

44. Lampstand. Between 1923 and 1927. Variant of no. 43, with a different base. Wrought iron, forge-welded with welding powder. Photograph (ill. 44,1); detail (ill. 44,2).

44,2

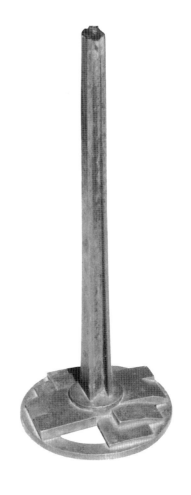

44,1

54. Centre light. Between 1923 and 1927. Hammer-finished steel and strips of clear and frosted glass.

55. Wall-light no. 46. Between 1923 and 1927. Hammer-finished sheet steel, with quartz strips.

70. Spherical centre light. About 1926/27. Unbeaten sheet steel, frosted glass.

76. Desk lamp for the Cité Universitaire, Nancy. 1930–1932. Folded steel. (See no. 258). Photograph (ill. 76,1); sketch (ill. 76).

54

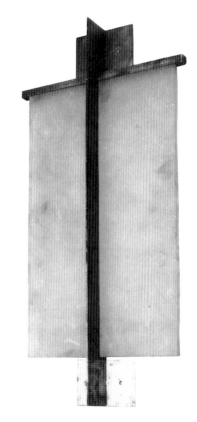

55

76,1

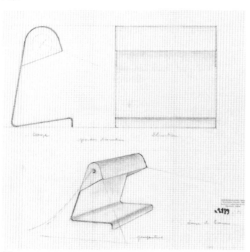

76

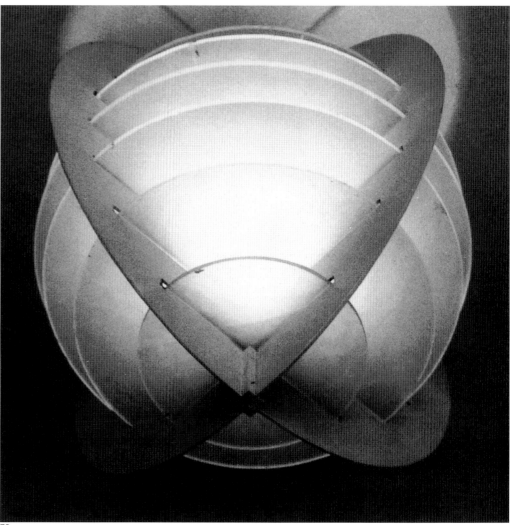

70

22

81.1,2

81.1,3

81.2,2

81.7

81.8,2

81. Work carried out for the Maison Robert Chevalier, Epinal. 1926/27. Charles Hindermeyer, architect. Chanaux and Pelletier, interior designers.

81.1. Main entrance door. In electrically welded square bar, with forge-welded decorative plaques. For this door, Prouvé was already using his new welding equipment, but he still forge-welded the decoration. The project for this door was exhibited at the exhibition of the Comité Nancy-Paris in 1926; the door had a decoration of diagonally superimposed plaques that have now been removed. Present state (ill. 81.1,2); detail (ill. 81.1,3).

81.2. Interior door. Designed by the architect. Hammer-finished and varnished metal. The two doors seen from inside (ill. 81.2,2).

81.3. Staircase railings. Electrically-welded square bars, positioned obliquely. Jean Prouvé (1983): "There was one bar this way and one bar that way to create a play of light a model for a competition probably or to show an architect what we were proposing." In fact, the rails and balustrades were constructed differently from the model; in the Chevalier house, Prouvé used the principle of "oblique positioning".

81.5. Two umbrella stands. Stainless steel.

81.6. Spherical centre light. Sheet steel and frosted glass (see no. 70).

81.7. Garden railings. On the rue Gilbert side. Constructed in a similar way to the staircase railings.

81.8. Garden gate. Arc-welded sheet steel. Photograph of the original state taken in the 20s; sketch by Prouvé (ill. 81.8,2). Jean Prouvé (1983), while making the sketch: "To keep the metal firm and ensure that it did not look as if it had been badly planished, I cut it like that. It is not folded steel, but strips of metal welded at intervals. You can just see the hardly visible marks across the surface. It is arc-welded. It is welded where the metal stands raised, because it is easier to weld at such points. It is very difficult to weld a depression ... I designed the handle and modelled the first one myself. It was later mass-produced by an ironmonger." (For the handles, see nos. 108 and 109.)

83. Work carried out for the Magasins Réunis, Nancy. Rebuilt between 1926 and 1928. Pierre Le Bourgeois, architect. Les Magasins Réunis were founded by a native of Nancy, Antoine Corbin (1835–1901). About 1910, his son Jean-Baptiste Corbin (1867–1952) made extensive changes to the Nancy store. The reconstruction, on the site of the former Art Nouveau buildings, which were destroyed during the war, made use of reinforced concrete. It was a modern commercial building, with internal courtyards. As a friend of the artists of the Ecole de Nancy, Corbin gave their artistic movement support and put the top floor of the new shop at their disposal. Corbin's house is today the Museum of the Ecole de Nancy.

83.1. Lift doors. Stainless steel.

83.2. Octagonal lift cage. Cover strips in folded stainless steel sheet.

83.3. Balustrades to shopping galleries. Bowed sheets of stainless steel placed between steel barring.

83.4. Guardrail. Situated on the landing between the ground floor and the first floor. Highly polished, welded stainless steel.

83.5. Staircase railings. Railing of a staircase leading to the first floor, in stainless steel, with chromed brass handrail; start of railing (ill. 83.5,1). Railing of a staircase leading to the basement; construction similar as for railing leading to the first floor.

83.6. Staircase railing. Railing of a staircase leading to the first floor. Aluminium tubing on flat-bar uprights. Attributed to Prouvé.

83.7. Frames of overhead windows. Attributed to Prouvé.

83.8. Centre lights.

83.1,2

83.5,1

83.2

83.6

96.1,1

96.1,2

96. Work carried out for the Hôtel de l'Ermitage, Vittel. 1928/29. Fernand César, architect. For Prouvé, who was 27, the commission from the Nancy architect César (who was appointed architect of the Etablissement Thermal de Vittel in 1925) was of considerable importance. Prouvé made use of his talents as a draughtsman and sketched a large number of proposals that he then put to the architect. The work at Vittel is an example of the transition period: Prouvé made the rail of the main staircase in wrought iron, was already using welding equipment, designed metal building-fittings (that are still in use today), and made original objects in stainless steel. Here he began to develop his mastery of working sheet metal.

96.1. Main staircase railing. Hammer-finished and welded bars (the horizontal bars are the dominant motif); handrail in nickeled brass, two standard lamps in hammer-finished metal at the foot of the staircase, on the ground floor. Photograph (ill. 96.1,1); detail (ill. 96.1,2); five sketches by Prouvé for the stair rail, variants A, B, C, D, E, with lamp standard, different motifs (ill. 96.1,3 to 96.1,7); seven sketches by Prouvé showing variants for the staircase railing, seen from the entrance hall, with different motifs (ill. 96.1,8 to 96.1,14); six sketches for the staircase railing, with motifs of horizontal bars, similar to the rail actually made (ill. 96.1,15 to 96.1,20).

96.2. Lift protection grills. Composed of square tubing, rolled sections and pressed sheet metal.
96.3. Lift-shaft protection grill for the small lift.
96.4. Revolving entrance doors. Sheet steel. Attributed to Prouvé.
96.5. Large bay windows. On the ground floor, with sliding sashes, pivot frames and fixed sections.
96.6. Window bays with swing door "in pressed sheet". Frame in metal sections covered with pressed steel pieces, welded and screwed to the frame.
96.7. Door handles. For the doors Prouvé developed a handle of which he published a model with chromed tubing, but the handles at Vittel are glass batons. The exterior doors of the bays no. 96.6 have different handles on the outside.
96.8. Interior doors. Single doors with fixed sections, similar in execution to 96.6.
96.9. Glazed landing doors.
96.10. Three glazed partitions. Folding partitions between the ground-floor salons, two sections, or the whole, of which can be opened.

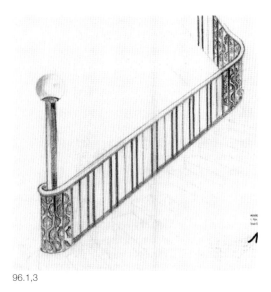

96.1,3

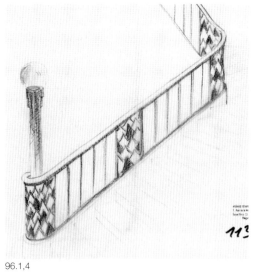

96.1,4

96.1,5

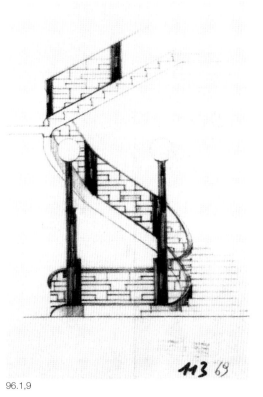

96.1,9

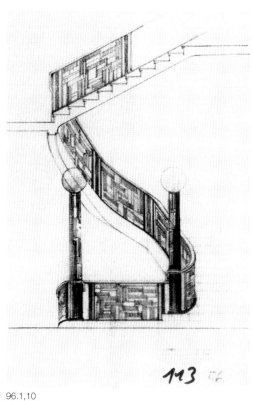

96.1,10

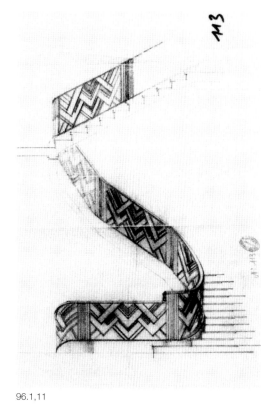

96.1,11

96.1,15

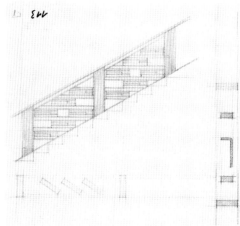

96.1,16

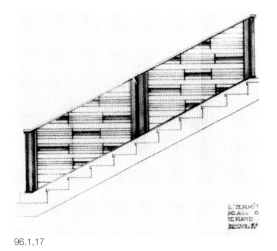

96.1,17

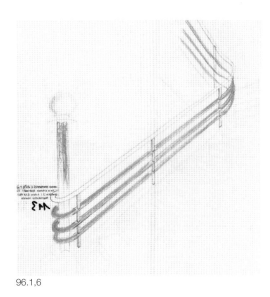

96.1,6

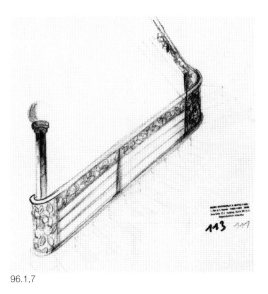

96.1,7

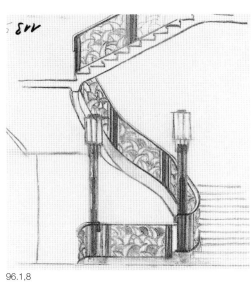

96.1,8

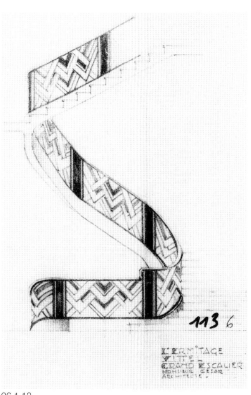

96.1,12

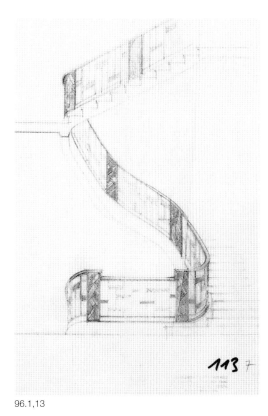

96.1,13

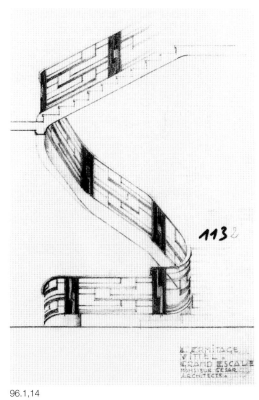

96.1,14

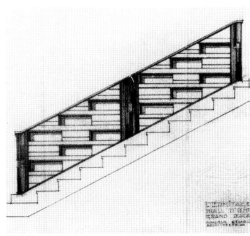

96.1,18

96.1,19

96.1,20

96.11. Letter box. Polished stainless steel. Jean Prouvé (1983): "... yes, it's stainless steel ... I suggested stainless steel and I arranged the opening like that, so the post wouldn't fall out ...". Photograph, about 1930, of the box closed (ill. 96.11,1).

96.12. Walking-stick stand (or umbrella stand). Polished stainless steel. This stand used to be in the Golf Club basement. Photograph (ill. 96.12), about 1930.

96.13. Showcases. Stainless steel sheet. We photographed this showcase at the Hôtel de l'Ermitage in 1984 (ill. 96.13,1). An example was shown at the first exhibition of the Union des Artistes Modernes, 1930, in Paris. In the J. Prouvé Collection there are several construction plans for the showcases at the Ermitage (type G, H and 1). Prouvé probably made a large number of showcases for the Hôtel de l'Ermitage: four on the main staircase, twenty-six for the gallery of the salons, six for the cloakroom.

96.12

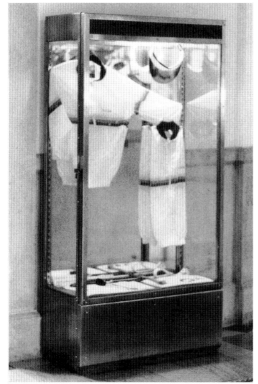

96.13,1

96.11,1

101.1,1

cause me much trouble ... I must have thought it up in about a quarter of an hour. I said, 'I'm going to make it like that.' ... I visualised it and then went ahead with it like that ... I had this large grill to make and in it there had to be an entrance ... These strips established the position of the entrance, and all the rest became clear to me. The door stands out in contrast because it is composed differently ... The composition consists of a highly emphasised door, with all the rest a sort of net. I also emphasised the door handle ... It was a double door. From one direction light was let in freely, from the other it was blocked. From here you could see through it, from there you couldn't. I was aiming at a kind of light effect, because the grill stood in front of a glazed entrance ... The door was not glazed, it was a protective grill ... And then, it formed a sort of ladder. Just as a ladder is made rigid by the stops let into it ... the fact that it slopes makes it stronger than if it were upright. It is a play of obliquely positioned bars and others placed square to them at different intervals ... The aim was to make something very lively with a great deal of light playing on it. As we often see, the play of light makes things seem to shimmer. Above all, this play of light was three-dimensional, whereas most older grills were merely two-dimensional silhouettes. It was a play of metal ... All the metal is hammer-finished, that is to say, the elements are not rolled, but forged ... They look like wrought iron. It is ordinary steel ... metal that has been polished and clear-varnished ... At this period I was working with conventional tools, but I was composing works in a different style ... Mallet-Stevens was enthusiastic ... he was very satisfied."

101.1. Interior grill. Polished and clear-varnished flat bars. Present state after modifications (eight flat bars added to the door), interior view (ill. 101.1,1); details of the grill, present state, view from outside (ill. 101.1,3); sketch drawn during the conversation of 1982 (ill. 101.1,4).

101.2. Interior grill for the staircase. Similarly executed.

101.1,3

101.1,4

101. Grills in the Villa Reifenberg, Paris. 1927.
Robert Mallet-Stevens, architect. Jean Prouvé (1982): "... One day I got together a small collection of photographs, and very tentatively – because I was shy, never blew my own trumpet, was always very careful what I said – I said to myself, 'I'll go and see those people (Le Corbusier, Mallet-Stevens ...) and perhaps they'll give me some work.' And the first person I went to see in Paris was Mallet-Stevens ... He was being bombarded with requests for work. So I found Mallet-Stevens' door closed to me, that is, I was received by his office manager, who did not know me at all ... Guévrékian ... Then, in desperation, I said, 'Look, I've come all the way by train from Nancy ... It's cost me a lot of money, what am I going to do?' 'All right, show me what you have done!' he said. He went away. Five min-

utes later I was with Mallet-Stevens ... he was looking at the photos. He received me as he received everyone, very kindly, almost deferentially. He was a quite exceptional man. 'I'm extremely interested in what you're doing', he said, 'I need a large grill for a house I'm building.' He then explained in less than five minutes what he wanted. Naturally, I replied, 'Right, Monsisur Mallet-Stevens, I'll go back to Nancy, make you a drawing, and give you an estimate.' 'No, stop a minute', he said. 'I don't want a drawing or an estimate, I want a grill!' That's how it happened, and that's how I came to make the Reifenberg grill ... When I delivered it to him, he didn't know what he would get. Once it was in position, he was totally enthusiastic about it. He was surprised to discover a way of looking at metal that he had never seen before ... I remember it didn't

101.2

103. Work carried out at the Maison Robert Mallet-Stevens, Paris. 1927. Robert Mallet-Stevens, architect.
103.1. Staircase railing. Polished stainless steel flat sections, placed diagonally.
103.2. Radiator casing. Polished stainless steel angle sections.

 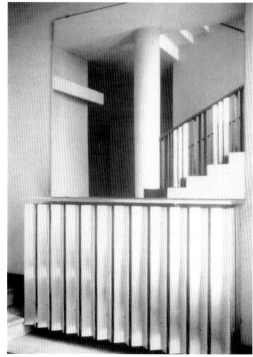

103.1

103.2

108. Door handle levers. About 1928.
108.1. Lever handle. Stainless steel. The lever is balanced by a fly-weight. The handle is a single bar, such as were in commercial production at the time. Jean Prouvé (1982): "I designed the handle, modelled it and made the first example..."
108.2. Lever handle, variant. There is a variant with two holes in the fly-weight. Jean Prouvé used these handles, for example, for the gate of the Maison Chevalier (see no. 81.8) and for the lift doors at Bains-les-Bains (see no. 107.5, Complete Works).
108.3. Lever handle, variant. We discovered a variant on the French window of the Maison France at Ferdrupt (see no. 203).

109. Door handles. 1930s. Aluminium. The J. Prouvé Workshops used moulded aluminium door handles made by the Société Bezault, and similar in shape to those in stainless steel (see no. 108).

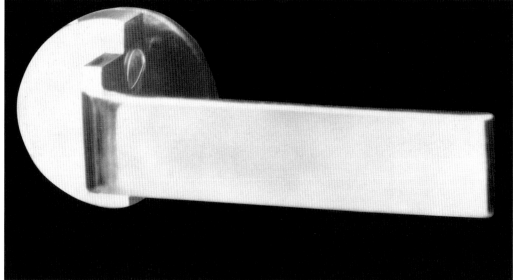

108.1

108.2

108.3

109

113,5

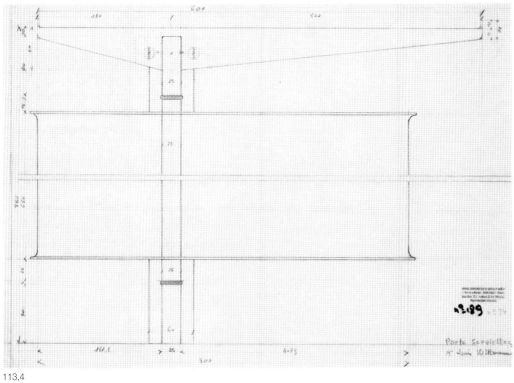

113,4

113,6

113. Hinged towel-holder. About 1930. Stainless steel. Prouvé made a pair for Louis Wittmann. The towel-holders are fixed to the wall, the upper part in 3 mm stainless steel sheet forms a shelf, the towels hanging from two round rails attached to the lower part, which is in folded stainless steel sheet; it folds away by swivelling around a chromed tube. Construction plan (ill. 113,4); photograph (about 1930) showing, left, a closed towel-holder, and, right, one that is open (ill. 113,5); detail (ill. 113,6).

114,1

114. Armchair with independently adjustable seat and back. About 1930. A unique piece commissioned by Louis Wittmann. The frame is in folded steel sheet, as are the seat and the back, which pivot on a common axis by means of cog-rails that are part of the circular arm-rests. The scat, back and armrests are covered by leather cushions. Jean Prouvé (1983): "... Wittmann, ... I made a completely round armchair for him ... and then a very fine table ... and some hinged towel-holders for the bathrooms ..." Only one photograph (about 1930) is preserved, published in the Studio Year Book Decorative Art in 1932 (ill. 114,1); sketch by Prouvé drawn for the periodical Intérieur in 1965 – the dating 1925 is inaccurate (ill. 114,2).

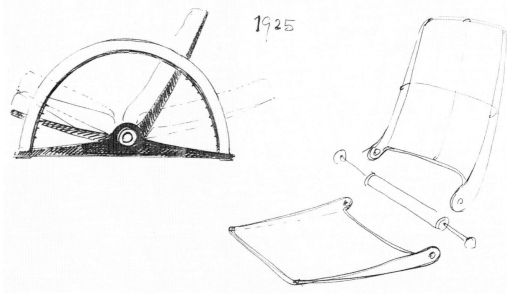

1925

114,2

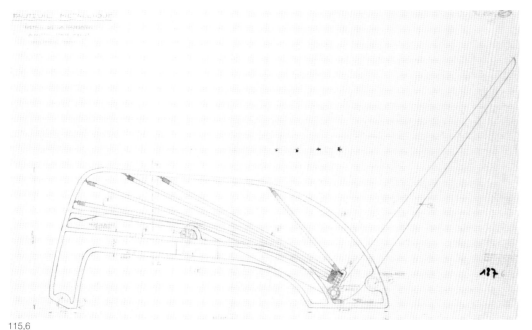

115,6

115. Armchair with reclining seat and back.

About 1930. This armchair was shown in 1930 at the first exhibition of the Union des Artistes Modernes (see no. 119). The frame was constructed of welded U-shaped sections 20 x 14 with sheet steel plating; the left and right-hand sides are joined by means of two chromed tubes. The seat and back in folded sheet steel are furnished with ball bearings that use the channel sections as a rail. A system of two sets of five springs moves the seat and back into normal position; they are held there by a clamping spring. The armrest consists of a leather-covered rubber tube; the seat and back have leather cushions. Three photographs (ill. 115,1 to 115,3); detail of frame, when the chair is lowered (ill. 115,6).

115,2

115,1

115,3

116. Fully reclining armchair. 1930. Prouvé made several examples of this armchair. The frame is in folded steel sheet with built-in rails that, by using ball bearings, articulate it. The ten springs found in armchair no. 115 have been replaced by a system using two springs that move the chair from the lying-down to the sitting position. The seat has a framework of steel wires across which is stretched a foam-filled woollen material. The wooden armrests are covered with textile material. Photograph (ill. 116,1); photographs taken in 1983 of the example at Prouvé's home, which, as Jean-Marie Helwig, a former colleague of the author, showed, was still in perfect working condition (ill. 116,3 and 116,4).

116,1

116,3

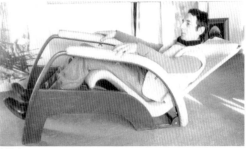

116,4

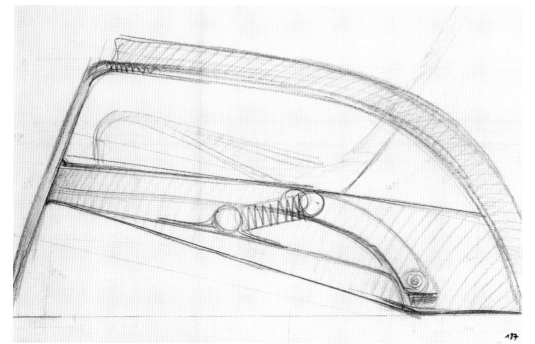

117a,1

117a. Sketches for an adjustable armchair.

About 1930. Large-scale sketch by Prouvé (ill. 117a,1). Jean Prouvé (1983): "... I've explained how I made this kind of furniture. I used to make a rough sketch and pass it to the workshop. My brother then made it. We didn't make a lot of drawings. We built the furniture and then made any changes needed." I should add that for his furniture Prouvé often made large-scale drawings in coloured pencil. The earliest furniture was made by Pierre Missey, who, like Prouvé, was an artist in wrought iron. It was only later that Pierre Prouvé made models from his brother's drawings. Pierre Missey: "Prouvé used to make a drawing (of a piece of furniture) ... a prototype was made to see how it looked, then modifications were made ... Then a final plan was drawn. That was the routine."

118a. Reclining chair.

About 1930. The frame constructed of two flattened and curved steel tubes, joined by welded pieces of pressed steel sheet. The two parts of the chair frame and of the back are in pressed and welded sheet; they are joined by two narrow tubes. Both move on pivots; the seat and back are stretched canvas. Pierre Missey made these chairs by hand. To achieve curves, he cut teeth in the sheet metal, shaped it and then welded it together again. Photograph of the chair, side view, taken at the "UAM from 1929 to 1958" exhibition at the Paris Musée des Arts Décoratifs, 1989/90 (ill. 118a,1); large-scale drawing of the chair with details of the pivots (ill. 118a,2).

118a,1

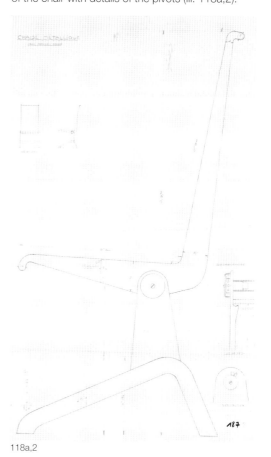

118a,2

119

119. **The Jean Prouvé Stand at the first exhibition of the Union des Artistes Modernes (UAM).**
From 11 June to 14 July 1930 at the Paris Musée des Arts Décoratifs. Prouvé exhibited: a metal reclining chair (see no. 118a), two metal chairs with lifting seats (see no. 120a), a metal armchair (see no. 115), a showcase (similar to case no. 96.13), some of the stands for Cournault's glass paintings (see no. 112, Complete Works) and several objects that were displayed in the showcase. He also showed eleven photographs of recent works, the model for a stainless steel door (see no. 164, Complete Works), a door in curved sheet metal for the Shell Company (see no. 170), and several plans were displayed on the wall. It was on this occasion that Prouvé visited the "Werkbund" and "Bauhaus" exhibition at the Grand Palais. Prouvé's early furniture is in radical contrast to the ideas of these movements.

120a. **Metal chair with lifting seat.** About 1930. The frame of the back is constructed of two flattened steel tubes, with elements in pressed sheet steel and welded steel tubes; the lifting seat frame is in pressed sheet steel and welded tubing. Seat and back are stretched canvas. The chairs are stackable. Pierre Missey: "... yes, the shaping of the tubes – necessarily done by hand – was achieved by filling them with lead or sand." This chair is different from variants nos. 120b and 120c (Complete Works): the flattened tubes are on the same plane as the sheet metal of the frame and the back is a single piece of stretched canvas. Photographs of the chair about 1930 (ill. 120a,1 and 120a,2).

120a,1

120a,2

120b. Metal chair with lifting seat, variant. About 1930. The frame is similar to that of no. 120a, but the assembly of the flattened tubes and the pressed sheet steel is different in detail. In 1930 Prouvé made a set of six chairs for his sister Marianne; they are slightly different: the flattened tubes have a different curvature. The back is made of two pieces of red canvas. Jean Prouvé (1983): "... I made these chairs specially as a present for my sister who was getting married ..." Photograph taken at the Basle exhibition (ill. 120b,1); photograph of the set of chairs Prouvé made for his sister (ill. 120b,3); photograph of four chairs stacked in a gallery in Paris (ill. 120b,5).

120b,3

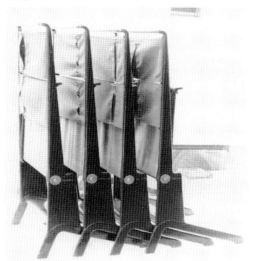

120b,1

120b,5

121a,1

121a. Table. About 1930. Nickeled steel, the top in stretched rubber. Prouvé here used principles from aircraft construction: he stretched rubber across a system of five "herring bones" of sheet steel welded to a central steel tube (see 121a,1, view from below). The base – which is not very stable under torsion – consists of a vertical tube, reinforced by two sheet metal channel sections and welded to a horizontal tube, covered by an U-shaped sheet of folded metal;

two flattened and curved tubes form the feet. The rubber was held between two flat bars and stretched by four stretchers. All the metalwork was nickeled, as were the chairs no. 118c (Complete Works) that came with the table. When we saw and photographed this table in Wittmann's home in 1985, the rubber had been replaced by sheet metal and the whole table was painted green. Jean Prouvé (1983): "... That's right ... at Wittmann's ... a very fine table.

A table ... I'll draw it for you on the back ... then there were two feet here ... that's it, and the top, the top here was stretched rubber. It's at Wittmann's house." Recent photograph (ill. 121a,1).

122,1

122. Small folding table. About 1930. The frame is constructed of a steel tube with four sheet metal "herring bones" and a stretching system similar to that of table no. 121a, plus three flat bars which press the rubber against the tube. A hinge is mounted on this tube on a similar system to that used for doors mounted on a tube (Prouvé's patents of 1929 and 1931). When we visited Louis Wittmann's house, we discovered this small table fixed to the wall in the garden pavilion, the owner's favourite workplace. The stretched rubber had been replaced with sheet metal. Photographs of the table with the leaf in horizontal position (ill. 122,1) and vertical position (ill. 122,2).

122,2

133. Work carried out for the extension of the Brasserie Excelsior, Nancy. About 1931. Alexandre Mienville, architect.

133.1. Railing of staircase leading to basement dining-rooms. Entirely in matt-polished stainless steel: column of standard lamp in rolled sheet, curved sheet at the bends and beginning of the staircase, handrail in tubing combined with a flat section, three tubes parallel to the handrail, a column in flat section. After the difficulties encountered earlier (see the door of the Maison Gompel no. 102, Complete Works), Prouvé no doubt wanted to avoid welding and find different solutions to assembly problems: with four years experience behind them, Prouvé and his colleague Pierre Missey were able to master the difficulties of shaping stainless steel. The modernity of this staircase railing is in sharp contrast to the decor of the hall. Recent photographs (ill. 133.1,1 and 133.1,3–133.1,4).

133.2. Entrance door. Attributed to Prouvé by Coley.

133.1,1

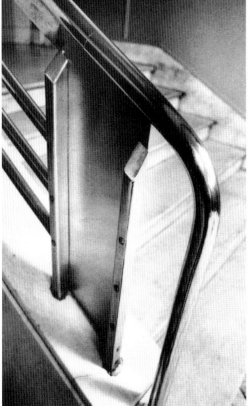

133.1,3

133.1,4

146,1

146,2

146,3

Lift cages. Prouvé began making lift cages about 1928, and during the 30s the J. Prouvé Workshops made two or three cages a month for several companies, especially Otis-Pifre, one of whose directors was a friend of Prouvé. The specialised team that assembled the cages consisted of a fitter, two mates and a welder. On-site mounting of the cages was the responsibility of the companies who commissioned them. This is why there are very few photographs of installed lift cages in the J. Prouvé Collection; on the other hand, there are many sketches, construction plans and copies of plans drawn by the lift companies. Prouvé very early on applied his principles to lift cages: forms of uniform strength, the bending and folding of sheet metal, rounded forms and the "monobloc" principle.

Prouvé was later to extend these principles, used very early in lift cages, to the construction of whole buildings in shaped sheet metal.

146. Lift cage. 1928/29. Model registered 14 November 1928. Jean Prouvé (1983): "...That's the frame of the cage ... We were already concerned to construct them better than the earlier ones ..." Photograph of the frame (ill. 146,1); detail of the plan that corresponds to the photograph (ill. 146,2); modified plan of the 1.7 x 0.85 m lift cage – the U-shaped section upright is pressed sheet in a form of uniform strength, the T-brace between the upright and the console is sheet, the console a beam of uniform strength (ill. 146,3).

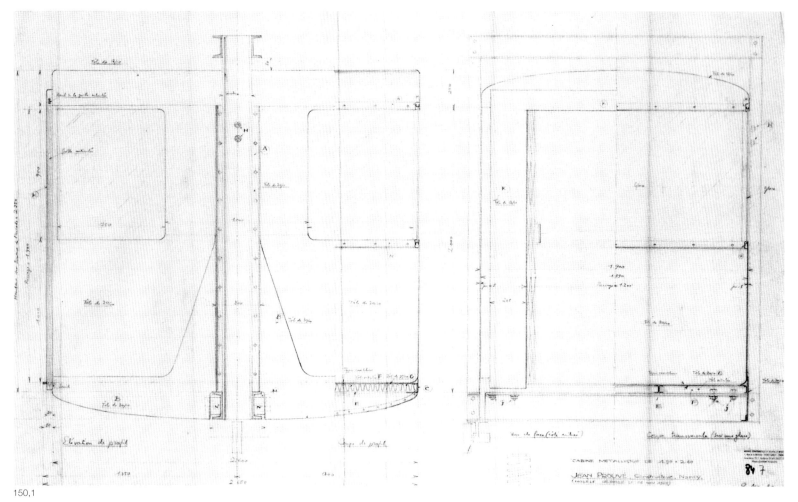

150,1

150. Lift cage. 1930. Metal cage 1.90 x 2.60 m for Otis-Pifre Lyons. 3 mm and 2 mm sheet steel, floor in corrugated sheet and folding gate. Elevations and section (ill. 150,1); view of the cage (ill. 150,2).

152. Lift cages for the Cité des Informations at the Exposition Coloniale, Paris. 1931. Jean Bourgon, architect. Prouvé made four metal lift cages for this building. Two photographs, taken during the 30s in the J. Prouvé Workshops at 50, rue des Jardiniers, Nancy, show one cage in sheet aluminium and another in the background (ill. 152,1).

152,1

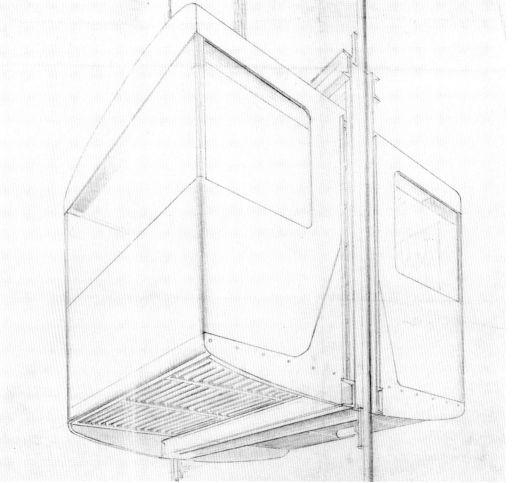

150,2

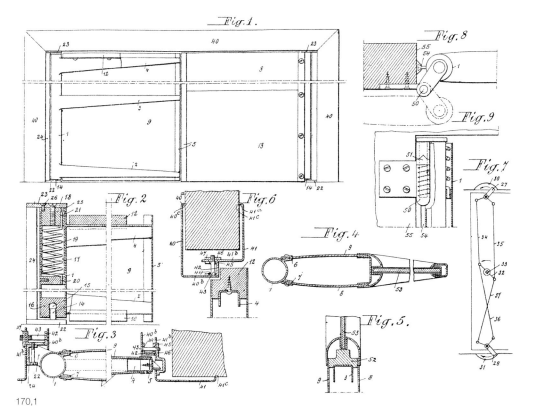

170,1

170. Doors in curved sheet metal mounted on a tube. 1929–31. The system for interior doors is the first example of Prouvé's developing an industrial product. He entered a patent on 9 February 1929 (ill.170,1) which was granted on 15 November 1929 as no. 669.430. On the drawing for the "single-action metal door (one leaf)", already patented (ill.170,7), we find all the details, including the stainless steel handle (see no. 109).

174. Patent no. 721.104 "Improvements in the construction of metal doors and windows". Entered 6 August 1931, granted 29 February 1932. After the doors for Shell, the J. Prouvé Workshops made doors in flat plate, as described in this patent.

175. Patent no. 709.085 "Improvements in the construction of metal doors and windows". Entered 9 January 1931, granted 3 August 1931.

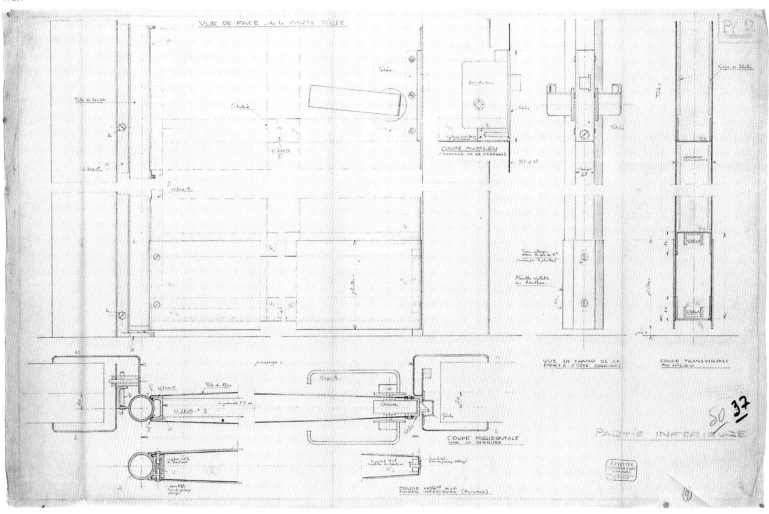

170,7

179.2

179. Work carried out for the Etablissements Citroën, Garage Marbeuf, Paris. About 1929. Albert Laprade and Léon Bazin, architects. This building is notable for the large glazed bay, 19 x 21 m, kept rigid by two vertical posts of uniform strength, and for the interior courtyard behind the bay which has five levels of galleries for the cars. The large glazed bay was suggested by M. Ravazé, architectural adviser to the Etablissements Citroën.
179.1. Rails and balustrades. Photograph from the 30s (ill. 179.1), with the words: "Balustrades and rails Garage Marbeuf, Paris".
179.2. Large plate-glass windows for the glazed bay. Probably made by Prouvé.

179.1

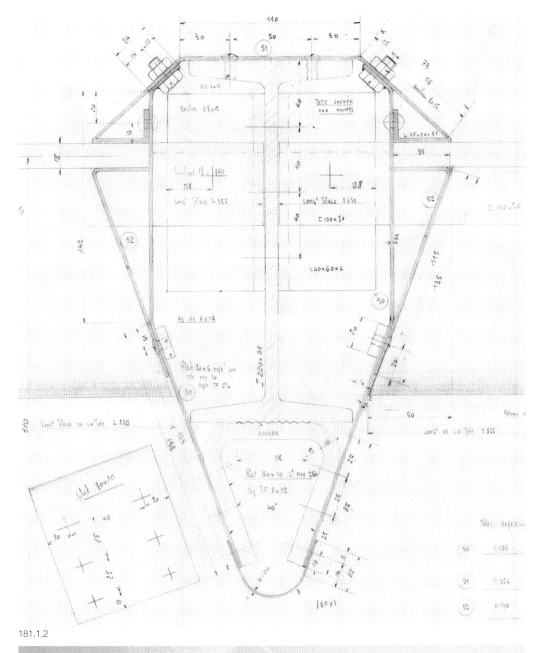

181.1,2

181.1,3

181. Work carried out for the Citroën showroom and garage, Lyons. 1930/31. M. Ravazé, architect. Jean Woelflin, outside consultant for structural calculations. This was one of the first large projects undertaken by the new workshop at 50, rue des Jardiniers, Nancy. Prouvé had there his first oil-pressurised lifting-table press (3 m fold) and other new machines.

181.1. Large window-wall. Jean Prouvé (1982/83): "... Yes ... I know Woelflin calculated the strength of the joints ... From the construction point of view it was very interesting, because it was made entirely of folded sheet ... I used to go to the site in Lyons ... Uniform strength already ... all the crosspieces ... and there's the folded-sheet stanchion ... The screws? To screw the sheets together. At that time we had no large folding presses, so we fixed the sheets together ..." The four folded sheets are screwed together (see no. 181.1,2). Photograph of the showroom about 1931 (ill. 181.1,1); detail of plan 961, showing the large post in I "220", encased in folded and screwed sheet (ill. 181.1,2); photograph of the large window-wall in 1984 (ill.181.1,3). Unfortunately the large interior courtyard has been destroyed by the building of a new floor.

181.1,1

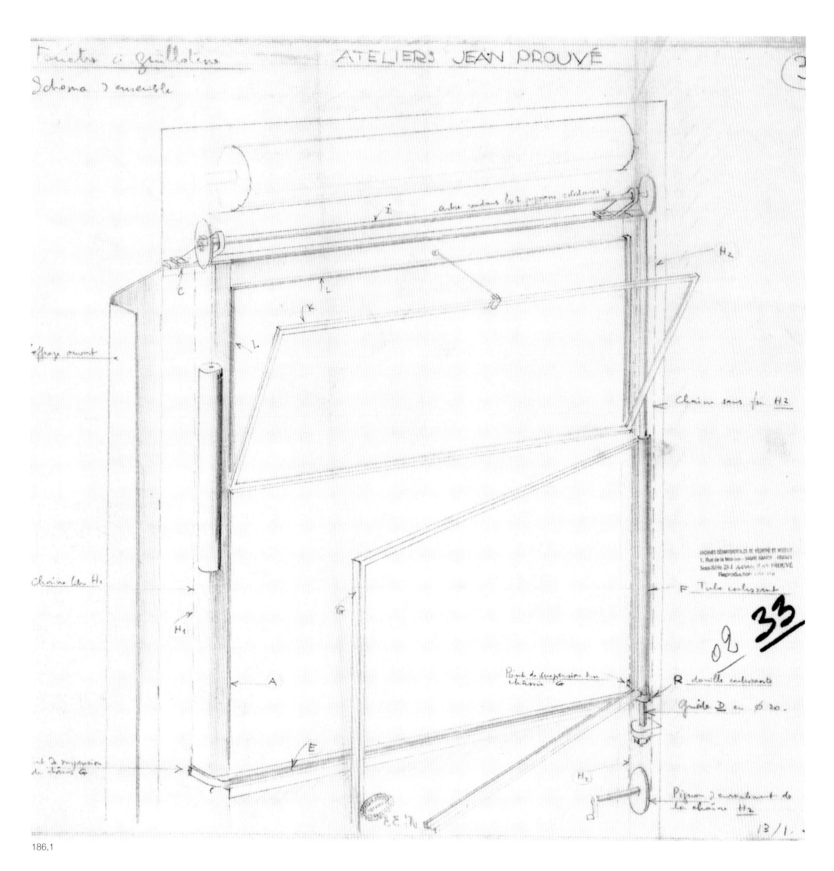

184. Patent no. 700.2R "Sash window". Applied for 8 August 1930, granted 26 February 1931.

186. Sash window. 1931. Patented window S. G. D. G., with inward-opening upper frame and side-hinged lower frame. Arrangement diagram (ill. 186,1), drawn by Prouvé on 13 January 1931, in which all the elements of the new system can be clearly seen: on the right, the continuous chain with the sprocket and the crank handle; above, the cross-bar to keep the two sprockets firm; on the left, the free chain with the counterweight and the open box.

189. Patent no. 717.866 "Improvements in the construction of soundproof panels". Applied for 28 May 1931, granted 15 January 1932.

190a,7

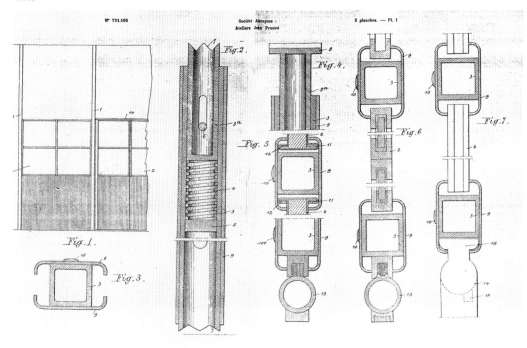

190b

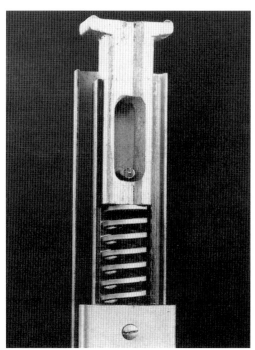

190a,8

190a. Movable partitions. 1931/32. Prouvé began to develop these partitions at the beginning of 1931. There are fifteen undated and unnumbered study drawings in the J. Prouvé Collection. Prouvé entered a patent in August 1931 and in the same year began to manufacture 350 linear metres of these metal movable partitions for the Messageries Hachette building in Paris (see no.191). According to Jean Boutemain and Jean-Marie Glatigny, these partitions provided the financial basis of the J. Prouvé Workshops. It was a standardised industrial product that was easily adaptable to a variety of buildings; there were standard plans, layout plans for the fitters. The J. Prouvé Workshops bought square tube, small sections for the windows and cold-drawn sheet sections; these sections were cut, drilled and welded in the Workshops (Emile Marchal, 1991). Jean Prouvé (1983): "They were the first movable partitions to be fitted by tension springs. They were not fixed to the ceiling by anything other than the springs ... detachable, that's right ... everything was movable: the frames could take the place of the panels, and the panels of the frames. You could even place one panel above another, which made possible a great variety of arrangements ... that was made for the Messageries Hachette ... a big commission. There was a competition that I won ... in 1931." Model photographed in the workshop about 1931 (ill. 190a,7); photograph of a spring jack about 1931 (ill. 190a,8).

190b. Patent no. 721.105 "System of metal partitions with interchangeable components".
Entered 6 August 1931, granted 29 February 1932.

47

191. Work carried out for the Messageries Hachette, Paris. About 1931, then 1935 and 1939. Jean Démaret, architect.

191.1. Movable partitions. This is the first time the system of movable metal partitions (patent, see no. 190b) was used. The J. Prouvé Workshops made 350 linear metres of partitioning. Plans 809 to 812 are probably proposals (prototype for a space 2.00 x 2.00 m). The J. Prouvé Collection holds a large number of documents, especially plans of arrangement and details, dating from 1931, 1935 and 1939; they probably concern modifications and the provision of additional elements. Contemporary photograph of the prototype erected in the building during the competition (ill. 191.1,1); two photographs of the partitions about 1931 (ill. 191.1,2 and 191.1,3).

191.1,1

191.1,2

191.1,3

203.7,1

203.7,2

203.7,3

203. Work carried out at the Maison France, Ferdrupt. 1931. Charles Hindermeyer, architect; Chanaux, interior designer. Prouvé talked to us in 1982 about the gateways and gates of the Maison France; we visited and photographed the house in 1984, and M. France showed us other work done by Prouvé, as well as sculptures by Victor Prouvé and Ernest Wittmann, and Chanaux's furniture.

203.1. Gateways. Double gates constructed of steel sections and sheet mounted on tubing.

203.2. Grills. Five grills on the wall running along the Route Nationale, constructed of 35 x 15 mm flat plate horizontals, and 15 x 15 mm and 8 x 35 mm vertical sections, placed at 45°, electrically welded; door of the caretaker's house, similarly constructed.

203.7. Cloakroom. The discovery of the house cloakroom in polished stainless steel sheet was a complete surprise. It is one of Prouvé's master-pieces. This cloakroom has a built-in washbasin with a stainless steel lamp-fitting above it; the floor is carpeted. Overall view (ill. 203.7,1); detail with stainless steel sheet diffused-light fitting (ill. 203.7,2); detail of the frames of the large mirrors, and of the polished stainless steel hatrack with aluminium hooks (ill. 203.7,3).

204. Work carried out for the Hôpital Grange Blanche, Lyons. 1930–34. Tony Garnier, Durand and Faure, architects. The work done for this hospital occupied the J. Prouvé Workshops for some years, and in the J. Prouvé Collection there are about three hundred documents related to it: studies, construction plans, discussion notes. The first plans for lift cages date from 1930.

204.1. Operating theatres. The J. Prouvé Workshops (about fourty collaborators) manufactured twenty operating theatres made entirely of folded sheet, load-bearing components, sash windows, doors and partitions, which were transported to the hospital by rail and lorry. They assembled the first theatre, took note of the criticisms of the architect, Tony Garnier, and then produced the others in series. Jean Prouvé (1982/83, looking at the photographs): "It was very difficult to do because ... Garnier was very demanding about the quality of the work ... You entered the theatres through sliding doors ... Obviously I was responsible for all the details, the door handles ... It needed a lot of planning ... they gave me an empty space and I filled it ... I constructed this post, they filled in the window breast, all in sheet metal ... The windows are double-layered with a gap between them ... they all had opening and closing mechanisms (my brother-in-law and colleague André Schott was a skilful engineer) ... You changed the handle to open the outer and inner windows. That was real engineering, Grange Blanche!" Operating theatre, photograph of 1984 (ill. 204.1,1); interior view of one of the ground-floor theatres with inner and outer sash windows and glass roofing, about 1933 (ill. 204.1,2); photograph of the site about 1933, in which are clearly visible the double partitions and the double glazed roofs of the ground floor and first-floor operating units (ill. 204.1,3).

204.1,1

204.1,3

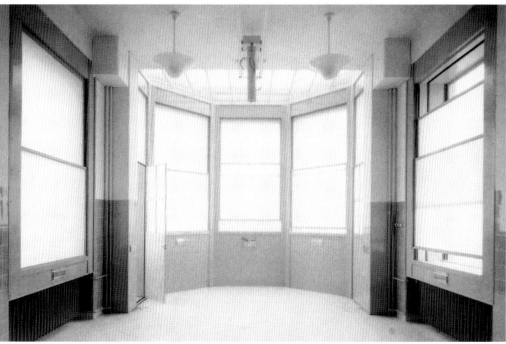

204.1,2

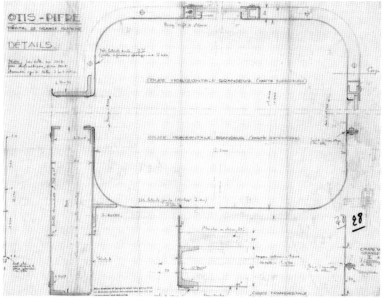

204.2,1

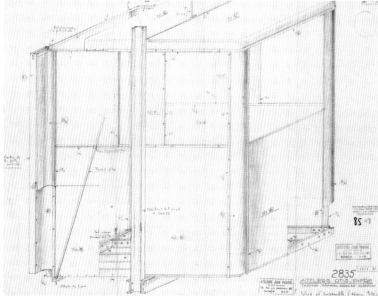

204.2,2

204.2,3

204.2. Lift cages. Planning for the lift cages of the Hôpital Grange Blanche (Otis-Pifre lifts) began in 1930: plans 757, 757.1, 757.2, 757.3. The J. Prouvé Workshops made twenty-three cages: fifteen standard A cages, four special B cages, three special C cages and one D cage. When we visited the hospital in 1988, there was still one Prouvé cage in Pavillon D. Unnumbered plan, probably drawn by Prouvé, dated 23 December 1930 (ill. 204.2,1); plan 2835, drawn by Prouvé, dated 13 January 1931 (ill. 204.2,2); photograph taken about 1933, which shows the two braces (30 mm diameter) drawn in the plan (ill. 204.2,3).

204.5. Work carried out for the operating unit of the Neuropsychiatric Building. In 1933, the J. Prouvé Workshops provided the operating unit of the Neuropsychiatric Building with double sash windows (plans 2803a and 2808) and sheet metal radiator casings (plan 2683). For this unit, the J. Prouvé Workshops developed a remarkable system of partitions with rounded corners; the principle was that the vertical joints never coincided with the corners. In 1933 this was something new! Jean Prouvé (1982): "A memory of the period of discoveries ... We made them immediately, probably not very economically, but with our digitally controlled folding machines of today ..."

205. Designs and work carried out at the former Palace of the General Government of Algeria, Algiers. 1931–34. Jacques Guiauchain, architect; Perret-Frères, contractors. The J. Prouvé Workshops did many studies and a great deal of work for this project; there are three hundred plans and sketches in the J. Prouvé Collection. Between 1932 and 1934, Prouvé's colleague Emile Marchal spent eighteen months in Algiers; the J. Prouvé Workshops used to send him plans, which he then discussed with the architect. He directed the installation of the components sent from Nancy, which were put in place by three assembly men and twelve Algerians. According to Bignon and Coley, the work was worth 14,000,000 francs; the problems caused by fragmented consignments and late payment led to a loss of 40,500 francs. When we visited the building in 1989, it housed the Central Office of the National Liberation Front and was in good condition – as was most of Prouvé's work. The lift cages had been replaced a few months previously and some partitions had been removed. Detail of a list headed "dispatch to Algiers" (see ill. no. 205.1, Complete Works).

205.1. Main entrance door. Glazed door in steel and stainless steel. There are several similar entrance doors in the building.

205.2. Staircase railings. Prouvé made several sketches for the rail of the principal staircase. The more modern proposals in stainless steel did not find favour, and more conventional railings were made. The bottom of the principal staircase rail, in steel section with a stainless steel handrail, is in perfect condition after more than fifty years. Sketch of a proposal in the modern style (ill. 205.2,1); photograph of the rail (ill. 205.2,2). There are two similar rails at the intersection of the wings of the building.

205.4. Large window bay. Sketch by Prouvé showing the hall with the large window bay (beam of uniform strength), on the garden side and with the principal staircase (ill. 205.4,1); photograph of the large bay in folded sheet looking on to the garden (ill. 205.4,2).

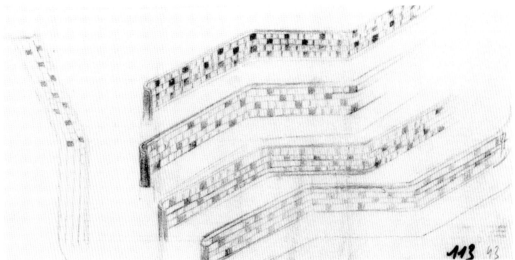

205.2,1

205.2,2

205.4,1

205.4,2

236,4

236,3

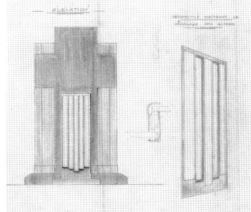

236,1

236. Door of the Hanus-Dillon family mausoleum, the cemetery at Charmes. About 1932. M. Rivenc, architect. André Hanus, owner of the Grande Brasserie de Charmes, had shares in the J. Prouvé Workshops. The door is made entirely of 1.5 mm stainless steel sheet, folded and polished, screwed on to steel flats 40 x 15 mm and 20 x 15 mm; the glazing is staggered. Even today this door seems astonishingly modern in style. During a conversation on 16 March 1989, Pierre Missey recalled making the door and remembered that there were difficulties with it: the metal shrank more than expected under polishing, and this caused fitting problems. Detail of plan 1433 with a sketch of the detail drawn by Prouvé (ill. 236,1); photographs (ill. 236,3 and 236,4).

255. Work carried out for the Musée de Zoologie, Nancy.

1932/33. Jacques and Emile André, architects. The André brothers and Jean Prouvé co-operated well together; the Musée de Zoologie was one of their first joint ventures.

255.1. Doors. The J. Prouvé Workshops made four glazed entrance doors that started as a series of plans for doors with a motif of diagonal bars with wrought-iron plates. They were constructed of a frame in sections and flat bar and cover strips of folded sheet, mounted on tube hinging, with aluminium finger plates and cast aluminium handles. Three of the four doors have been removed. Photograph of the entrance door to no. 32, rue Sainte-Catherine in 1986 (ill. 255.1,6); photograph of the door to the garden in 1991 (ill. 255.1,7).

255.2. Staircase railings. There are three staircase railings in this building. Photograph of the start of the main staircase, with stainless steel tubing handrail (ill. 255.2,1).

255.1,7

255.1,6

255.2,1

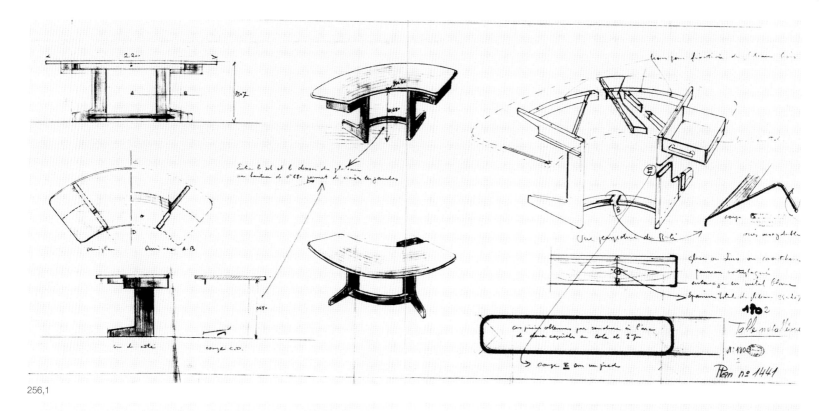

256,1

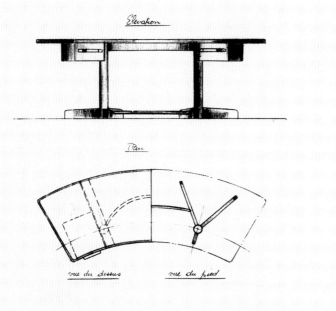

256,2

256. Metal table (curved desk). 1932. This is probably Prouvé's first desk. It has a curved laminated top covered with plate glass, linoleum or rubber, with a white-metal surround, a frame of 3 mm folded sheet steel, arc-welded; the pedestal is covered with stainless-steel plate, the drawers are sheet metal. Plan 1441 (ill. 256,1) is a typical Prouvé drawing: the perspective section contains all the technical details, but with added functional points: "a height of 0.680 m between the ground and the top of the desk will allow for crossing the legs". Plan 1442, drawn by Jean-Marie Glatigny, is a variant with a different pedestal (ill. 256,2). We do not know whether the J. Prouvé Workshops made a prototype, but Prouvé later made several variants of curved desks.

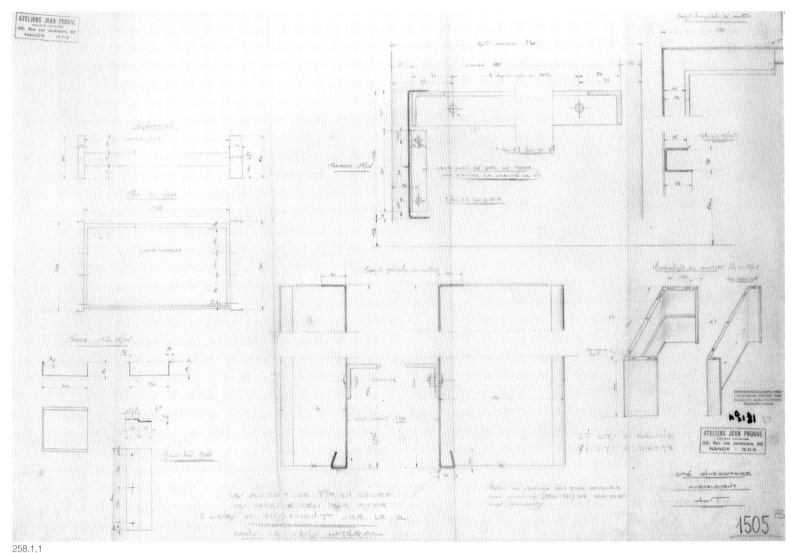

258.1,1

258. Furniture for the Cité Universitaire, Nancy.
1930–32. Prouvé (1982/83): "... That's the armchair for the Cité Universitaire competition ... We entered an armchair, a bed, a table, a chair and a bookshelf. I landed a quarter of the competition, a quarter of the rooms and these were the only pieces of furniture that withstood student use ... that was perhaps 1930 ..." Prototypes for the competition were made in 1930, probably in the workshop in the rue du General Custine; the production run came from the Workshops of the rue des Jardiniers in 1932. This run consisted of fifty-five chairs, sixty sets of shelving, sixty tables and fifty-four beds; the exact number of armchairs is not known (see no. 258.5). The furniture has been replaced and dispersed; a few examples exist in private collections. Model room with prototypes: photograph about 1932 of a student room with Prouvé's original furniture (ill. 258,3); plan 1671 with number and references for the wooden items.

258.1. Bed for the Cité Universitaire. Folded
sheet head and footboard, folded-sheet frame sides (not yet closed triangular sections!). At the head, a shelf 35 x 125 cm projecting beyond the sides to form a bedside table with a metal drawer and intermediate shelf; at the foot, shelf 16 x 95, waxed oak shelves, rounded edges. Height 60 cm, mattress springing 193 x 93 cm. Plan 1505B, twenty-seven left-hand beds, twenty-seven right-hand beds (ill. 258.1,1). There are many variants, often misdated: divan bed no. 10 (prospectus about 1935), "Cité" bed of the 50s.

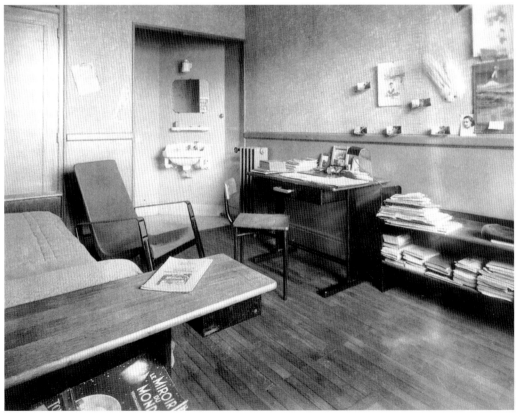

258,3

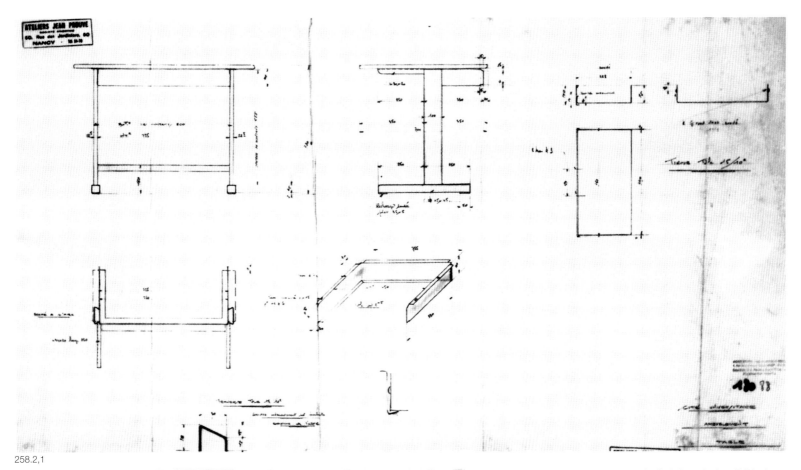

258.2,1

258.2,2

258.2. Table for the Cité Universitaire. Folded sheet base and drawer, two uprights in the shape of an open "C", feet in 45 mm square tube, folded-sheet pedestal, cast aluminium handle (Bezault). Height 73 cm, massive oak top 70 x 100 cm. Plan 1506 (ill. 258.2,1); photograph of the table with chair (ill. 258.2,2). Prouvé used one of these tables during the last months of his life. There are many variants, often misdated: table no. 20 (prospectus about 1935), "Cité" table no. 501 of the 50s.

258.3,2

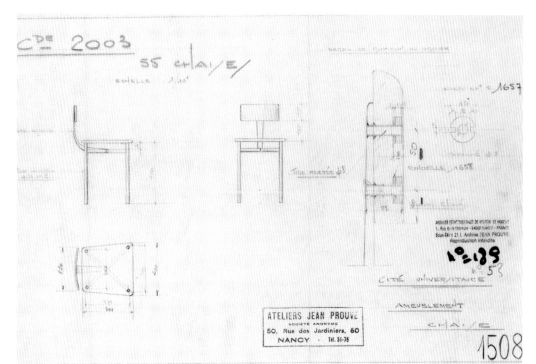

258.4,1

258.3. Shelving for the Cité Universitaire. Made differently from the prototype. Height 70.6 cm, width 100 cm; uprights of 1.5 mm folded sheet, 22.5 cm deep, spot-welded, two waxed oak shelves. Photograph taken in 1990 (ill. 258.3,2). Variants were made later.

258.4. Chair for the Cité Universitaire. Frame in 25 mm diameter welded boiler tube, massive oak seat and back. The back is fixed by two special nuts to an arm in form of uniform strength, in folded sheet or compressed tube. Plan 1508 (ill. 258.4,1); photographs of the chair in 1992 (ill. 258.4,2 to 258.4,5).

258.4,2

258.4,3

258.4,4

258.4,5

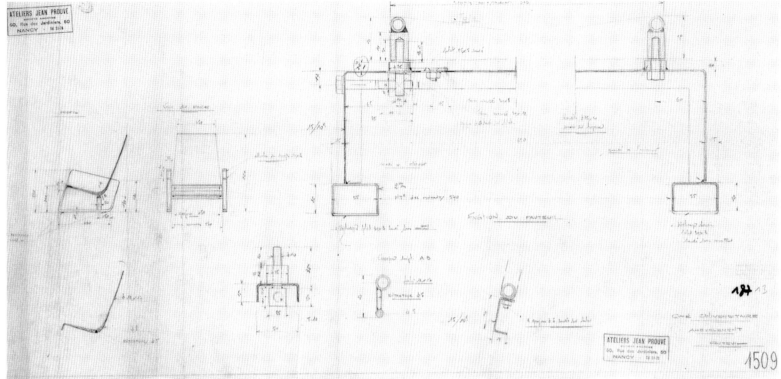

258.5,1

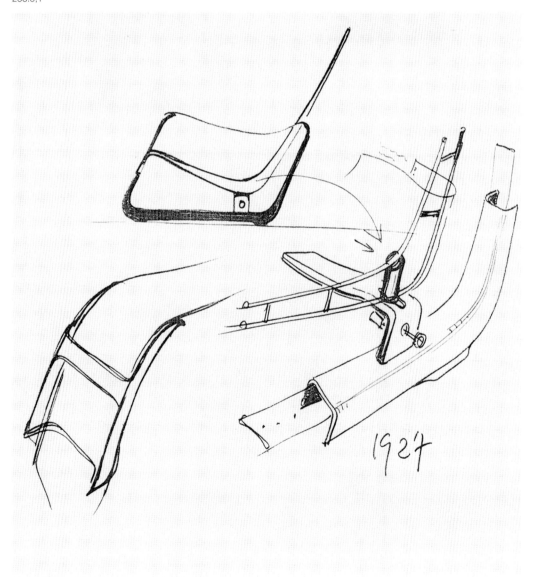

258.5,3

258.5. Armchair for the Cité Universitaire. The frame is entirely shaped sheet metal; the open channel uprights (uniform strength) are surrounded by canvas arms, but not completely as in the variants. The frame of the seat and back is of 12/17 mm tube, reinforced by 8 mm diameter round bar, joined by 5 mm struts and with stretched canvas. The canvas is stretched by means of rubber strips; screw adjusters regulate the tension (screw visible on the left side). Plan 1509 (ill. 258.5,1); sketch explaining the principle, drawn by Prouvé in 1964/65 for the magazine *Intérieur* – the dating 1927 is incorrect (ill. 258.5,3). There are several variants of this comfortable and elegant armchair produced in the 30s (ill. 258.5,4) and reproduced in our own day.

259,1

259. Armchair. After 1932. Variant of metal armchair no. 258.5: the arms (canvas or leather straps) completely surround the uprights; they are adjusted by a buckle. The crosspiece joining the sides is curved towards the bottom. Photograph of the frame alone (ill. 259,1).

260. Armchair. After 1932. Variant of metal chair no. 258.5. The vertical uprights are of closed-section folded sheet. Plan 4099, drawn 30 January 1935 by Jean-Marie Glatigny: armchair without screw adjustment but with seat tension springs; photographs taken at Prouvé's home in Nancy of a variant with an adjustment screw and leather arms (ill. 260,2 and 260,3).

260,2

260,3

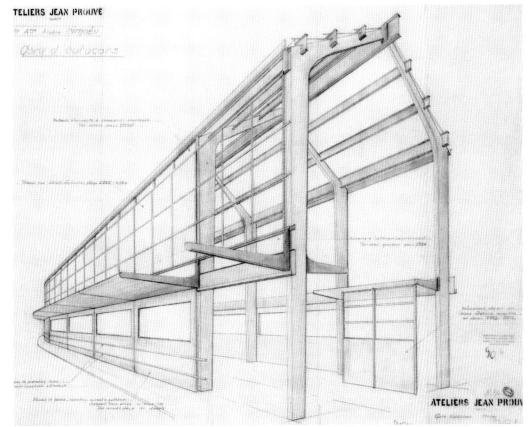

270.1,1

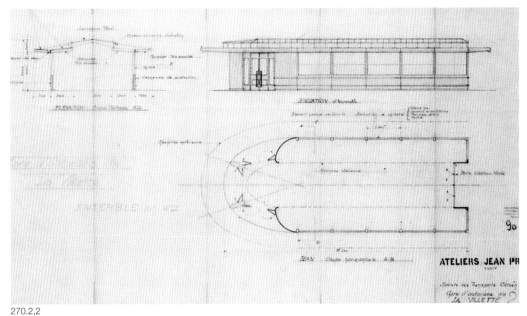

270.2,2

270. Design for the coach station at La Villette, Paris. 1933. Société de Transports Citroën, Maurice Ravazé, architect. The work was never carried out. This design, the first for buildings made entirely of folded sheet metal, was very important for Prouvé. Jean Prouvé (1982/83), while talking about the Maison du Peuple at Clichy (1936–39): "In fact, panels like this had already been designed in my workshops for the coach station buildings ... at La Villette. I remember completely doing all the drawings for the Citroën buildings, using the same techniques and achieving an effect rather unusual for the period." There are thirty-one plans related to this project in the J. Prouvé Collection. It consists of two buildings, the coach station proper and the waiting room with facilities for the sale of tickets. We do not know exactly why this project was not realised.

270.1. Design for the coach station. Plan 2341, drawn by Jean-Marie Glatigny, with portal frames in folded sheet closed sections of uniform strength, a large window-wall above, sheet metal awnings and panels on the ground floor (ill. 270.1,1). This unit consists of an outer layer of folded sheet with two channels, and an inner layer, the sash (unframed glass, as used later by Prouvé) is lowered into the window-breast. The width of the panel was probably limited by the lifting-table press which could only fold 3 m. Plan 2343, with detail of stanchion/panel later used at Buc; detail of plan 2338, one of the first examples of functional integration: frame, rainwater pipe and heating pipe are integrated with the sign. Prouvé designed other units: door, booking office, ...

270.2. Design for the waiting room. The design office drew two variants for this building. Plan 2539 shows a rectangular building with a low-pitched roof and an enormous advertisement hoarding, but there were already different designs in plan 2479 and plan 2480 (ill. 270.2,2): pairs of folded sheet "crutches" with inner and outer awnings and a central lantern light. Prouvé used similar "crutches" for IRSID (Institut de Recherche de la Sidérurgie Française, Saint-Germain-en-Laye) in 1949, for the pump room at Evian in 1954, etc. Plan 2540 of 9 June 1932: extended section; we should note that all the façade elements are interchangeable. In the J. Prouvé Collection, there are also two plans (plans 3073 and 3074) for metal building-fittings for the North and South pavilions, which are of traditional construction.

1

2

1. The Town Hall of Boulogne-Billancourt 1933–35. Interior
   view, condition in 1998 (see no. 340).
2. The Town Hall of Boulogne-Billancourt 1933–35. Counters in
   1998, after the restoration (see no. 340).

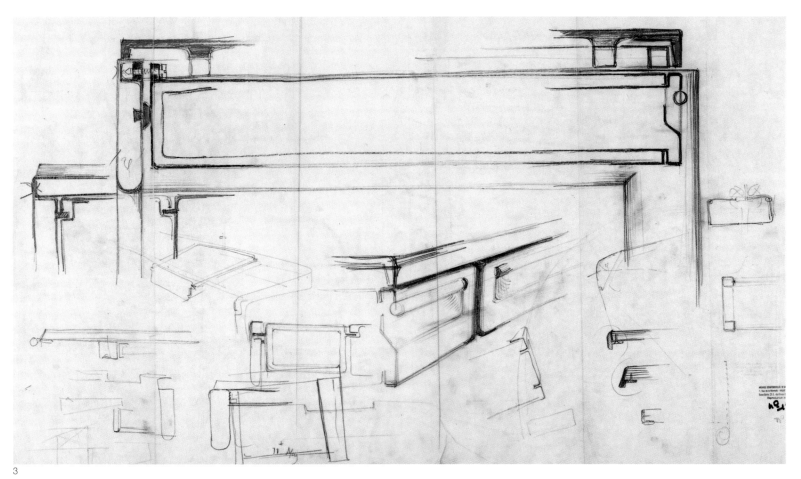

3

4

3. Furniture for the Compagnie Parisienne de Distribution
   d'Electricité, 1934/35. C.P.D.E. desks, sketch by Jean
   Prouvé (see no. 396).
4. Furniture for the Compagnie Parisienne de Distribution
   d'Electricité, 1934/35. C.P.D.E. typing table (see no. 397).

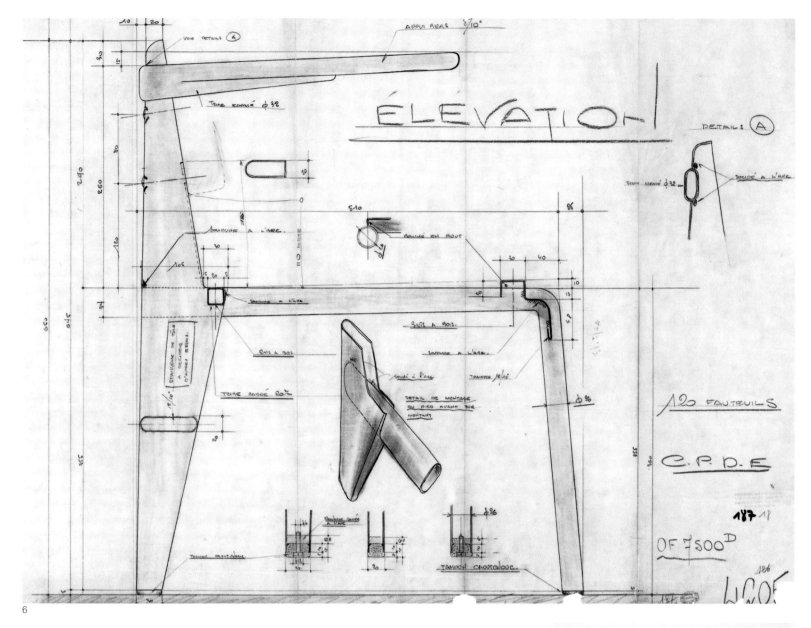

6

5. Furniture for the Compagnie Parisienne de Distribution
d'Electricité, 1934/35. C.P.D.E. armchair (see no. 403).
6. Furniture for the Compagnie Parisienne de Distribution
d'Electricité, 1934/35. C.P.D.E. armchair, drawing of 1935
(see no. 403).
7. J. Prouvé Workshops brochure, after 1934 (see no. 404).
8. Office chair with seat and back in solid wood. Drawing of
1934 (see no. 404).
9. Office chair with seat and back in solid wood. Design for
back legs, undated sketch (see no. 404).
10. Chair no. 4, 1935 (see no. 405).

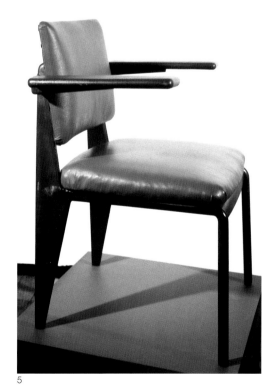

5

7

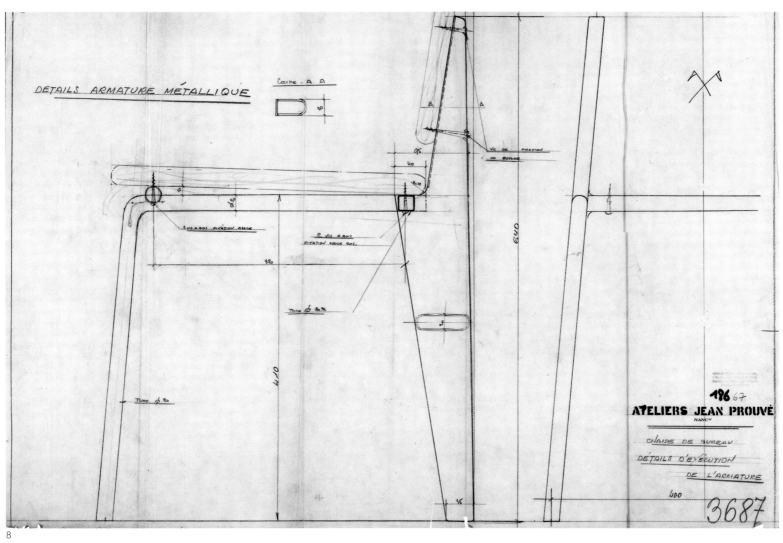

DÉTAILS ARMATURE MÉTALLIQUE

COUPE. A.A

ATELIERS JEAN PROUVÉ
NANCY

CHAISE DE BUREAU

DÉTAILS D'EXÉCUTION

DE L'ARMATURE

3687

8

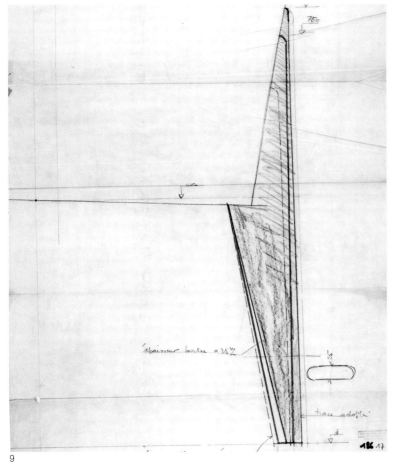

9

10

11

12

13

11. Lecture hall seats for the Ecole des Sciences Politiques, Paris, 1934 (see no. 442.a).
12. Lecture hall seats for the Ecole des Sciences Politiques, Paris, 1934. Detail (see no. 442.a).
13. Furniture for the boarding school of the lycée of Metz, 1935. Metal beds, photographed in 1987 (see 534.1).
14. Furniture for the boarding school of the lycée of Metz, 1935. One of the beds, exhibited at the Galerie Jousse-Seguin in 1996 (see no. 534.1).

14

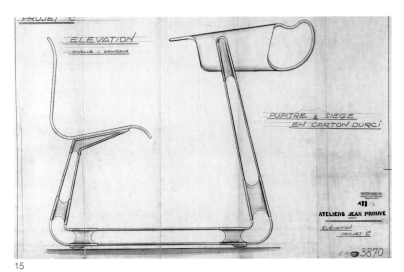

15

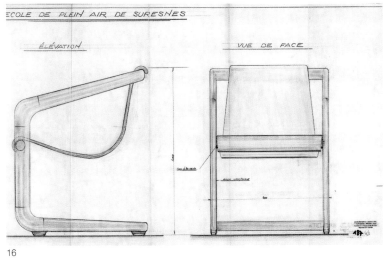

16

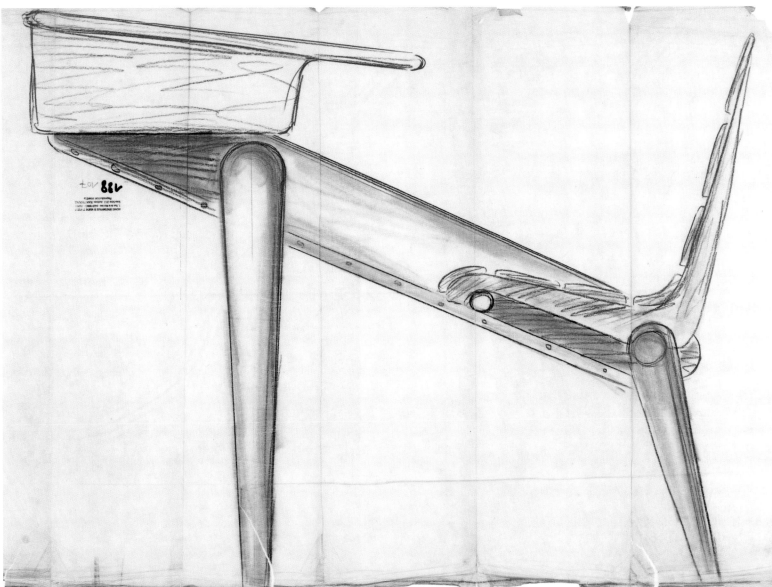

17

15. Designs for furniture for the Open-air School of Suresnes,
1934. Single-seater pupil's desk in stainless steel
(see no. 483).

16. Design for furniture for the Open-air School of Suresnes,
1934. Nursery school armchair in stainless steel
(see no. 485).

17. Two-seater classroom table, 1935. Sketch by Jean Prouvé
(see no. 545.5).

18

19

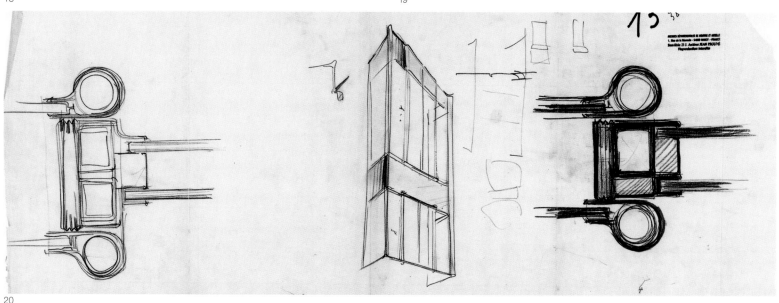

20

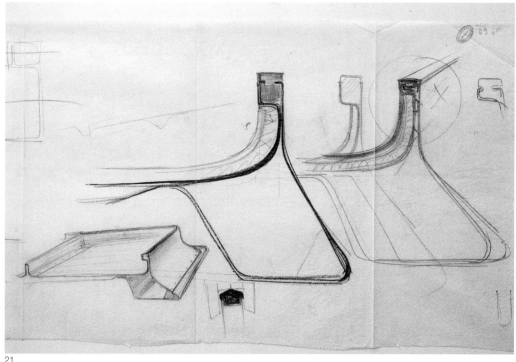

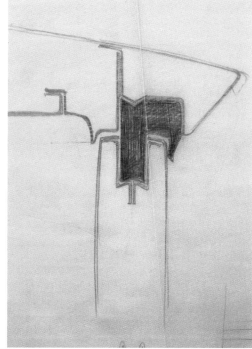

21

22

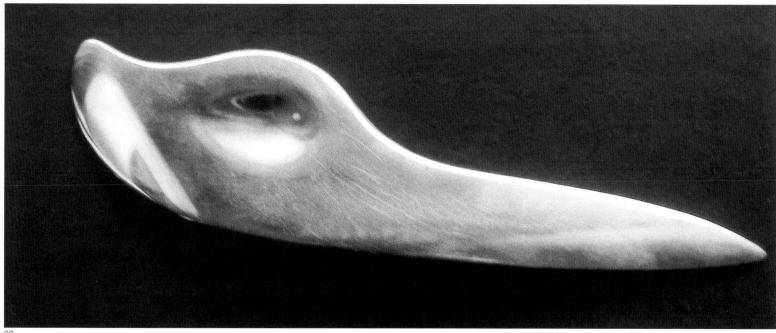

23

18. Design for a newspaper kiosk, 1935. Sketch by Jean
    Prouvé (see no. 565,2).
19. Sanatorium bed with integrated bedside table, 1936
    (see no. 612.1).
20. French Legation in Ottawa, 1936–38. Bow-window in
    bronze, sketch by Jean Prouvć (scc no. 716.3).
21. B.L.P.S. demountable house, 1937/38. Detail of the floor,
    sketch by Jean Prouvé (see no. 715.5).
22. B.L.P.S. demountable house, 1937/38. Detail of
    assembly (see no. 715.6).
23. Stainless steel paper-knife (see no. 731).

24

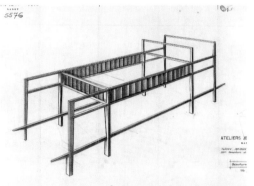

25

24. The Maison du Peuple at Clichy, 1935–39. Condition in
    1998, during the restoration (see no. 704).
25. The Maison du Peuple at Clichy, 1935–39. Design for the
    folded sheet frame, sketch by Jean Prouvé (see no. 704,4).
26. The Maison du Peuple at Clichy, 1935–39. Facade of the
    shopping gallery, condition in 1998, after the restoration
    (see no. 704).

26

27

28

29

27. The Maison du Peuple at Clichy, 1935–39. Facade of the shopping gallery, condition in 1998, after the restoration (see no. 704).

28. and 29. The Maison du Peuple at Clichy, 1935–39. Facade of the shopping gallery, condition in 1995, before the restoration (see no. 704).

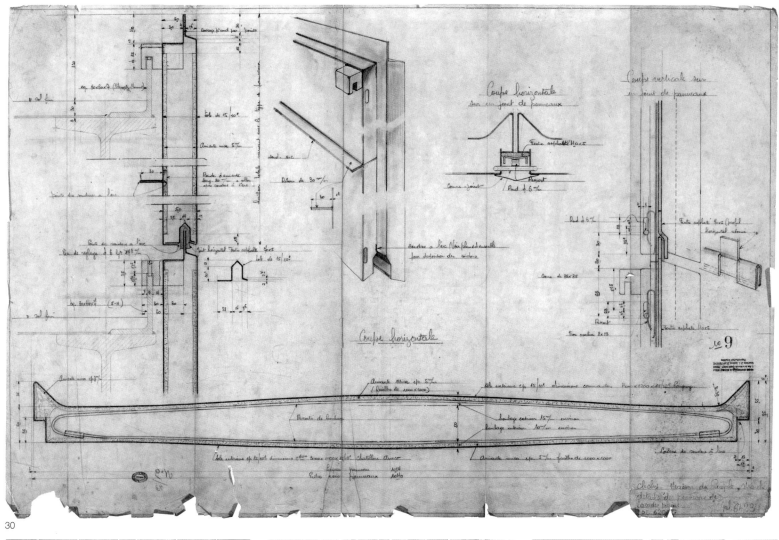

30

31

32

33

35

36

34

30. The Maison du Peuple at Clichy, 1935–39. Facade of the offices, construction plan drawn by Jean Boutemain on 15 June 1937 (see no. 704,26).
31. The Maison du Peuple at Clichy, 1935–39. Facade of the offices, condition in 1995 (see no. 704).
32. The Maison du Peuple at Clichy, 1935–39. Facade of the offices with awning, condition in 1982 (see no. 704).
33. The Maison du Peuple at Clichy, 1935–39. Detail of the facade in 1998, after restoration (see no. 704).
34. to 36. The Maison du Peuple at Clichy, 1935–39. Facade of the offices, condition in 1998, after restoration (see no. 704).

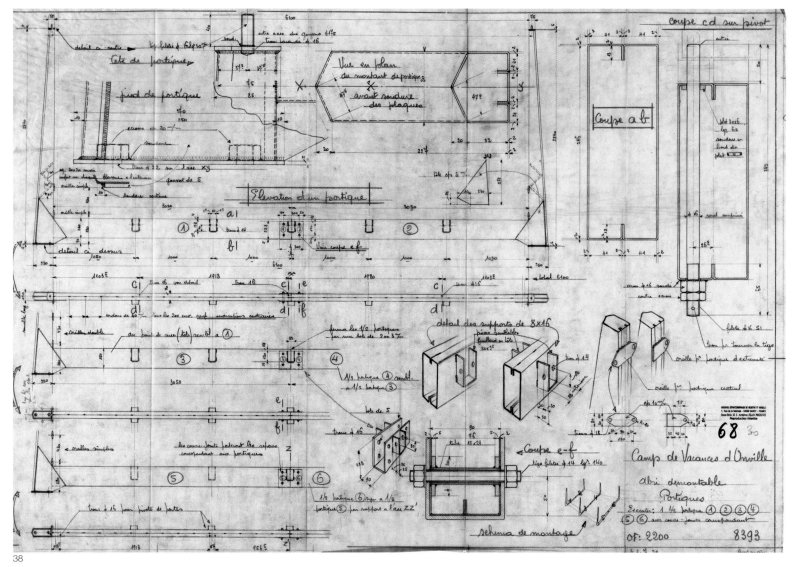

38

37. Rolling table, special order, about 1939 (see no. 815).
38. Holiday camp of Onville, 1939. Construction plan for the
    portal arches (see no. 828,4).
39. Demountable barracking for le Génie, 1939. Plan 8594
    (see no. 850).
40. Entrance box for the Ferembal factory, 1943/44.
    Photograph taken during an exhibition of the works of Jean
    Prouvé in Ludwigsburg in 1998 (see no. 943).

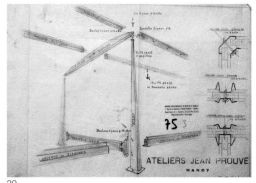

39

40

37

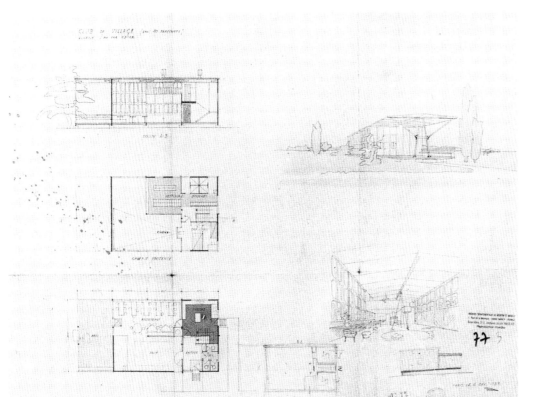

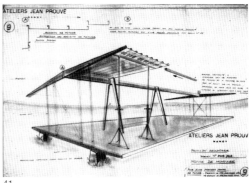

41. Works carried out for the Société Centrale des Alliages Légers (S.C.A.L.) in Issoire, 1939/40. Installation of portal frame pavilions (see no. 854,16).
42. Works carried out for the Société Centrale des Alliages Légers (S.C.A.L.) in Issoire, 1939/40. Club pavilion, drawing by Pierre Jeanneret, sketch by Jean Prouvé (see no. 854.b,1).
43. Works carried out for the Société Centrale des Alliages Légers (S.C.A.L.) in Issoire, 1939/40. Club pavilion, detail of the portal frames (see no. 854.b,3).

41

42

43

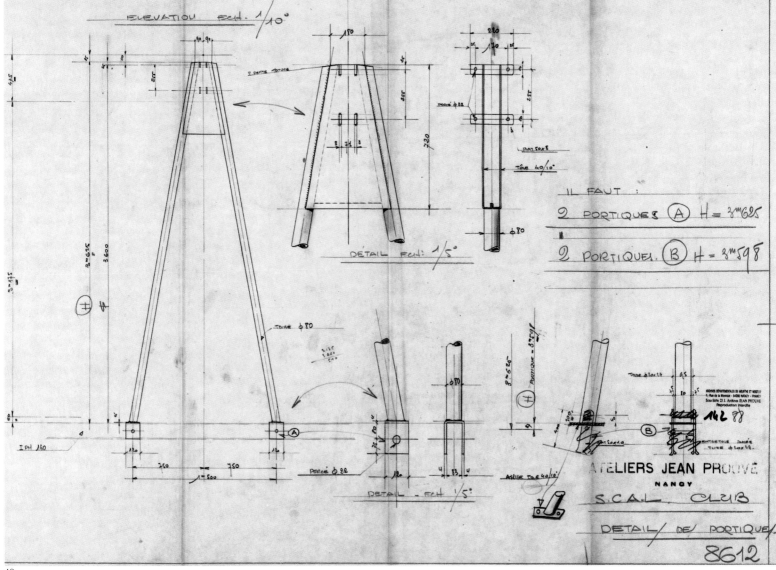

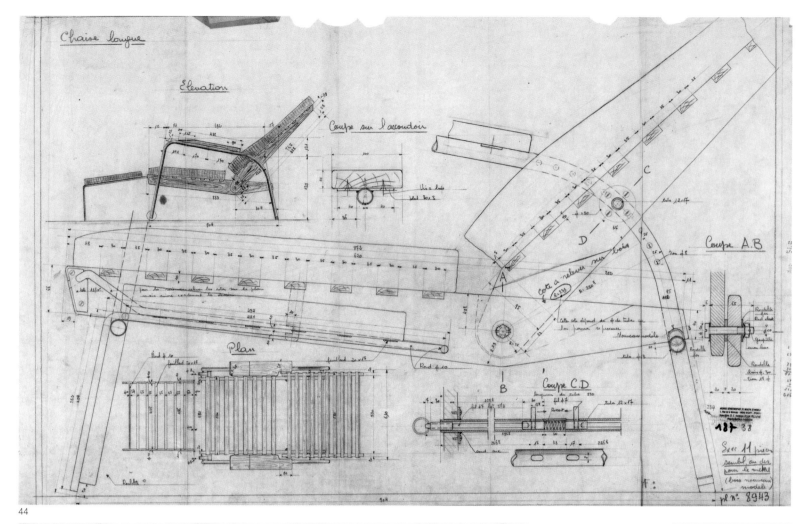
44

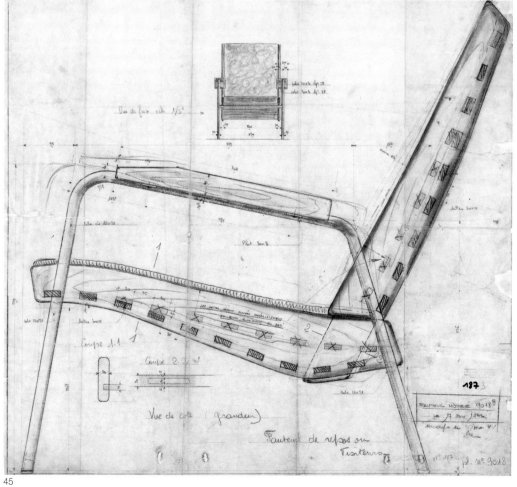
45

46

44. Chaise longue, 1941. Construction plan (see no. 883.e,8).
45. "Easy, or visitor's, chair", 1942, modified in 1943 and 1944 (see no. 912,2).
46. One of the first easy, or visitor's, chairs between 1942 and 1944 (see no. 912,4).
47. Chair entirely in wood, 1942 (see no. 915,2).
48. Chair entirely in wood, variant (see no. 915,3).
49. Table with plate-glass slab, 1944 (see no. 963).

47

48

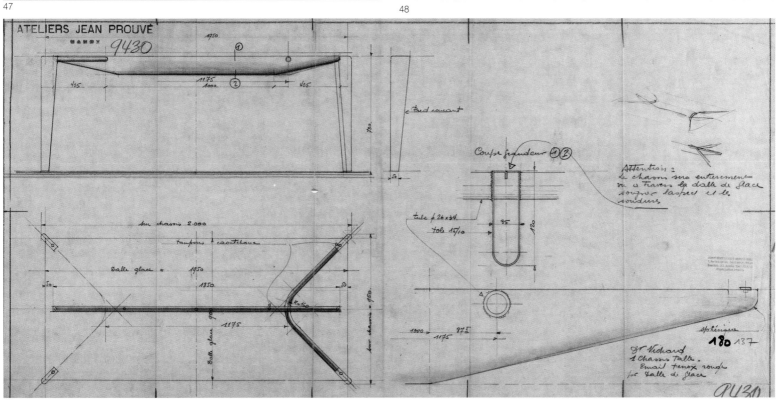

49

288. Designs and works for the Compagnie Parisienne de Transport building, Paris. 1933/34. At a price of 173,400 francs, this was a medium-size job for the J. Prouvé Workshops, which, according to Jean-Claude Bignon and Catherine Coley, made a considerable loss on it. Photograph of the building taken in 1987 before alteration (ill. 288). The J. Prouvé Workshops designed and made a number of components: seventy-seven sash windows with fixed parts, six curved bays, side-opening windows; twenty pivoting bull's-eye windows, a steel and stainless steel entrance door on the boulevard Diderot, the entrance vestibule, lift shaft protection and the rail, folded sheet electricity cable housing, a design for the glazing of the stairwell, a design for a metal door.

288

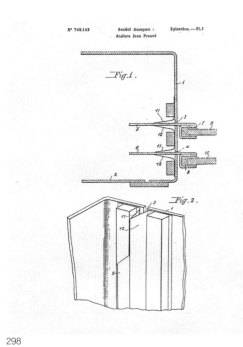

298

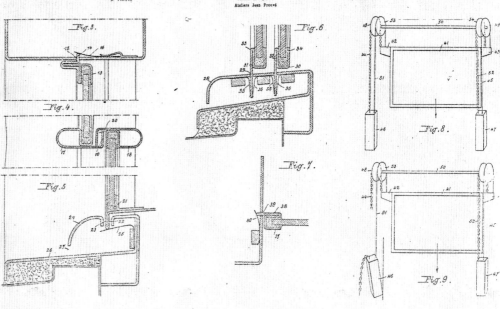

298. Patent no. 784.143, improvements to sliding windows. Patent application entered on 28 December 1932 and published on 29 June 1933.

337,1

337. Caves de la Craffe in Nancy. 1933–35. The frontage and awning in folded sheet, and internal conversion to a design by the J. Prouvé Workshops. Jean Prouvé in a conversation with Jean-Marie Helwig (1982/83): "…it was designed in a special way. There was an old wooden shop, with a wooden shop window and mouldings, and the owner wanted to modernise his business completely. He ordered this window from me and it was made in a single piece…the awning was ordered at the same time. That is a drip moulding for the water to flow away… I think the only joints we had were here, because of the transport problems. There was a joint here, you see, and a joint there. There were two sections, the upper and the lower, and that's a door to the cellar…It's a shop (designed) like the body of a vehicle, absolutely. It's quite near the station, I don't know whether it still exists. It's a 'false frontage' window: we didn't demolish the old shop, we just covered it up. It was one of the first occasions on which I used stainless steel…these bars here are round bars in stainless steel…the same height as people, and acting as a protection. …and it was painted in burgundy red. Then we had the idea of putting a trellis here to hang the bottles on". Contemporary photograph (ill. 337,1). The construction plans date from 1934.

340. Designs and works carried out for the Town Hall of Boulogne-Billancourt. 1933–35. Tony Garnier, architect, with the collaboration of the architect, M. Debat-Ponsan. The building was opened on 15 December 1934 by André Morizet, senator and mayor. Photograph of 1998 showing the central hall with the administrative departments distributed over four levels (ill. 340,1).The building and the works carried out by the J. Prouvé Workshops were carefully restored by the architect Dominique Châtelet during the 90s. In the J. Prouvé Collection there are approximately 170 plans. Studies and work carried out by the J. Prouvé Workshops for this Town Hall: design for a lantern above the main staircase and glazed ceiling;

340,1

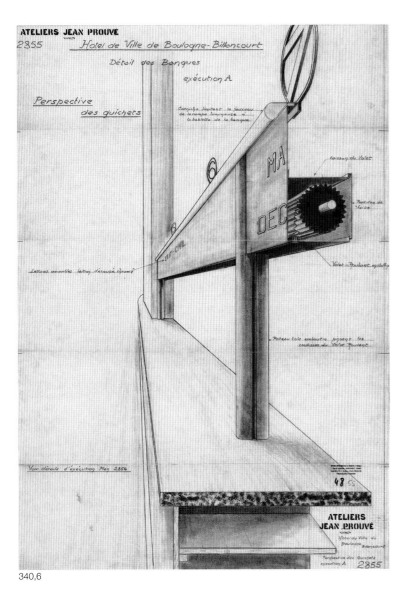

340,6

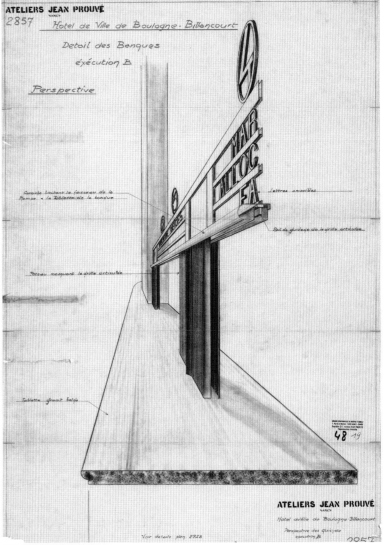

340,7

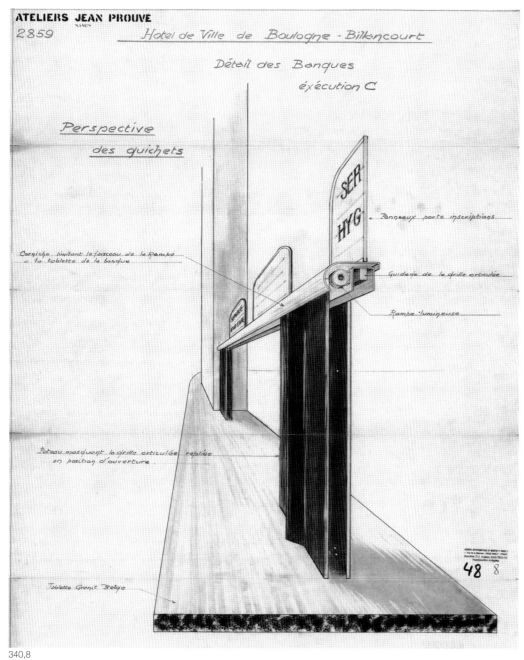

ATELIERS JEAN PROUVÉ
NANCY

2859

Hôtel de Ville de Boulogne-Billancourt

Détail des Banques

éxécution C

Perspective
des guichets

340,8

340,10

design for external building fittings, carried out by Schwartz-Haumont; design for a revolving door, a garage door, non-operable windows for the service stairs, low metal partitions. For the counters, which were open at the start, Jean Prouvé proposed three variants drawn in perspective: plan 2855, version A, with rolling blind (ill. 340,6); plan 2857: version B, with articulated grill and movable letters (ill. 340,7); plan 2859, version C (ill. 340,8). At the start of 1935, the J. Prouvé Workshops studied the possibility of closing in the counters with sliding plate glass or sash windows. The banks and windows were closed in during the years 1936/37: photograph of the counters after restoration (ill. 340,10).

For the movable partitions between the hall, the wedding hall and the council room (approximately 8 m high), the J. Prouvé Workshops made many studies and reached a practicable solution. In the J. Prouvé Collection there are several sketches by Jean Prouvé. On plan 3084, drawn by Jean-Marie Glatigny (ill. 340,12), we can see the principle of the box frame (perforated 8/10 sheet) and the "Plymax" covering, gilded according to the architects' instructions; contemporary photograph (ill. 340,14); letter box; stair windows and swing door between the hall and the stair; construction plan 3893: transom bar of uniform strength, dated November 1934 and drawn by Jean Boutemain (ill. 340,15); shaft protection for book lift; lift shaft protection (unfortunately demolished); filing cabinets and lockers delivered in 1936/37.

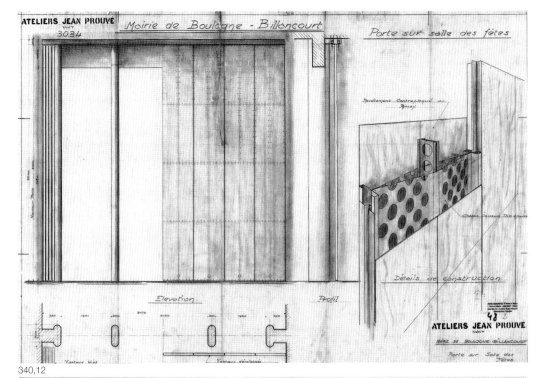

340,12

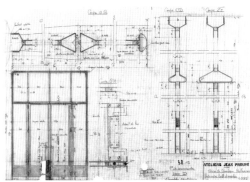

340,15

340,14

353,8

353,1

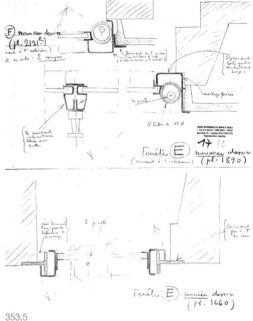

353,5

353. Designs and works carried out for the Cité de la Muette, Drancy. 1932–39. The public housing office of the Department of the Seine, Henri Sellier, client. Eugène Beaudouin and Marcel Lods, architects. E. Mopin, design office; collaborator, V. Bodiansky, engineer. The Cité de la Muette, an important example of modern architecture, has a sinister past: a Nazi concentration camp during the Second World War, it was from here that trains left for Auschwitz. There is a commemorative monument on "the Square", the only part of the Cité that still exists. The buildings were constructed in mixed steel and concrete prefabrication, in accordance with the Mopin process. For the J. Prouvé Workshops this was the largest order of the 30s and the start of the collaboration between Marcel Lods and Jean Prouvé. The J. Prouvé Workshops designed and made metal building fittings for all the constituent parts: towers and buildings in comb formation (folded sheet frame made by Schwartz-Haumont), stepped buildings, central boiler house and factory, as well as for the Square and the alterations of 1938/39. According to Jean-Claude Bignon and Catherine Coley, the J. Prouvé Workshops were not alone in this work: "At Drancy, ADCLO (5,000 metal door frames) and Schwartz-Haumont…" The design office produced approximately seven hundred designs and plans for Drancy, and these are preserved in the J. Prouvé Collection. In the framework of this book we can present only a few examples. Prouvé's first studies were for the towers and the buildings in comb formation, contemporary photograph (ill. 353,1). For the towers the J. Prouvé Workshops designed and carried out: two hundred and eighty sliding windows type A; a hundred and forty sliding windows type H with shutters, manufactured by the Compagnie Industrielle et Minière du Nord et Alpes; a hundred and forty windows type E, side-opening kitchen bays, two sketches by Jean Prouvé "old and new design" (ill. 353,5); window sashes types G and J; two hundred and eighty bathroom sashes type L; large bays for the stairwells; kitchen doors; ground floor doors; two hundred and eighty doors for the community rooms; a hundred and fifty lift doors; various doors, rails, etc…

Among the designs and works by the J. Prouvé Workshops for the buildings in comb formation we find: sliding windows type A; French windows type B with shutters (photograph taken at the U.A.M. exhibition at the Musée des Arts Décoratifs in 1988/89, (ill. 353,8); three hundred and ten window sashes type F, twenty window ensembles type I for the workshops; three hundred window sashes type K; glazed swing doors; fifty stair doors; folded sheet garage doors; large bays for stairwells; balconies; six hundred kitchen doors; various doors, balcony rails, etc… For the boiler house the J. Prouvé Workshops designed window sashes, sliding windows and balustrades; they probably also made window bars. For the factory the J. Prouvé Workshops designed doors, balustrades, various protective components, sliding doors, but most of the designs probably remained unrealised. For the stepped building the J. Prouvé Workshops designed or made: doors on the staircase, two hundred and forty-nine sash windows; side-opening windows; approximately 600 m balustrades; seventy-five kitchen entrances and gas housing; various doors. In 1938/39 the J. Prouvé Workshops were again involved in designs or works that related to finishing the alteration of the buildings into a barracks for the riot police: main stairway, windows and doors, rails and protective elements, etc. For the building called "the Square", the J. Prouvé

Workshops designed and carried out: a hundred and eighty-four sliding French windows type AP with two sliding leaves; three hundred and sixty-eight sliding windows type BP with sliding shutter; glazed doors; stairwell bays, etc. In 1938/39 the J. Prouvé Workshops took part in a study for the fitting up of this building for temporary teaching purposes.

392. Studies and works carried out for the "Vienne-Rocher" building of the Compagnie Parisienne de Distribution d'Electricité S.A. (C.P.D.E.). 1934/35. Urbain Cassan, architect (on the relationship between Urbain Cassan and Jean Prouvé, see Jean-Claude Bignon and Catherine Coley 1990, p. 99). On this project for the C.P.D.E., the J. Prouvé Workshops were in competition with several large companies and they made a considerable effort: the design office drew approximately a hundred and thirty plans. Prouvé proposed a complete design in the form of a perspective with description of the component parts (ill. 392,1). Plan 2944 is a study by Jean Prouvé for a "panel" partition very different from that of the Prouvé patent (see Complete Works, no. 190), perhaps influenced by the architect Urbain Cassan. Plan 3002 is a proposal for a panel partition in sheet, joined to the suspended ceiling by diamond pointed components, and fixed with a central screw "E". Jean Prouvé also proposed a system of cupboards in sheet linked to the ceiling and the partitions. The partitions and cupboards were manufactured by the S.A. des Forges de Strasbourg (Snead patent), and perhaps partly by the J. Prouvé Workshops (see Jean-Claude Bignon and Catherine Coley 1990, p. 87). The company Borderel et Robert made the radiator covers. On the fifth floor, for the offices of the directors – MM Dessus and Sartre – the J. Prouvé Workshops made, after numerous studies, sliding doors in stainless steel "…of a revolutionary technique, the steel used being very thin sheet (6/10 mm), shaped by folding, so as to create resistance-welded tubular sections" (Prouvé: Une architecture par l'industrie, p. 182). Construction plan 4055 (ill. 392,7). In a conversation with the author in 1989, Jean-Marie Glatigny, who made the study, commented "…not of the best quality…from the point of view of watertightness… at that time stainless steel was not being worked". In another conversation with the author at Gleisweiler in July 1991, Jean-Marie Glatigny explained that the stainless steel sheets were folded on a rubber lifting table to prevent imprints on the sheet. Plan 4747, dated September 1935 and headed "equipment for 2 bays with 5 leaves sliding on staunchness strips" shows how to ameliorate the problem. When the author visited in October 1988, the doors were still in existence; they were in good condition, but sashes had been added, recent photographs (ill. 392,9 and 392,10). For the office of the Chairman of the C.P.D.E., the J. Prouvé Workshops carried out thirteen sliding doors in stainless steel sheet, after presenting a prototype; the open leaves retracted into the wall. Among other studies relating to this building: design for the office, including furniture, of M. Dessus; design for a letter carrier; design for a movable grill for a lighted rail; construction of a glazed double door in folded sheet.

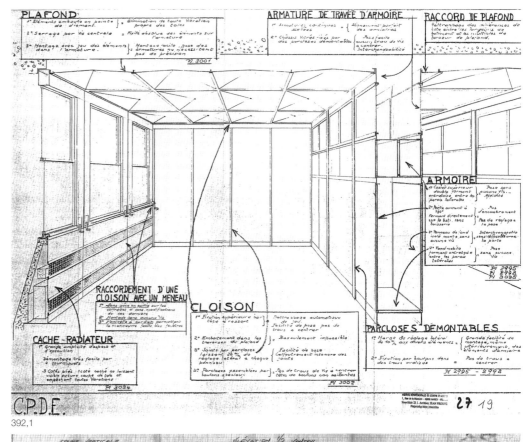

392,1

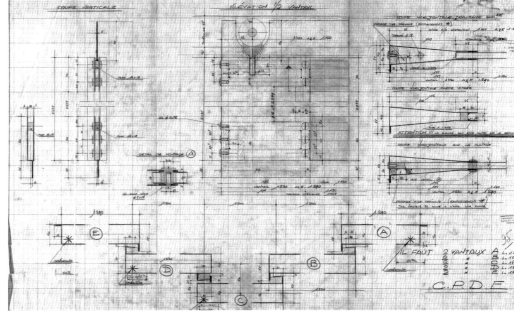

392,7

392,9

392,10

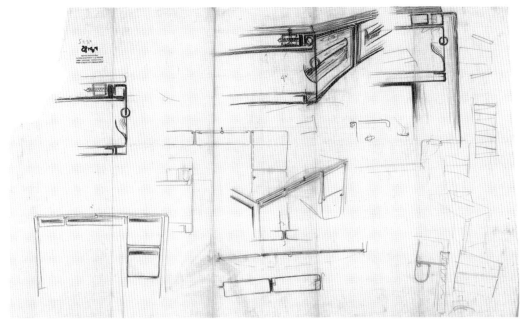

396,2

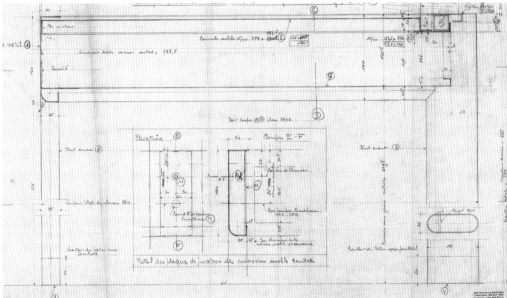

396,5

396,7

396. Variably equipped desks for the Compagnie Parisienne de Distribution d'Electricité S.A. 1934/35. The J. Prouvé Workshops took part in the competition for furniture for the offices of the C.P.D.E. at the corner of the rue de Vienne and the rue Rocher (see no. 392). In the J. Prouvé Collection there are approximately thirty drawings, two of which are sketches by Jean Prouvé in black, red, and blue pencil (ill. 396,2). There were apparently two prototypes, and four plans are still in existence relating to the second prototype (horizontal section of the drawers). From August to December 1934 Jean-Marie Glatigny drew about twenty construction plans, among others, plan 3905: frames of desks 2, 3 and 4, cross-section (ill. 396,5). A sketch drawn on 10 December 1934 gives the dimensions of frame no. 1 (1400/840/755), of frames no. 2, 3 and 4 (1680/840/755), and the frame of the typing table (1400/550/755). For the C.P.D.E., the J. Prouvé Workshops delivered, in collaboration with the Compagnie Industrielle et Minière du Nord et des Alpes, eight hundred desks (without stainless steel shoeing). When we visited the "Vienne-Rocher" building (see no. 392) on 6 October 1988, we were shown the only desk remaining in the building; the top had been replaced, the frame repainted (ill. 396,7). It was desk no. 4, which had been advertised in the J. Prouvé Workshops brochure (with stainless steel shoeing) with the following text: "Warp-resistant one-piece frame consisting of electric-welded tubular sections. Legs directed on two perpendicular planes to ensure the rigidity of the desk in all directions. Stainless steel shoeing welded without projections, to avoid chipping of the enamel and rust stains on the floor. Interchangeable equipment – on both sides of the central drawer, runners allow use of a sound-damped compartment 0.10 or 0.65 high. These compartments fit all drawer combinations (see reverse) and protect them from dust. Drawers with shaped fronts, smooth stainless steel handles. Multiple locking by a single lock.

Metal top covered with linoleum, with flush framing, or plate glass resting on a sound-damped metal top. Frame and drawers in stove enamel. Dimensions: length 1.66; width 0.80; height 0.78. Standard drawers, effective dimensions:
A – central drawer, 0.68 x 0.08 (on runners)
B – side drawer, 0.34 x 0.08 (on runners)
C – business drawer, 0.34 x 0.28 (on rollers)
D – partitioned drawer 0.34 x 0.60 (on rollers) with shelves, paper basket and telephone flap.
Standard combinations
No. 1 – 1 A drawer – 2 B drawers
No. 2 – 1 A drawer – 1 B drawer – 2 C drawers
No. 3 – 1 A drawer – 2 C drawers – 1 D drawer
No. 4 – 1A drawer – 3 B drawers – 1 D drawer."
As was his habit, Jean Prouvé made several variants: desks with or without stainless steel shoeing, drawers with or without locks. The design office even drew a variant with legs in polished stainless steel, plan 3608 of 30 August 1934, which was probably not made. For the C.P.D.E. desks, the J. Prouvé Workshops developed a device for receiving movable baskets, and movable letter baskets, made in Duralumin. Pierre Prouvé told us in 1988 that the Chairman of the C.P.D.E. personally decided the colours of the furniture.

397,1

397. Typing table for the Compagnie Parisienne de Distribution d'Electricité S.A. 1934/35. Frame similar to that of no. 396 and movable top (dimensions 1400/550/755–670 at the point where the typewriter stands). Photograph (ill. 397,1), taken at the Musée des Arts Décoratifs, Paris, in 1984 with an armchair (see no. 403); plan 3932A, dated December 1934: C.P.D.E. typing table (details, ill. 397,2). This model has no stainless steel shoeing.

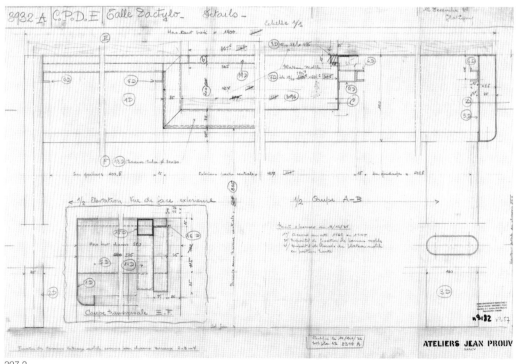

397,2

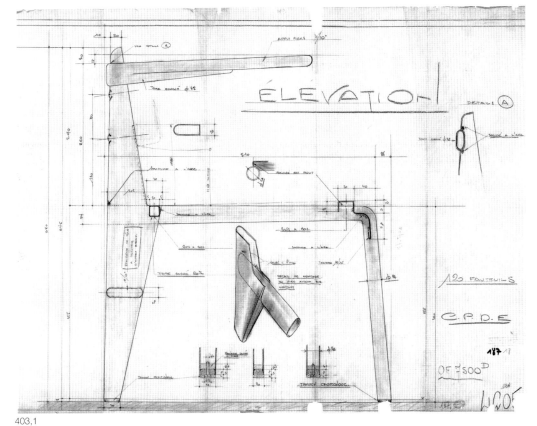

403,1

ATELIERS JEAN PROUVE
4273

Fauteuil de Bureau

ATELIERS JEAN PROUVE

403,4

403. Chair with arms for the Compagnie Parisienne de Distribution d'Electricité S.A.

1934/35. On plan 4205 (ill. 403,1), headed "120 chairs C.P.D.E." and drawn by Robert Feck on 12 February 1935, the folded sheet back legs have a tapered section (the document carries the entry: "thickness of sheet to be decided after tests"); the front legs are in 26 diameter tube; the cross-piece between the front legs is in folded sheet, arc-welded; the arm supports are in 32 diameter crushed tube, arc-welded to the uprights of the back legs; the legs have rubber studs; the covering is leather. In march 1935 Jean-Marie Glatigny drew presentation plan 4273 (ill. 403,4) for an armchair with seat and back in leather. In 1981 Jean Prouvé commented:

"…this chair has quality, it's very comfortable…you see, very early on we started making furniture like that…it was taken up by the great American manufacturer Knoll".

One of these armchairs was exhibited at the Musée des Arts Décoratifs, Paris, in 1984, another piece in an exhibition in Munich in 1990 (ill. 403,6). A similar detail appears on plan 7951 of 1939 (see Complete Works, ill. 788,2). We must not confuse the armchairs of 1934/35 with the "Bridge" armchairs of the 40s and 50s.

403,6

404. Office chair. 1934. A little before the studies for the C.P.D.E. armchair (see Complete Works, 402 and in this volume 403), or parallel with them, the J. Prouvé Workshops began to develop "chair no. 4". Altered after the war, this chair was enormously successful (demountable "cafeteria" chair no. 300, semi-metal chair no. 305, Complete Works) and became a piece of true serial production furniture. The first undated and unnumbered sketch presents the essential characteristics: back legs of uniform strength, to achieve balance, and front legs in tube. The model of plan 3687 (ill. 404,2), headed "office chair, construction detail of frame", has the same characteristics, with a seat and back in solid wood, as can be seen in a recent photograph of this chair with seat and back in solid oak (ill. 404,3). On a full-scale colour sketch showing the back legs of "the present serial chair", the depth of the legs to the ground has been decreased from 35 to 30 mm and the height of the upright increased from 750 to 800 mm, with a thickness of 20 to 25 mm (ill. 404,4).

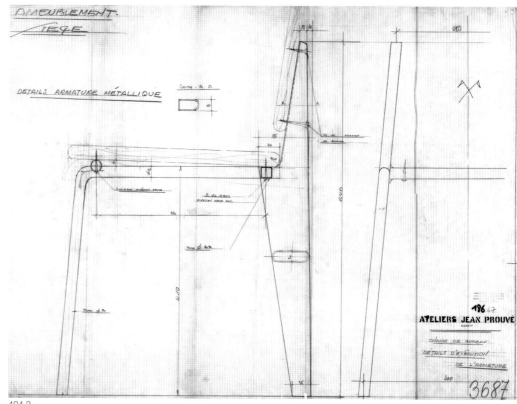

404,2

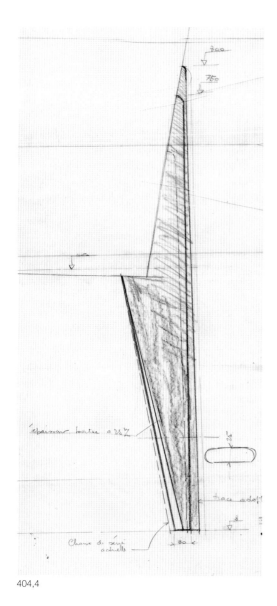

404,4

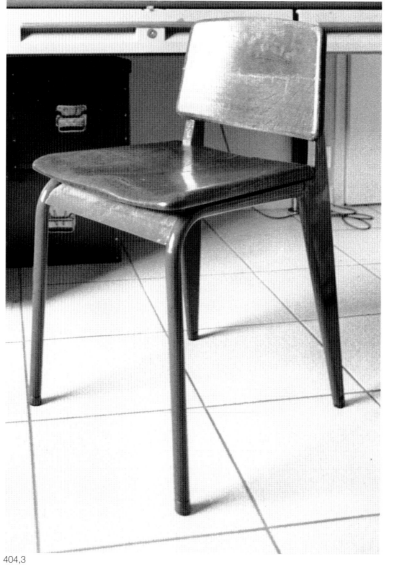

404,3

405,3

405,4

405. Chair no. 4. 1935. The result of the development of the office chairs, explained in no. 404, is model no. 4. It is described as follows in the J. Prouvé Workshops brochure: "Light and rigid one-piece frame; the section of the back legs prevents any bending by leaning backwards. The front legs are in light tube. Seat and back in curved plywood". It was called chair no. 4, because it was the fourth model, after the reclining chair (see no.118a), the metal chair with lifting seat (see no.120a), and the chair for the Cité Universitaire of Nancy (see Complete Works, no. 258.4). Chair no. 4 is often wrongly dated. It must not be confused with the demountable "cafeteria chair no. 300" or the semimetal chair no. 305 of the 50s. The plywood seats and backs were manufactured by Luterma, an Estonian company, and most carry the maker's name underneath. The seats are fixed to the frame by two bolts on the folded sheet cross-piece and two clasps fixed to the back legs. The back is fixed to the uprights of the back legs by two bolts. This chair no. 4 was manufactured in serial production and public bodies such as the lycée for boys in Metz (see Complete Works, no. 534.8) were equipped with it. In his lectures at the Conservatoire National des Arts et Métiers (C.NA.M.), Jean Prouvé explained all the construction details (see Archieri and Levasseur 1990, pp. 162/163). During conversations the author had with Jean Prouvé's colleagues, Jean-Marie Glatigny explained that folding of these legs was carried out with a piece of 40 mm rubber, and Pierre Missey said the legs were welded from within. Photograph of chair no. 4 (ill. 405,3); the same chair seen from below with the cross bar between the folded sheet legs and the trade-mark "Luterma" (ill. 405,4).

442.a,4

442.a. Lecture hall seats for the Ecole des Sciences Politiques, Paris. 1934. In sheet steel and solid oak. There are fourteen plans relating to these seats in the J. Prouvé Collection. Unnumbered plan corresponding to the prototype (ill. 442.a,1); photographs of the seats taken in 1988 (ill. 442.a,4 and 442.a,5). The J. Prouvé Workshops made lecture hall seats until the 50s.

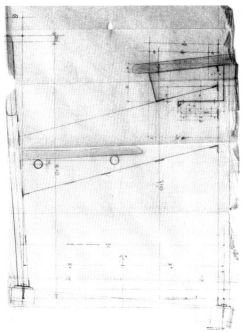

442.a,1

442.a,5

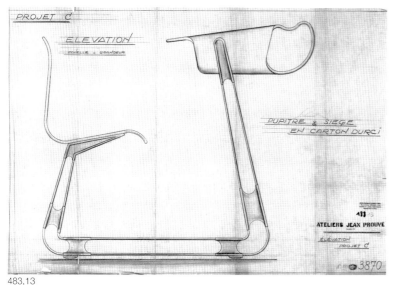

483,13

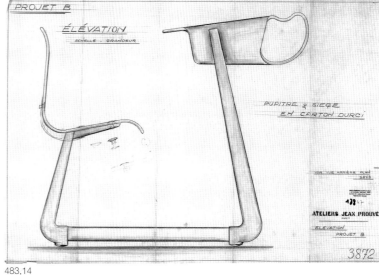

483,14

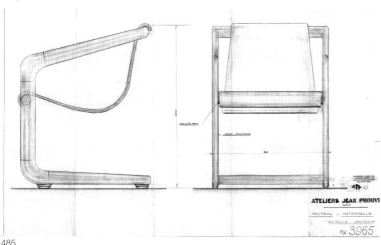

485

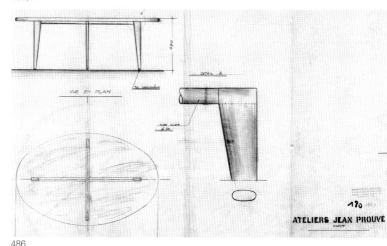

486

482 to 491. Study for furniture for the Open-air School of Suresnes. 1934. Eugène Beaudouin and Marcel Lods, architects. This considerable study and bid by the J. Prouvé Workshops had no outcome. The furniture was made by two companies. This is perhaps the context in which, on 19 February 1936, Marcel Lods wrote to Jean Prouvé in connection with a publication by Albert Laprade: "My dear Prouvé, here is one of the very precious and rare off-prints that I have managed to get from the Administration de l'Encyclopédie. I am giving away only one of them: this is it; I think it belongs by right to you. Very sincerely, Marcel Lods". (For the details of this business see the Commentary in the Complete Works.)

483. Study for an individual school desk. In the J. Prouvé Collection there are seventeen plans relating to this desk, which is similar to the individual desk of 1936 with a Rhodoïd top (see no. 599). The study led to three variants: design A, with a plywood desk and seat and adjustable base in folded sheet; design B, with a hardened board desk and seat and adjustable base in folded sheet; design C, with a hardened board desk and seat, base in stainless steel with sheet brackets. Plan 3870, design C (ill. 483,13); plan 3872, design B (ill. 483,14).

484. Study for a chaise longue. Sheet metal frame, tubular section of uniform strength, stretched canvas.

485. Study for a nursery school chair with arms. Stainless steel frame of tubular section of uniform strength – very different from the models of Mart Stam, Marcel Breuer, Mies van der Rohe, etc. – seat probably moulded plywood. Plan 3965 (ill. 485).

486. Study for an oval table. Steel base with legs in tubular section sheet of uniform strength, joined by 30 mm tubes; top 1.4 m long, probably in wood. Plan 3966 (ill. 486).

487. Study for a refectory table. Base consisting of four feet in tubular sheet section, centre post in sheet (all of uniform strength), 2.5 x 0.7 m top in lamellated plywood covered with linoleum, aluminium section border. Plan 3967 (ill. 487,1); variant with foot rest and stainless steel legs.

488. Study for a desk. First desk design with legs of uniform strength, a principle to which Prouvé later returned. Stainless steel foot rest and legs, painted folded sheet drawer, top 1.3 x 8 m.

489. Study for a refectory bench. Legs in tubular folded section of uniform strength, joined by painted 30 mm tubes; seat (0.35 x 2.6 m) probably moulded plywood.

490. Study for an individual nursery school table. Folded sheet tubular section legs of uniform strength, and variant with foot rest; top 0.6 x 0.6 m.

491. Pieces in wood for the furniture of the Open-air School of Suresnes. Plan 3961, showing numerous pieces in wood, no doubt drawn to price a sub-contract.

534. Designs and works carried out for the boarding school of the lycée of Metz. 1935/36. Robert Parisot and Paul Millochau, architects. Design for a metal door, glazed bay, windows and French window. The J. Prouvé Workshops designed and made metal furniture for the boarding school.

534.1. Lycée of Metz, metal beds no. 102 and no. 113. 1935/36. During our visit to the boarding school of the lycée of Metz we saw, in the dormitory for young pupils, thirty-six blue beds with one or two drawers. Construction plan for the prototype (same number 5063): a bed no. 102 with two drawers (ill. 534.1,2); plan 5249: bed no. 102 with a drawer and bed no. 113 with two drawers, height 220 mm, detail of closed-section frame members (ill. 534.1,3); plan 5274: oak shoeing; photograph of the beds taken in 1986 (ill. 534.1,4).

534.6. Lycée of Metz, refectory table. About 1936. When we visited in 1986 we saw and photographed a table (ill. 534.6) with support in folded sheet and steel tube and a plywood top, published in the inauguration booklet (infirmary refectory).

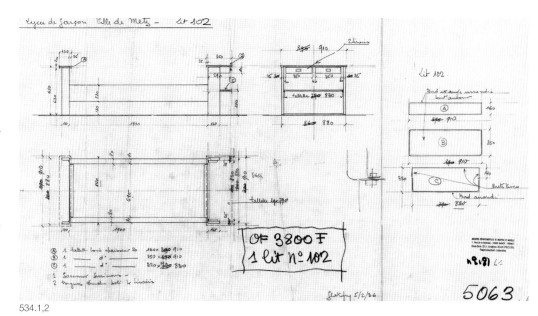

534.1,2

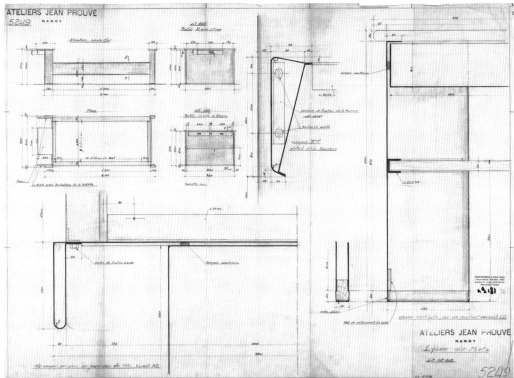

534.1,3

534.1,4

534.6

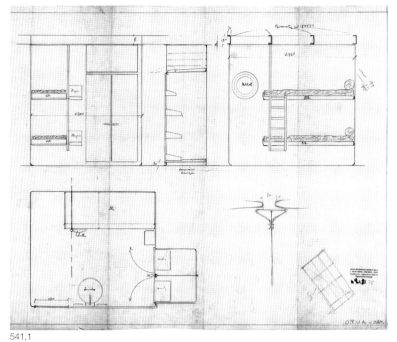

541,1

541. Prototype for a steamer cabin. 1934/35.
Marcel Gascoin, architect; Jean Prouvé, builder. For
the consultation exercise launched in 1934 by the
O.T.U.A. (Technical Office for the Use of Steel),
some members of the U.A.M. (Union of Modern
Artists), in association with builders, presented cab-
ins (among them, René Herbst, Pierre Chareau
and Robert Mallet-Stevens). The O.T.U.A. required
documents on the fire-resistance duration of the
prototypes; according to Jean-Claude Bignon and
Catherine Coley, the J. Prouvé Workshops themselves carried out these tests in Nancy. In 1934 the
models were exhibited at the Salon d'Automne.
The Gascoin/Prouvé prototype was also exhibited at
the Salon Nautique in April 1935. In August 1935 the
J. Prouvé Workshops advertised this cabin in the review *L'Architecture d'Aujourd'hui.* Unnumbered plan
headed: "O.T.U.A. – U.A.M." (ill. 541,1) plan 4559 of
July 1935: bunks in 8/10 stainless steel sheet for
steamer cabin, with weight calculation; photographs
(ill. 541,3 and 541,4).

541,4

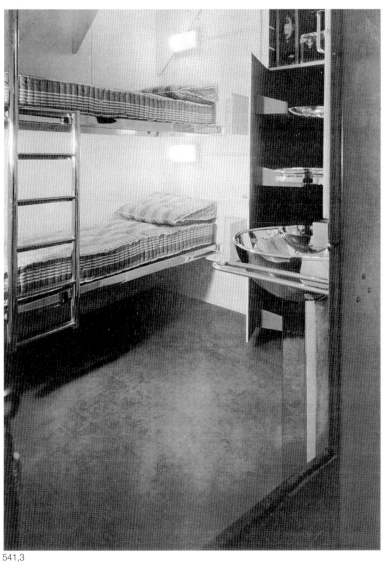

541,3

543. The Roland Garros Flying Club at Buc.

1935/36. Eugène Beaudouin and Marcel Lods, architects. Vladimir Bodiansky, engineer. The study for this building entirely prefabricated in folded sheet by the J. Prouvé Workshops consists of a hundred and forty-four plans drawn between June 1935 and August 1936 by Jean Boutemain and Robert Feck. The J. Prouvé Collection also holds several sketches by Jean Prouvé and some photographs. In 1982 Jean Prouvé explained to us:

"The Flying Club of Buc was ordered by Mlle Deutsch de la Meurthe. She was passionately fond of flying, a pilot herself, and she took on responsibility for a flying club at Buc, near Versailles. As architect she chose Marcel Lods, with whom I already had a relationship, because we had already begun to work on Clichy. (Author's note: In fact, Clichy was carried out later, but Jean Prouvé had already worked with Marcel Lods at Drancy, see no. 353.) Lods was totally sympathetic to the industrialisation of building construction. He already knew how I worked, what I could do for him and make of an architectural document, I had in hand only a plan of the volumetric mass of the building. Of course there were internal lay-outs, on two levels in places, while part of the building was open to its full height. It was a simple rectangular parallelepiped, but it had to be built very quickly and be a demonstration of contemporary architecture. All the construction of the ensemble, down to the windows, all the cladding,

543,2

543,1

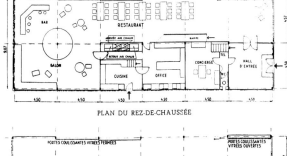

PLAN DU REZ-DE-CHAUSSÉE

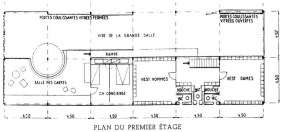

PLAN DU PREMIER ÉTAGE

Fig. 12. Vues en plan.

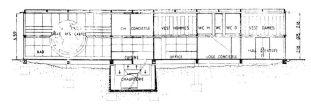

Fig. 13. Coupe longitudinale.

Fig. 14. Coupe transversale. On note la disposition particulière de la cheminée.

543,3

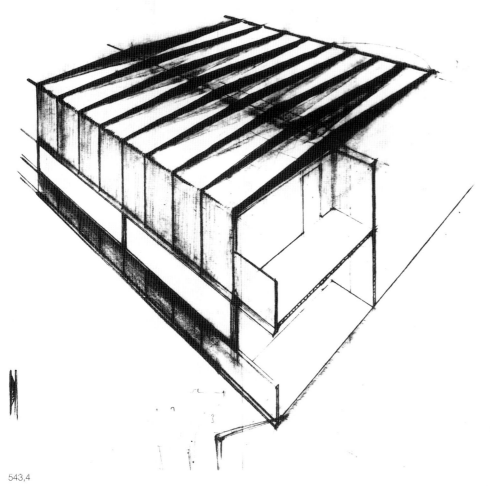

543,4

all that was made in my workshops in the rue des Jardiniers – I hadn't yet moved to Maxéville. And we had to work fast; that means that everything started with sketches I made that went directly to the workshop. They made it possible to make a prototype of a slice of the building that Lods came to see. He was totally in agreement, and we then set about designing seriously and had to draw the whole construction of the building which was carried out completely in folded sheet. There is not a single commercial laminated section, which was currently used at that time. It was not a question of principle, my machinery enabled me to do it. So we had to invent everything, and we did so with great boldness. The load-bearing frame is in 4 mm thick sheet steel. We'll see the details later, when I describe this frame".

Photographs of the building about 1936 (ill. 543,1 and 543,2); plans and sections (ill. 543,3); sketch by Jean Prouvé (ill. 543,4); sketch of the structural frame (ill. 543,5); assembly of a section of the building "unloaded" in the workshop (ill. 543,6).

543,6

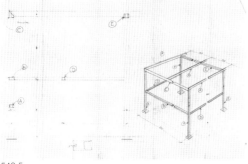

543,5

Jean Prouvé: "This photograph (ill. 543,7 and 543,8) is interesting because it shows the building during the course of assembly. You can very easily see the structural arrangement of beams, posts and the roof – the roof constituting a horizontal beam – and then a series of panels put in place. You can see the size of these panels. While the building was being built there were always a lot of people moving round the site, because it was strange to them and they were interested. It was very inconvenient, but we had to allow it. The structural frame, the external partitioning, the facades, the interior partitioning, the ceilings, were not commercially supplied. All the floor beams, the floors themselves, and the ceilings were made of metal sheets. The structural frame sheet was 40/10 thick (author's note: 3 mm), while the external panels were in 15/10 sheet and the internal partitions were, I think, 10/10 or 12/10 thick, so it was very thin sheet. All these sheet metal components were shaped and assembled in totally new ways that were invented for this building…

Just now I gave you a quick description of the section of the posts… You can see they consisted of three folded sheet components: a deep nose and two sides, folded to create the rebate for the panels. All this electrically welded. The inward space provided by the channel iron had a carefully thought-out purpose, which was to create ducts for the passage of liquids, which could run through the space from floor to floor. This space was finally blocked by a sort of small sheet flap that made it independent of the building (ill. 543,9).

543,8

543,7

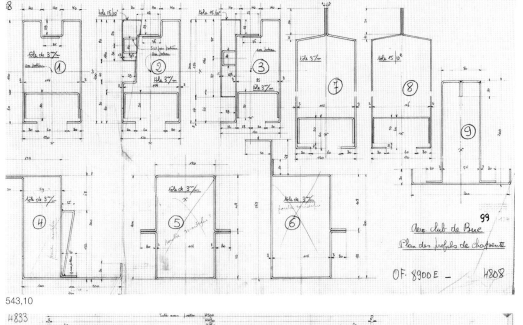

543,10

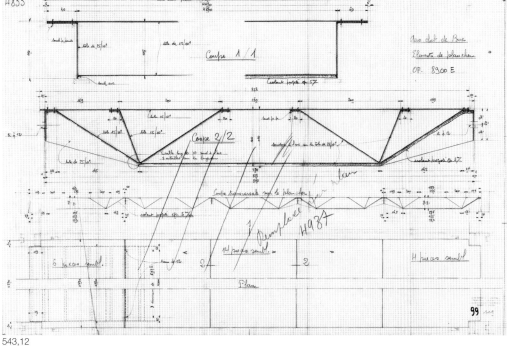

543,12

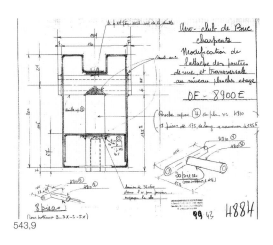

543,11

543,9

This leads me on to tell you about the joints between the beams and the posts. You see there a section of a post; you saw just now the section of a folded sheet beam (ill. 543,10). The beams had to be housed in the posts, because this was necessary for the strength of the building. It was a difficult joint to make, because the beams were hollow and the posts were also hollow, and we had to find a way of creating a continuity between these beams and these posts. For this continuity we had the idea of welding sockets of fairly large diameter into the posts. They were sockets in the form of a sort of perforated barrel and were welded to both sides of the post. We assembled the two sides of the posts between them, and the beams were fixed by bolts which went through these sockets, these barrels, and this made for a continuity of strength between beams and posts. Construction in hollow sections leads to arrangements like this. You cannot just join something to the outside of a tube; you have to think up a way of creating a continuity to the inside of the tube, and we did so by this device of the barrels… The welding could only be done outside on the thickness of the sheet, because it was necessary to close the post. You can't see that from the photograph, but the barrel projected a little from the sheet, so that the bolt thrust should be on the spur/barrel and not on the sheet metal. Thus there was a thickness that allowed welding."

Photographs of the site (ill. 543,7 and 543,8); plan 4884: post (detail, ill. 543,9); plan 4808: welded frame sections in folded sheet of 3 mm, 1 to 3 posts, 5 to 9 beams (ill. 543,10); photograph of the detail of the frame structure showing a corner post and the end floor beam (ill. 543,11); plan 4833: floor components in folded sheet (ill. 543,12).

Jean Prouvé: "You can see how the roof was designed, consisting of large sheet pans of 1.10 x 4.50 m. They were pans with a joint cover and you'll notice these pans are slightly concave, which means that the sheet metal is hanging and finds its position by hanging like a tarpaulin; merely installing it made it rigid… This photograph shows the acroters, that is the beams, the plates, the beams that link the frames to the apex outside the building. These are hollow and you can see very well in this photograph an assembly barrel. The welding is very visible there, which shows you the barrel is off-set and that there is welding between the sheet metal and the end of this barrel. So these are hollow elements the design of which provides for necessary water flow, creating throats and all that is needed for effective facades and roofs. You see there the underside of the roof and the stiffeners which are in quite complex section. There is a reason for that: these are stiffeners that can act as warm air circulation ducts and are constructed to do so. Rather than construct ducts and ceiling supports, we thought that the ceiling support itself could be the duct… The channel iron of the base of these sections provides housing for the ceiling elements. We housed the ceiling elements and that did not pose any problem… These partitioning strips between the roof and the ceiling were the ducts that circulated the warm air. So there was a warm air current that followed a certain route, and the route was marked out by these strips… The building was heated by the ceiling heating and radiation. There was another innovation at the time. An important thing to note about this building, is that the toilets – and this was completely new at the time – were entirely manufactured and fitted out in the workshop. They were the cubicles you see here before assembly. They were stored on site and you can see that each cubicle has a porthole in the front panel. They were linked in pairs by a sleeve for the lighting and there were ventilation holes above. These cubicles were very attractively constructed in lacquered sheet, delivered with the floor covered by linoleum or rubber and the sanitary ware installed in the factory, and then they were placed next to each other. I think it was one of the first times such things had been seen … We believed that a cubicle should be a totally watertight component, able to be flooded; so there was a threshold under the door. It had to be able to be jet-washed and have no partition joints that dirt could get into. It was a real little bit of car-body building. I think there were four or six toilet cubicles at Buc".

Detail of the roof pans with joint covers (ill. 543,13); construction plan 5031: roof (detail, ill. 543,14).

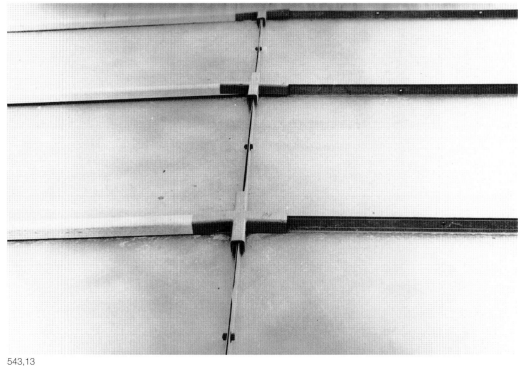

543,13

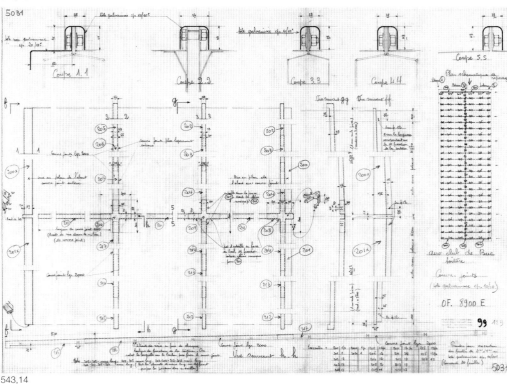

543,14

Jean Prouvé: "The facade panels consisted of an inner and an outer sheet… You have a sketch, I made it from memory however, which shows you how these facade panels were made up. You can see that they are placed between posts, on the axis of the posts, in a rebate at the bottom of which was arranged a plastic joint, and that the double-sheet panels had convex edges that enabled them to be fitted with this plastic joint, to achieve water and air tightness. These panels – the sheets having been welded together – were shaped for the vertical joint

bends and to create the throats it was necessary to make to prevent water entering between the panels. These throats had a double function: not only to divert water, but at the same time to stiffen the panel. Although the panel was vertically stiffened by the post, it was necessary to give it a certain horizontal rigidity. This is why the facade panels were delivered in quite unusual sizes, because they went from post to post… It was necessary to weld leaves of sheet metal between them, electric welding that naturally led to shavings, then to planing to achieve

a suitably smooth surface. We used a craft system of planing, because there was no machine capable of planing such sizes".

Of the Flying Club at Buc, Marcel Lods said in 1974: "At that time we were at the stage of prefabricated concrete elements assembled on site. It was possible to advance thanks to the work done by Jean Prouvé. I had met him and he had told me that we should study light facades. We made an experiment for the Club-House, which, no one ever knew why, was demolished by the army.

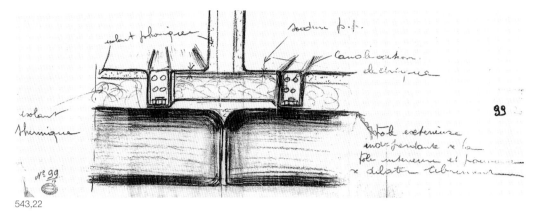

543,22

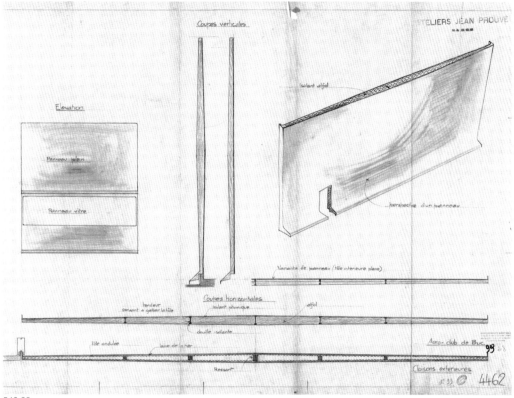

543,23

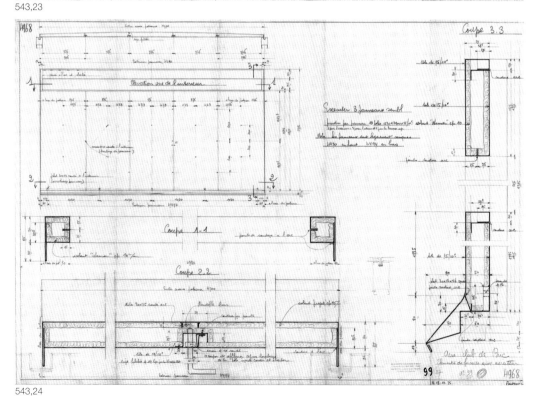

543,24

There were advantages: it was assembled very quickly, very well, and there were mistakes. When it was finished I said to Prouvé: 'My friend, we're going to take a walk together, alone, and spend a whole afternoon analysing Buc. We'll note the mistakes made in order to put them right'. And we set off with our little notebooks in hand. The first correction was in the facade panels. For myself, I am panic-stricken by joints; a building moves, it expands in summer and contracts in winter. At that time we did not have the wonderful plastic materials for joints that we have today. You made joints with cement and when the building moved, the joint broke. So I had a terrible fear of joints. I used to say: 'joints, I'll have no more of them,' and I arrived at this solution: the joint hidden behind the points of support. That led us to panels 4.50 m long by 2.25 m. The joints were few and limited to the posts. To make a faultless sheet panel of 4.50 m, that was too large. At Clichy we reduced the module to 1.04 m, because we were no longer frightened of joints… In fact, there were never any leaks…"

Jean Prouvé: "… In the main, it worked well. The frame was rigid and it must be said that we did not fail, in our calculations of strength, to take into consideration the large area external panels; we considered them as wind-bracing components, and they proved very effective. We think the inspection offices of the present time would not accept such an arrangement. We made it and it worked; it worked very well.

The whole of the facade facing the airfield was glazed, and consisted of windows which, you can see, were fitted into frames identical to the panel frames. Assembly was the same throughout. There was no special frame. You simply had to have the idea and, indispensably, make up a team whose ideas were in harmony. From the tracer of the draughtsman's work to the folder of the sheet metal, from the welder to the assembler of a component, everyone had to want to do it. I achieved that in my workshops.

…There was total agreement of ideas among those carrying out the work. The draughtsmen were passionately enthusiastic. Jean Boutemain, who did the drawings for Buc, is still alive. In retirement we get on well with each other, we're happy to meet and we have a great mutual respect for each other. He has marvellous memories of this time, and myself, I know what he contributed to this building. I know much more about him than he thinks I do, that's certain…"

Sketch by Jean Prouvé with an "open joint" between the external sheets (ill. 543,22). When Jean Prouvé noticed the problem of planing, his design office studied the possibility of curving the sheets, a principle already used for doors. On plan 4462 (ill. 543,23) two principles are sketched: tensioners with isolating bushes and mattress springs; another system was used: the panels were swelled with threaded rods " to be cut out when the panel has swollen". Construction plan 4698 (ill. 543,24).

543,25

Photograph of the assembly, showing the swelling and also the welding (ill. 543,25); photograph of the facade with joint covers that were not foreseen (ill. 543,26); photograph of the assembly of the glazed facade (ill. 543,27); photograph of the finished building with sliding doors and blinds (ill. 543,28). The J. Prouvé Workshops designed and made for this building the doors, the internal partitions, the footbridge, the stairs, cupboards, cloak-rooms, etc…

543,26

543,27

543,28

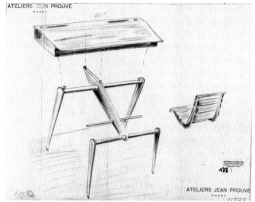

545.5,6

545. Designs and works carried out for the Ecole Nationale Professionelle (National Technical School) of Metz. 1935–38. Robert Fournez and Louis Sainsaulieu, architects.

This phase of the works included a boarding school added to the building of 1912/13, enlargement of the teaching rooms and workshops, and modernisation of the lecture halls and laboratories. Work on the site started in December 1934, the boarders returned in October 1936, but the works continued until 1938. In the inauguration booklet we read: "various metal furniture, J. Prouvé Workshops, Nancy (metal beds, Ets Matifas, Amiens; classroom tables, Ets Schmitt, Colmar)". The photographs of the inauguration booklet show Jean Prouvé's furniture: chairs no. 4 (see no. 405), chairs with arms (see no. 403), table (see Complete Works, no. 545.1); divan (see Complete Works, no. 545.15); two-seater classroom desks (see no. 545.5); beds (see Complete Works, no. 545.10). Jean Prouvé and his colleagues in the design office drew, between July 1935 and July 1938, ninety-three plans and many sketches for these works. The most important designs are described below.

545.5. E.N.P. of Metz, two-seater classroom tables. 1935.

It was probably for the National Technical School of Metz that Jean Prouvé first designed and carried out this classroom desk that the J. Prouvé Workshops made in a considerable number of variants until the 50s. Full-scale colour sketched by Jean Prouvé (ill. 545.5,1); plan 4722, drawn by Jean Prouvé on 13 September 1935 and enabling us to date the sketches (ill. 545.5,6).

545.8. E.N.P. of Metz, two-seater classroom table for adults with metal seat and back. 1936.

Two photographs of the prototype taken in the design office of the J. Prouvé Workshops, rue des Jardiniers (ill. 545.8,1). These photographs correspond to plan 5167 and to a photograph of a classroom published in the inauguration booklet. During a discussion of these photographs, Jean Prouvé said to Jean-Marie Helwig: "… You see it was entirely in folded sheet. It was very light sheet, not in reaction, but in contrast to the furniture in tube… That must have been after 1935… We made hundreds of pieces of furniture like that".

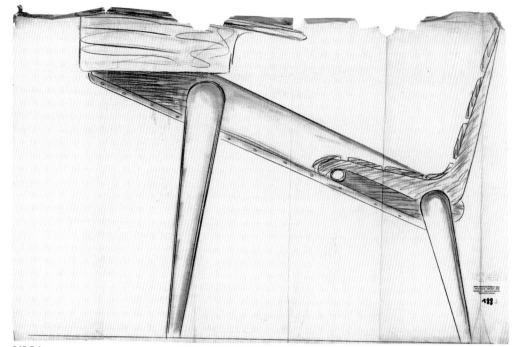

545.5,1

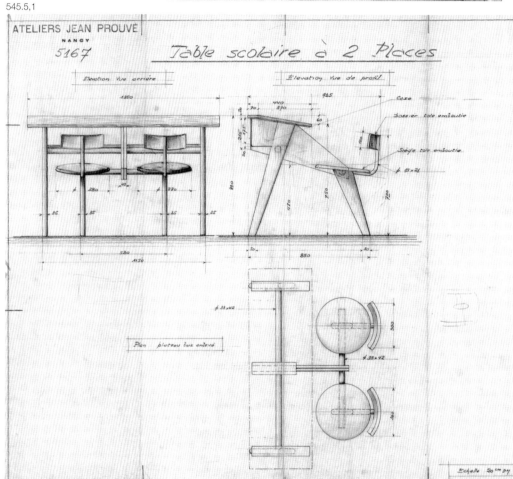

545.8,3

545.8,1

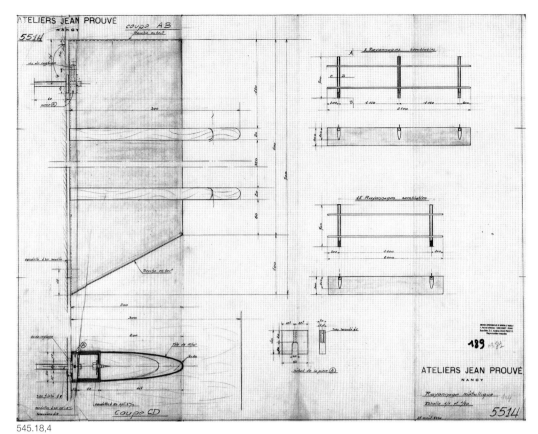

545.18,4

545.18. **E.N.P. of Metz, study and carrying out of shelving.** 1936. For the Ecole Nationale Professionelle of Metz, the J. Prouvé Workshops developed a system of shelving different from the shelves of the Cité Universitaire of Nancy (see no. 258.3). In this model the notched wood shelves rest in grooves made in the folded sheet uprights. Plan 5293: wall shelving (ill. 545.18,2); construction plan 5514: three shelves with three uprights and fifteen shelves with two uprights (ill. 545.18,4). Similar shelving in a private collection (ill. 545.18,7).

545.18,7

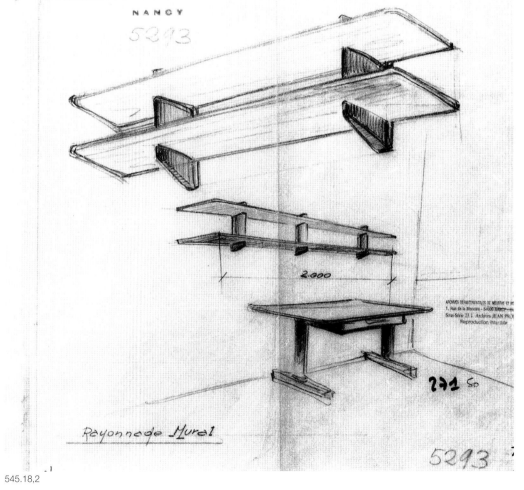

545.18,2

103

565. Design for a newspaper kiosk. 1935.
In December 1935 Robert Feck drew four presentation plans for this project. Plan 4932: horizontal section, framework in folded sheet filled in with thermal insulation panels and sash windows (ill.565,1); colour sketch by Jean Prouvé (ill.565,2).

565,2

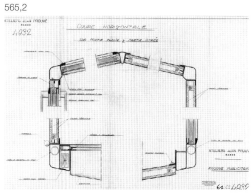

565,1

572,1

572. Designs and works carried out for the P.T.T. (Post Office) Ministry in Paris. 1936–39.

Jacques Debat-Ponson, architect. This was a large order for the J. Prouvé Workshops. The inventory of documents relating to this project includes a hundred and twenty plans, drawn between January 1936 and June 1939, mainly by Robert Feck. It is an example of very meticulous work made possible by a design office staffed by highly qualified collaborators: the 6.6 m high doors still work after more than fifty years! Jean Prouvé, always present, concerned himself with all the details, such as the handles. The J. Prouvé Workshops bid included all the metal building fittings, stair rails, balustrades, the glazed ceiling and grills, but – according to Jean-Claude Bignon and Catherine Coley 1990, p. 87 – the business was shared and the company Douzille provided three thousand two hundred metal door frames and 6,000 m² of side-opening casement windows. J. Prouvé Workshops designs that were not carried out: sash windows with two and three horizontally pivoting frames; side-opening windows and other metal building fittings; railings for the conference room; the gallery of entrance hall. Among the works carried out by the J. Prouvé Workshops were the four tubular doors of the main entrance on the Avenue de Ségur, 2.30 m wide, 6.61 m high (ill. 572,1). There are a large number of plans relating to this door, including: plan 5652, first sketch with a more modern proposal than that carried out (ill. 572,2); plan 5989 (ill. 572,3); construction plan 6965: horizontal section with indication of the numbers of detailed plans for glazing beading, vertical sections in drawn bronze, and the installation of locks and handles (ill. 572,5).

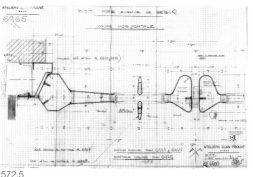

572,5

572,3

572,2

599. One-seater classroom desk. 1936. In 1934 Jean Prouvé had designed for the Open-air School of Suresnes, of which Eugène Beaudouin and Marcel Lods were the architects (see no. 482), a series of variants for a one-seater classroom desk. In March 1936 the J. Prouvé Workshops took up this design again and made a prototype. Photographs (ill. 599,4 and 599,6). During a conversation, Jean-Marie Glatigny told the author that Pierre Missey had made the desk, which he had welded from two shells and had afterwards polished. There are other documents relating to this desk: sketch of steel sheet pieces, 10/10 or 12/10 thick; quotation for two hundred of each model (ill. 599,7). This model was probably exhibited at the Salon d'Automne in the school furniture section of the Union des Artistes Modernes, organised by René Herbst, and in January 1937 at the Salon des Art Ménagers. The Georges Baumont Lycée Professionel Industriel made a reconstruction for the Jean Prouvé exhibition at the Pompidou Centre in 1990.

599,4

599,6

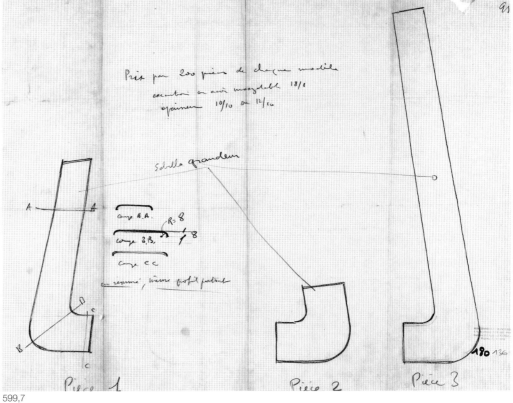

599,7

607,1

607. Wall-mounted telephone booth. 1936. There are eighteen plans and sketches in the J. Prouvé Collection. A prototype, of which there is a photograph (ill. 607,1) published by Jean-Claude Bignon and Catherine Coley, was made. Presentation plan 5209 (ill. 607,2); construction plan 5370, horizontal section (outer face of doors in bellied sheet) with the entry: "Bid 7300 francs – 1 booth"; plan 5373: details of the ceiling. After the prototype was made, new presentation plans were drawn: plan 5418: assembly diagram and variants of internal furnishing; plans 5419, 5420 and 5421: plans 5803 and 5805 of June 1936; plan 5823 of December 1936; plan 5917 of January 1937. This effort on the part of the J. Prouvé Workshops was certainly aimed at serial production, but it was not successful.

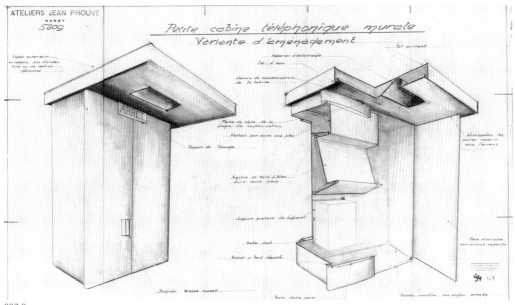

607,2

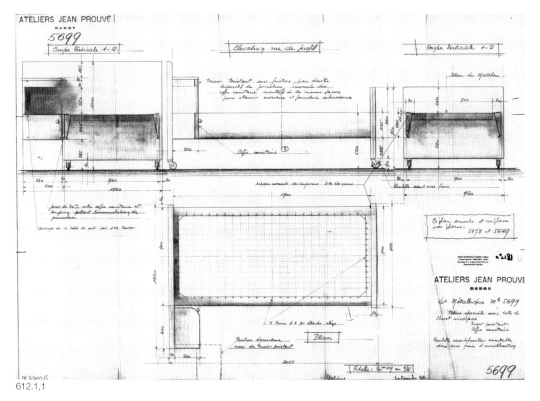

612.1,5

612.1,1

612.1. Sanatorium furniture, metal bed. 1936.
This is divan bed no. 14 of the J. Prouvé Work-shops brochure (see Complete Works, no. 536). An example of this bed was exhibited at the Galerie Jousse-Séguin, Paris, in March 1993. In a conversation in March 1993, Pierre Missey remembered the construction of the prototype. Several presentation plans were drawn by Jean-Marie Glatigny for this considerable study. Plan 5463, plan 5464, plan 5466, plan 5478, plan 5479 and plan 5649: variants of the bed with special headboard, with integral bedside table, hinged drawer and compartment for toilet articles; construction plan 5699 with the entry: "metal bed 5699 special headboard with bedside table incorporated, hinged drawer, compartment for toilet articles, rubberised wheels…" (ill. 612.1,1); name list for one hundred and sixty-four beds model 5699; photograph of one of the beds, taken on site in 1997 (ill. 612.1,5). Manufacture of the series was probably subcontracted.

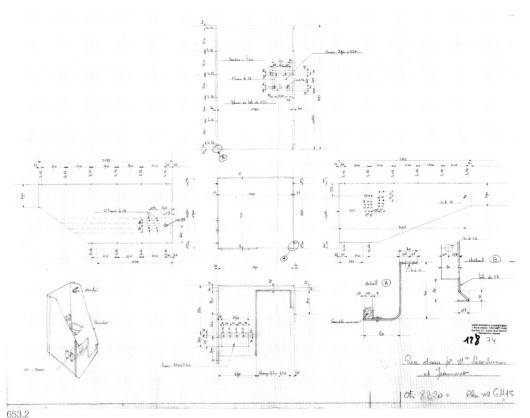

653,2

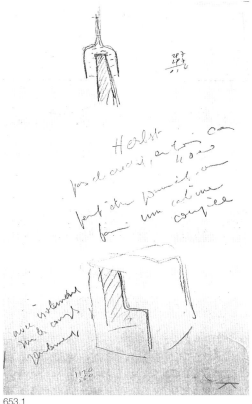

653,1

653. International Exhibition of 1937 in Paris, shower and WC unit. Le Corbusier and Pierre Jeanneret, architects. The prototype of a toilet cubicle for hotels was exhibited in the pavilion of the Union des Artistes Modernes (U.A.M.). Plan 6165: drawing by Jean Boutemain; blueprint of this plan with sketch and a note by Jean Prouvé: "Herbst, no credit… 4,000 francs, perhaps we could make an open-top cubicle" (ill. 653,1); construction plan 6415 drawn on 8 June 1927 by Jean Boutemain showing this open-top cubicle in 25/10 sheet (ill. 653,2).

654,1

654,2

654. International Exhibition of 1937 in Paris, designs and works carried out for the pavilion of the Union des Artistes Modernes. Georges-Henri Pingusson, Franz-Philippe Jourdain, André Louis, architects. Staircase with central string and straight flight of 8 m span, central string consisting of two welded 40/10 folded sheet shells, steps in 25/10 folded sheet, welded to the string; a railing with 26 x 34 mm tube spindles and handrail, fixed to the string and the steps, and 6 mm wires; contemporary photographs (ill. 654,1 and 654,2). This was the first time a folded sheet staircase had been designed so that its form was an expression of the material used. In the J. Prouvé Collection there are several drawings and blueprints with notes taken during discussions with the architects, including the example we give (ill. 654,3). The J. Prouvé Workshops probably made the internal and external balustrades. Plan 5923F, plan 6161 and plan 6298: stairway situated at the end of the gallery (probably a design not carried out); plan 5923A: design for folded sheet glazed facades; plan 5923B: design for a folded sheet band course; plan 5923D: design for spiral staircase; plan 5923E: plan for staircase for the reception centre. Three plans drawn by Jean Boutemain: plan 6159, plan 6160 and plan 6296 showing folded sheet two-leafed swing doors (sixteen leaves were delivered).

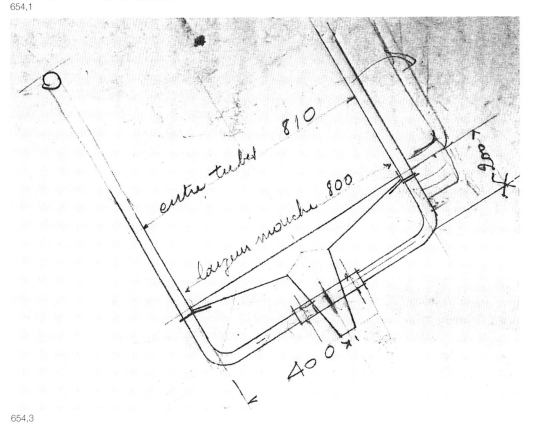

654,3

655. International Exhibition of 1937 in Paris, garden furniture for the pavilion of the Union des Artistes Modernes. Jacques André, the architect, was a friend of Jean Prouvé. The J. Prouvé Workshops made this garden furniture in perforated and folded sheet steel, steel tube and Rhodoïd, a material produced for the first time in 1933. Photograph of three pieces of furniture, taken on the terrace of the U.A.M. pavilion (ill. 665).

655.1. U.A.M. Pavilion, armchair. Photograph of 1937 (ill. 655.1).

655.2. U.A.M. Pavilion, table. Photograph of 1937 (ill. 655.2).

655.3. U.A.M. Pavilion, stool. Photograph of 1937 (ill. 655.3).

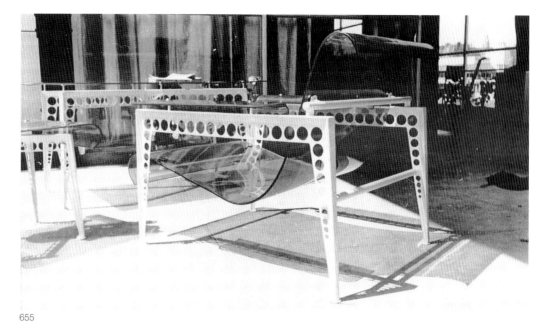

655

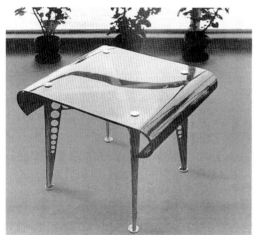

655.3

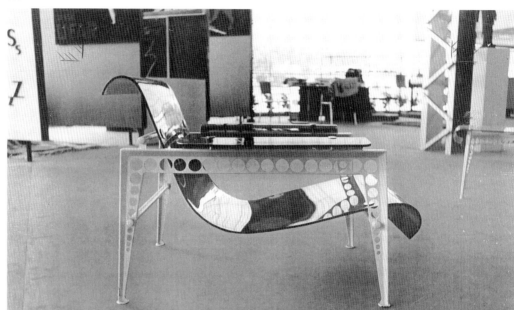

655.1

655.2

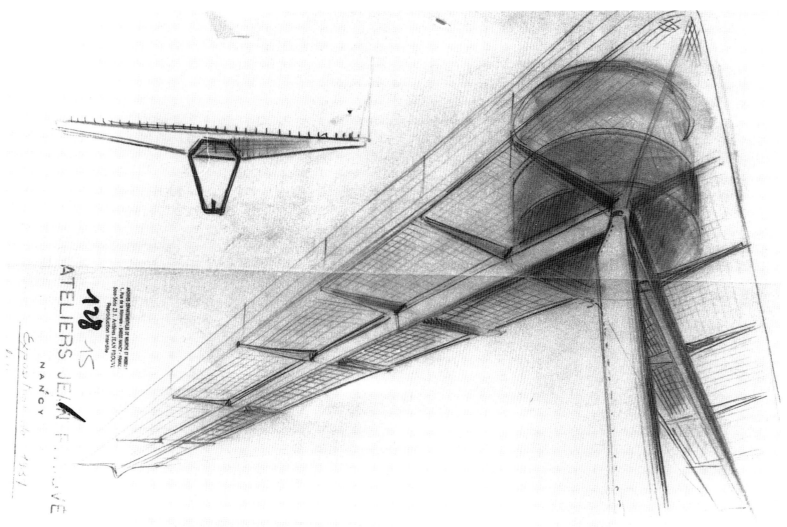

661,1

661. International Exhibition of 1937 in Paris, study for the Martenot clock. In the J. Prouvé Collection there are a large number of sketches by Jean Prouvé relating to this project, including: unnumbered sketch (ill. 661,1).

677

677. Five-position chaise longue. 1937. This piece of furniture is only known through six photographs. The safety catch can be lifted by the handle on the back and the position changed. This chair has a sheet and steel tube frame, metal spring bands and removable cushions. It was probably a prototype. A similar piecc of furniture was designed for a student sanatorium in 1939 (see Complete Works, no. 833). Retouched photograph (ill. 677).

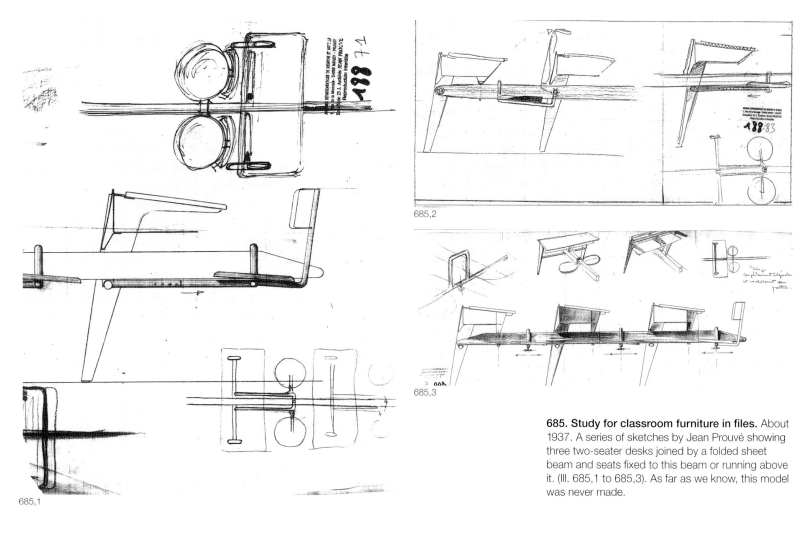

685,2

685,3

685,1

685. Study for classroom furniture in files. About 1937. A series of sketches by Jean Prouvé showing three two-seater desks joined by a folded sheet beam and seats fixed to this beam or running above it. (Ill. 685,1 to 685,3). As far as we know, this model was never made.

688. Classroom desks in files for the National Technical School of Metz. 1937/38. Plan 6908 of December 1937; plan 6980, cancelled and replaced by plan 7214, which corresponds to the photograph of the prototype (ill. 688,3); plan 6981: perspective corresponding to the model in the photographs; plan 6982: full-scale detail; plan 7214; construction plan 7228 (ill. 688,6), with all the details of assembly and the entry: "for a file of 5 two-seater desks you must…" and "… total of 80 places"; plans 7229 and 7230 showing the cut of the pieces, with the entry: "40 tops in solid oak, 1,150 400 x 20 mm".

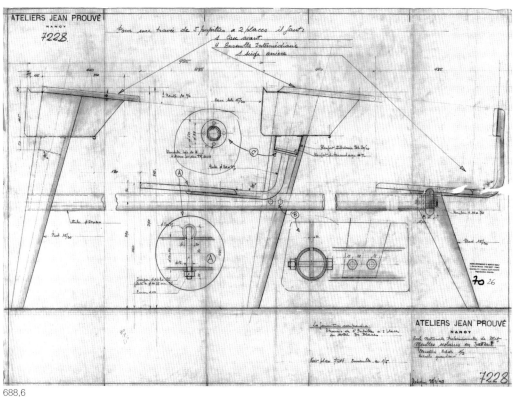

688,6

688,3

691,1

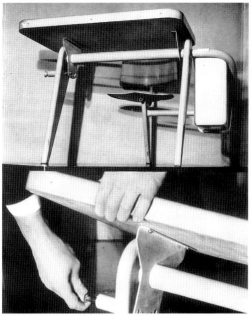

691,2

691. Classroom desk, single-place table for a child of 6 to 8 years. 1936/37. Jacques André, architect; Jean Prouvé, maker. Two contemporary photographs (ill. 691,1 and 691,2). This desk – a prototype – was presented at the exhibition of scholastic furniture organised by the office Technique pour l'Utilisation de l'Acier (O.T.U.A.) and the Union des Artistes Modernes (U.A.M.) at the Salon d'Automne in 1936, and also at the Salon de l'Habitation and the Salon des Arts Ménagers of January 1937.

693. Design for a movable and adjustable desk for a pupil of 5 to 8 years. 1937. Children could themselves move the table around on its wheels. Sketch by Jean Prouvé (ill. 693,1); unnumbered plan: elevation; plan 6467: elevation (ill. 693,2); plan 6468; photograph of a copy made in the context of the "J. Prouvé operation" and exhibited at the Centre Georges Pompidou exhibition of 1990 (ill. 693,3).

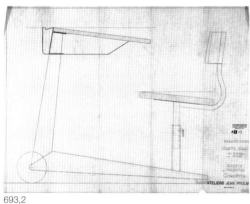

693,2

693,3

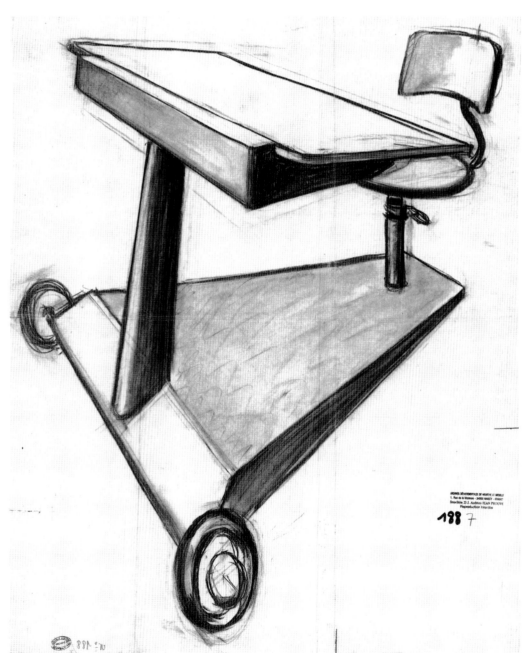

693,1

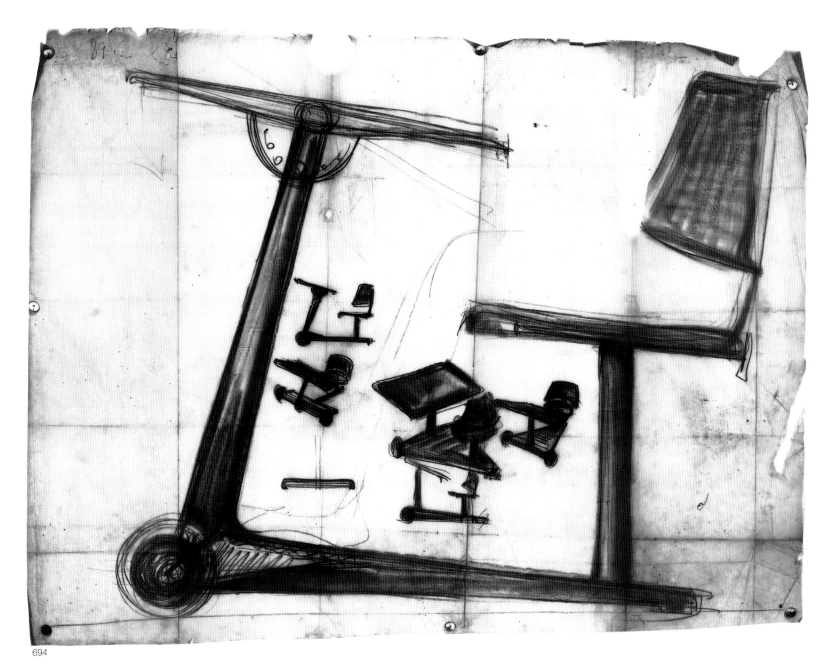

694

694. Design for a movable and adjustable desk.
About 1937. Sketch by Jean Prouvé (ill. 694);
variant of the preceding desk (see no. 693) with an
adjustable inclining top.

695. Design for a "Puteaux" classroom desk.
1937. Desk with adjustable height and seat
distance. Plan 6745 of October 1937 (ill. 695).

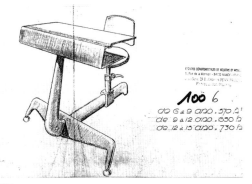

695

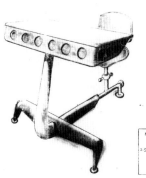

696,1

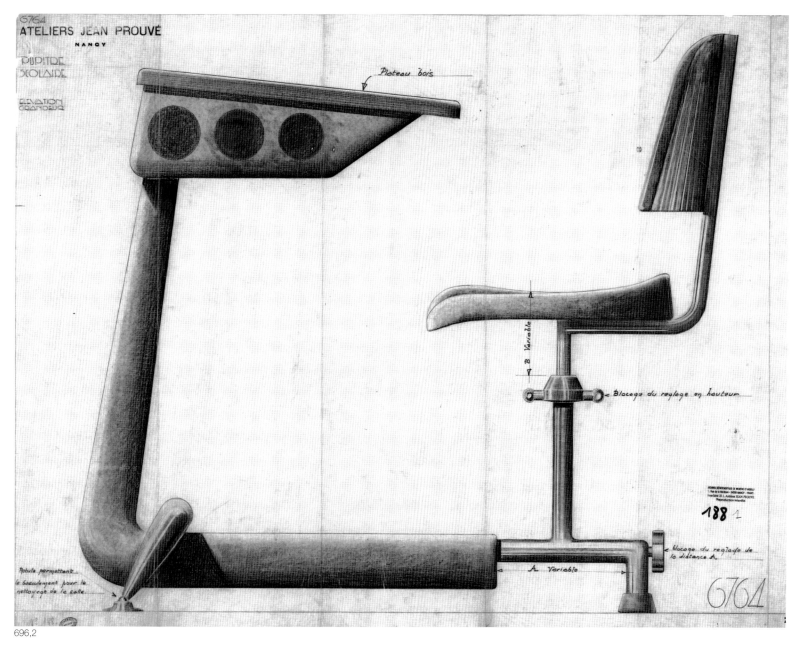

696,2

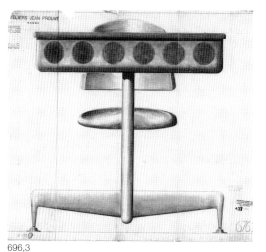

696,3

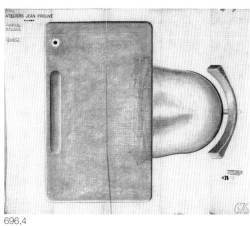

696,4

696. Design for a classroom desk. 1937. On 19
October 1937 R. F. drew a series of full-scale plans
with different adjustment mechanisms and a perforated shelf. Plan 6763: perspective (ill. 696,1); plan
6764: elevation showing the details of the adjustment catch and a "swivel allowing it to be tipped up
for cleaning of the classroom" (ill. 696,2); plan 6765:
full-scale front (ill. 696,3); plan 6766 (ill. 696,4) desk
with top, seat and back in wood.

700. Two seater classroom desk no. 51. About 1937/38. This desk is described in the J. Prouvé Workshops brochure: "Very rigid single-piece frame consisting of four legs in tubular sections, two cross-pieces and an encased central brace with no sharp edges. Electrically welded assembly; elimination of any component that might become loose with use. Stove enamelling. Metal shelves with rounded edges. Inclining top in solid oak, rounded edges; fixing allows full play to the wood. Front edge with shaped pen-tray. Seats and backs in folded sheet with rounded edges" (ill. 700). In connection with this desk Jean Prouvé told Jean-Marie Helwig: "All that led to considerable production. It was furniture I made in answer to a call for bids from the Ministry of Education and I had a fair number of orders… It was entirely in sheet metal, very light sheet, not in reaction against, but in contrast to, furniture in tube…"

702. Two-seater classroom desk no. 57. About 1937/38. The J. Prouvé Workshops brochure with the entry: "same frame (as no. 51), but with the front edge that forms the pen-tray in sheet metal and of a single piece with the compartments". Contemporary photographs (ill. 702,1, 702,2 and 702,3). Similar schoolroom desks were made during the 40s and 50s.

702,1

702,2

ATELIERS JEAN PROUVÉ
SOCIÉTÉ ANONYME
50, Rue des Jardiniers
NANCY   Tél. 70-31
MOBILIER EN ACIER

**PUPITRE
SCOLAIRE**

Pupitre à deux places N° 51

BATI MONOBLOC d'une extrême rigidité composé de quatre pieds tubulaires profilés, de deux traverses, et d'une entretoise centrale cuirassée sans aucune arête vive. Assemblage par soudure électrique ; élimination de tout montage susceptible de prendre du jeu à l'usage. Emaillage au four.
CASIERS métalliques à bords roulés.
PLATEAU incliné en chêne massif, bords arrondis ; fixation permettant au bois de jouer librement. Toilette avant avec plumiers souples.
SIÈGES et DOSSIERS en tôle d'acier emboutie avec rebords arrondis.

700

702,3

116

704,1

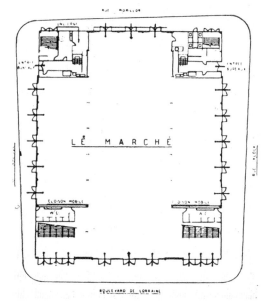

704,3a

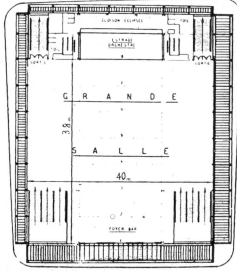

704,3c

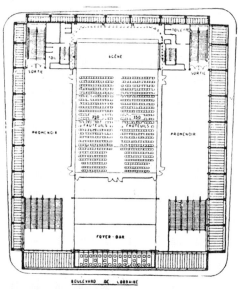

704,3b

704,3d

704. The Maison du Peuple and the covered market in Clichy. 1935–39. The town of Clichy, client; Charles Auffray, mayor. Eugène Beaudouin and Marcel Lods, architects, André Sive, collaborator from 1937; Vladimir Bodiansky, engineer. Etablissements Schwarz-Haumont, metal framework; Robert et fils, heating. On 30 December 1983 the building was listed as a historic monument, and between 1990 and 1991 the Ministry for Cultural Affairs commissioned a study. Restoration of the building began in 1995 under the direction of Hervé Baptiste, chief architect for Historic Monuments. After a long period without maintenance, this monument of functionalism, "a hymn to metal and folded sheet" and a symbol of the euphoria of the Popular Front, seems at last to have been saved. Catherine Dumont d'Ayot and Franz Graf discuss its restoration in *Faces* no. 42/43, autumn/winter 1997/98. The study made by the J. Prouvé Workshops consists of eight hundred and thirty-eight plans, drawn mainly by Jean Boutemain between August 1936, the date of the call for bids, and March 1939. The J. Prouvé Collection also holds several sketches by Jean Prouvé. Photograph of the building seen from the boulevard du général Leclerc (formerly the boulevard de Lorraine) in 1939 (ill. 704,1). Plans (ill.704,3a–d) published in *Techniques et architecture* in 1955 with the following commentary: "The schedule required the building of a Maison du Peuple, the great hall of which could accommodate 1,500 to 2,000 people – so that it would be possible to show films (500 seats) in part of the great hall – and to make available a number of offices for the use of local societies, trades-unions, etc. The solution adopted was made possible by the fact that the two main components, the Market and the Maison du Peuple, never operated at the same time. The whole area of the ground floor was left free. On the first floor, the central part consisted of an operable floor, the eight components of which could be moved towards the stage and stored on it. The cinema and the promenades and foyer bar could be separated by a sliding partition of articulated panels that folded away behind the stage. Finally, the glazed roof which lit the hall was fully openable". During a conversation in 1982, Jean Prouvé explained to Jean-Marie Helwig: "So we come to the Maison du Peuple and the covered market of the town of Clichy. The municipality of Clichy made a courageous decision, persuaded by Lods to construct a building in an entirely new spirit… You find there all the techniques already described for the building at Buc (see no. 543). Not for the whole building, because there were design stages. First of all, architect's designs that I saw again recently in the municipal archives of Clichy, that I had obviously forgotten and that have nothing to do with what the building became during the construction stages. To my mind, this building, because I was responsible not only technically, for the design, but for the construction, was clearly an unexpected opportunity to make a demonstration. I made the most of it, I can tell you. First of all I designed the building as a whole, and from the start it had one characteristic – the framework was totally enclosed. There were no structural elements projecting through the facades. I considered that very important from the point of view of thermal insulation. So there's a framework and an outer envelope, two kinds of casing, on the one hand the large glazed bays that predominate in the photograph, and panels (see ill. 704,1). The canopies, the awnings, were bolted with thermal gaps to the main posts, which means that, here

117

and there, there were elements projecting through the facade, but very widely apart…

Then the first study, after the architect's study of one of the complicated general proposals, because this building had to provide a market on the ground floor, an auditorium on the first floor – a multi-purpose auditorium – and then, on the rear facade, offices for trades-unions and the town-hall. So it was something of a rarity, that is, it was a building that had to fulfil several functions. There was one thing that was essential, because of the smells of a market that sold fish and other foodstuffs with more or less strong smells… **The first structure frame** was designed at my office. I designed it in folded sheet, using thick sheets because it was the structure of a large building with beams of uniform strength of quite sophisticated construction but well suited to the facades that were added. Unfortunately there were difficulties, muddles, and finally one of the collaborating engineers took fright at the idea of a folded sheet structure and he decided to make a traditional structure of commercially produced sections."

Design for the structure in folded sheet: sketches by Jean Prouvé, drawn in August 1936 (ill. 704,4 and 704,5); plan 5563: cross section (ill. 704,6); plan 5566: posts in 60/10 sheet, too thick for the J. Prouvé Workshops folding press (ill. 704,7); plan 5567: beams; plan 5568: folded sheet flooring; plan 5576: main framework in folded sheet; plan 5561: overall perspective (ill. 704,8).

Jean Prouvé (in a conversation with Jean-Marie Helwig in 1982): "… And there is the framework that I was saying there was nothing to be ashamed of. These are posts in rolled section. At the top you see the two large main beams, quite attractive in shape, which support the tracks of the operable roof (ill. 704,9). Then a system of posts, traditional beams in rolled section… I faced all that with sheet, but at the start there was a much more highly characterised frame…"

Jean Prouvé (extract from *Jean Prouvé, une architecture par l'industrie*, Benedikt Huber and Jean-Claude Steinegger 1971): "The framework in rolled steel joists made by the company Schwartz-Haumont included the sliding roofing and the operable flooring, for which Bodiansky found the most elegant solutions, both in principle and mechanical detail…"

704,5

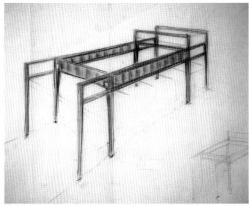

704,4

704,9

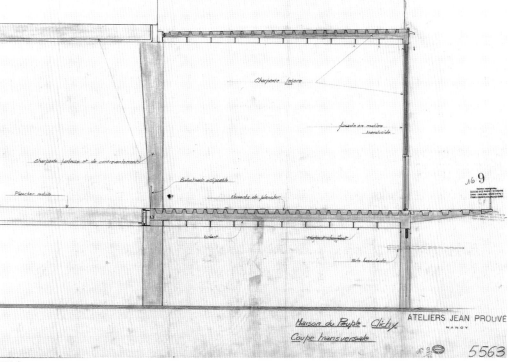

704,6

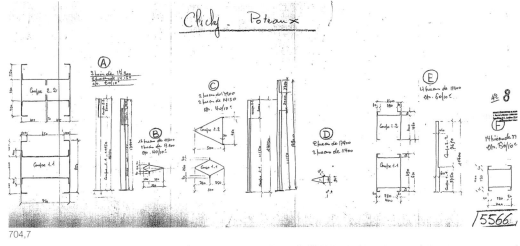

704,7

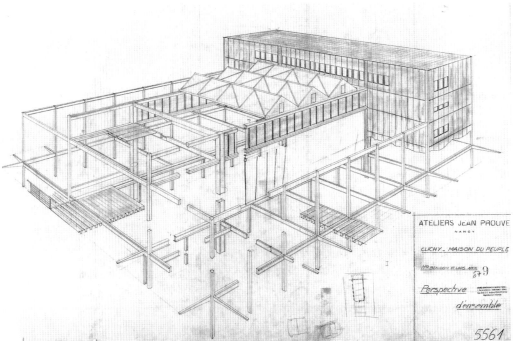

704,8

Jean Prouvé (in a conversation with Jean-Marie Helwig in 1982): "…On this photograph… (ill. 704,10) all the horizontal bars you can see are floor cuts that by a lift system are stored on top of each other and then put into place to fill in the gap. The floor sections were put into place, then they poured a slab of concrete on top and placed posts underneath because the slab was heavy, so this system of movable flooring was buried… These wide-span floors consisted of operable elements that could be stored away to open up completely a space above the covered market, the roof itself opening and consisting of three track-mounted skylights that could be moved aside, and so at the touch of a button it was possible to ventilate the market and open it to the sky. Equally, it was possible for entertainments to take place under the open sky. So, you can see there were mechanical problems in all that…"

The rolling skylight was made by the Etablissements Schwarz-Haumont; the facing panels by the J. Prouvé Workshops. Plan 5474: study for a skylight in folded sheet (ill. 704,11); photograph of the opened roof (ill. 704,12).

Jean Prouvé (in a conversation with Jean-Marie Helwig in 1982): "…the roofing consisted of three skylights that were mounted both on tracks and wheels and which, by an electric system… by moving outwards on the beams, could be opened up completely. This roof is still in working order today. When you press the button, it still operates… You can also see the large roof pans that made it possible to cover side rooms. All that was delivered below, already shaped, drilled, machined, and the installation was carried out very quickly…"

704,10

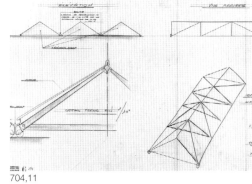

704,11

704,12

The great glazed facade of the Maison du Peuple was not a new problem for Jean Prouvé, who had already made the large window-wall of the Citroën showroom in Lyons in 1930/31 (see no. 181). In a blueprint of the architect's plan no. 109, dated 10 August 1936, we can see signs of the collaboration with Prouvé (ill. 704,13). In 24 August Jean Boutemain made a study for a transparent wall 4.20 m high with folded sheet posts, double sheets of Rhodoïd; and tube reinforcement. This study – plans 5523 to 5525 and 5582 – was not followed up. Construction was carried out in accordance with plan 7365, which carries the entry: "frames for Rhodoïd"; sketch by Jean Prouvé (ill. 704,14). Two plans, drawn by Robert Feck in December 1936 and carrying the entry: "rue Kloch facade – market gallery", are a study for folded sheet posts, sliding windows, and the folded sheet post that was actually used. Plan 5816 (ill. 704,15); plan 5817; construction plan 6794: folded sheet post (ill. 704,16); interior view of the large facade with panels in corrugated Rhodoïd (ill. 704,17).

Jean Prouvé (in a conversation with Jean-Marie Helwig in 1982): "… That is the mullion of the large window-walls (see ill. 704,16). It's a folded sheet section. Why these angles in the straight part? Simply to allow the knife of the press to pass through. You had to give three blows of the press to obtain the angle, and then afterwards squeeze the section to close it and make a tongue on which were screwed the plate-glass rebates, the shutter slides and the rebates for the interior transparent facing that I shall simply call the curtain. It's a plastic curtain. After forty years, these mullions are still there. All they need is the old paint scraping off and repainting. It's funny, but this mullion started a tradition. Afterwards you found all the builders using it, more or less altered, because there was a technical change and different sections became possible…"

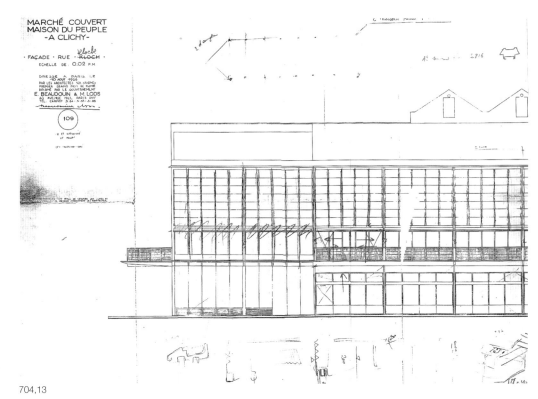

704,13

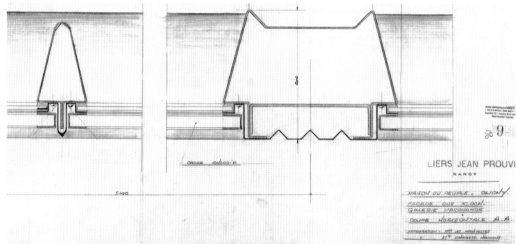

704,15

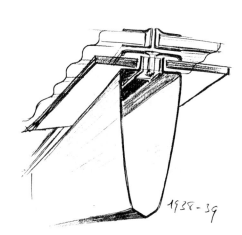

704,14

704,17

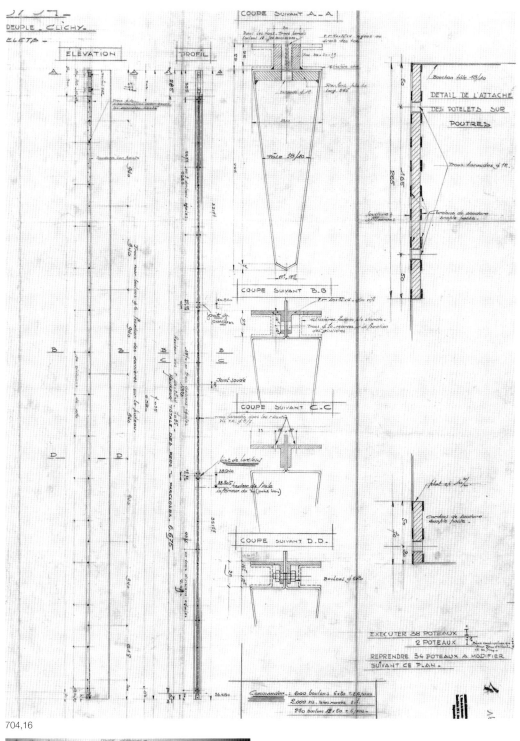

704,16

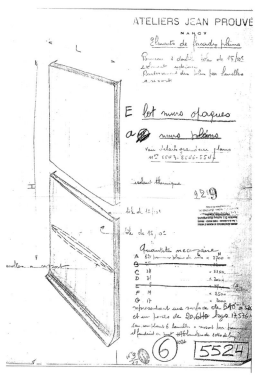

704,19

Non-load bearing facades hung on a load bearing frame had already been used in Chicago at the end of the 19th century (Reliance Building, architect, Burnham, 1895), and a remarkable example of a facade with two glass panes on a metal frame was made in 1903 at Giengen in Germany. The J. Prouvé Workshops had already made prefabricated facade components in sheet for the Flying Club at Buc (see no. 543). There had been difficulties then because of the width of the components and the welding of the sheets. For the Maison du Peuple of Clichy, Jean Prouvé designed a **curtain wall** consisting of narrow components attached to the floors, but the final answer was not discovered straightway. There follow a number of variants designed during this development: plan 5524 of August 1936, similar to the components of the Flying Club at Buc (ill. 704,19); detail of plan 5547: full facade panels – variant (ill. 704,20); plan 5547: detail of the joint (ill. 704,21);

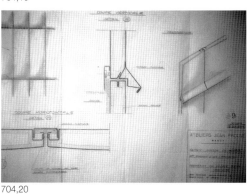

704,20

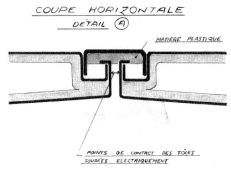

704,21

plan 5546: variant in which the "joint-cover" post is not yet integrated with the panel (ill. 704,22). On 19 January 1937 Jean Boutemain drew plan 5743: detail of the joint (ill. 704,23) and plan 5897 (ill. 704,24). The answer, which can be seen in a photograph of 1939 (ill. 704,25), had been found. Jean Prouvé's final solution is a significant example of combining several functions in the same component. The external folded sheet fulfils several functions:

– variations of temperature lead to expansion outwards and no change in size is registered at the joint;

– the folded sheet resists the horizontal forces and also prevents water from entering the joint;

– a visual purpose, because, since the sheet is bellied, we do not notice where it is not perfectly flat (see also Peter Sulzer 1990, pp. 129/130). Jean Prouvé (in a conversation with Jean-Marie Helwig in 1982): "… The facade is made up of panels very carefully designed form the technical viewpoint. First of all there was the question of panel size: the panels were a storey high and 1 m wide (1.04 m centre-to-centre). That was sheets 3 m high, I think, or 3.5 m. We could use sheets up to 4 m high and 1.2 m wide. This 1.2 m was useful for folding over the edges and making up the details… These panels seem bellied to you. They are bellied quite simply by those wonderful mattress springs which regularise the appearance of the sheet.

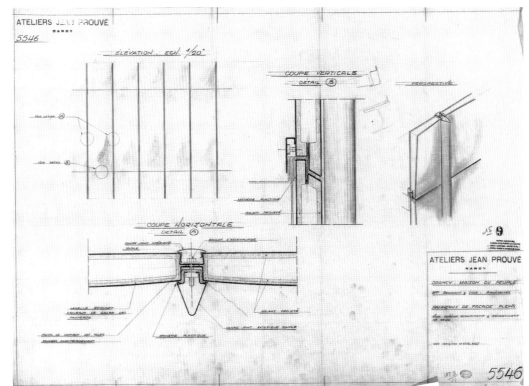

704,22

704,25

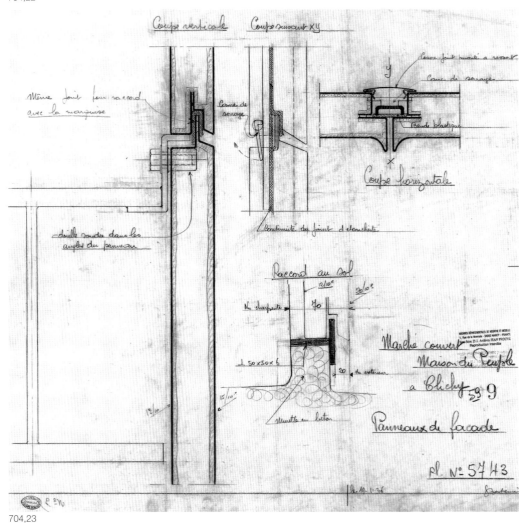

704,23

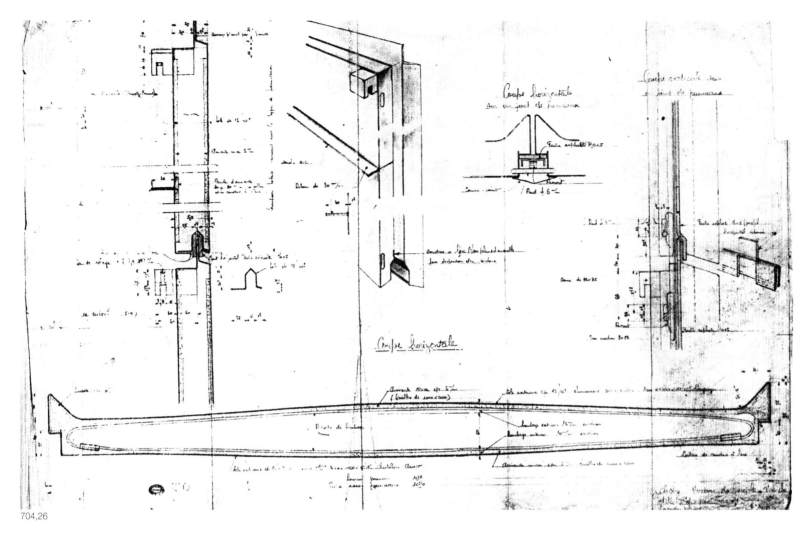

704,26

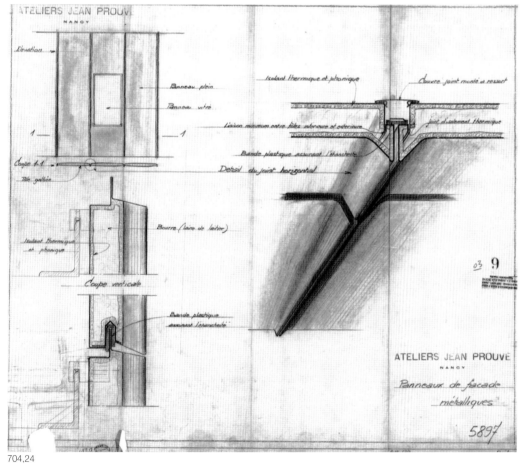

704,24

Nowadays we might find the bellying rather irritating, but it isn't ugly, however. It was quite attractive because it created a play of light. Obviously these days one would attach the sheets to supports, and would make sheets as flat as polished granite. But in those days it wasn't possible, so we had to use a bit of ingenuity…"

On 15 June 1937 Jean Boutemain drew two plans 6423 on which appears the final solution (ill. 704,26). The plan provides for leaf springs, but mattress springs were used – the idea of a workman. These springs can be seen in plan 6945, dated 21 December 1937, showing the last panels of the ground floor (ill. 704,27), with the entry: "sheet (external) 4.000 x 1,200 15/10 Longwy (steel-copper alloy, according to Jean Boutemain), two coats of 'Mica' 5 mm asbestos, slag wool".

Photograph of the installation (ill. 704,28); horizontal section at the joint (ill. 704,29); photograph of 1938/39 showing the watertightness test made by the town fire brigade (ill. 704,30).

Jean Prouvé (in a conversation with Jean-Marie Helwig in 1982): "…These panels that I gave you the size of were on average 60 mm thick. They were installed by two men. The lorry used to arrive from the factory with a supply of panels and park at the foot of the building. There was one man above and one below who attached the panel with quite a simple little device. A little electric winch took the panel up to the first floor and this panel was put in place by a single man, was hung like hanging an overcoat on a coat-peg. The hanging systems had an device for adjusting the vertical hang of the joints, because you can understand that with the manufacturing tolerances you would have had rather uneven facades, a bit all over the place, whereas what was needed was perfect alignment. This alignment was achieved by an adjustment device on each panel hook. It worked down to the last millimetre, micrometre you might say, so the result was perfect. These panels were delivered with a window glazed with plate glass and are in perfect condition… The section of the joint (see ill. 704,29) was very carefully worked. It seems quite simple, but it needed a lot of thought. You can see that on the outside the panels are not joined, there is a gap between the two panels. In fact, we wanted a wider gap than that. The reason for the gap: maintenance. You had to be able to rub down, paint, and clean. It was also necessary to consider the expansion of these panels, which are independent of each other. At 4 m high and 1 m wide, they change size in the heat or the cold. It's impossible to imagine a joint that could survive such alteration in size. So this was the trick: by folding we made a rebate which is a hollow groove, at the bottom of which we fixed between the two panels a strip of asphalt. This was like the sealant of an asphalt roof with an aluminium facing. You still find this today. We cut up these strips and fixed them to the panel, with the aluminium on the outside. So we had watertightness so long as the joint was pressed together. We thought of pressing them together permanently with screws, because the asphalt joint tends to creep rather… Then we decided that it was absolutely necessary to find a flexible joint that stays compressed in all weathers. That is why there is a slightly bent U-channel which fits against the asphalt joint, then a small piece the cross-section of which it would be interesting to see, because it is a spring, a sort of clip hooks on to the flange. These clips, set at every 50 or 60 cms, exert a flexible pressure on the joint-cover, and in more than forty years there has never been a single leak at Clichy. Water has never got in because the spring has always done its job. To fill in the gaps, when it was an office, we added a little external clip to hide all that, whereas for some storage and equipment rooms we left the joint visible.

The external shape, the purpose of which is to stiffen the 4 m high panel, has another role to play as well. In high winds and heavy rain, this shape creates an eddy of wind that prevents water entering the joint. At the time of handover we even put the Clichy building to a watertightness test with the help of the fire brigade, who came and drenched it with their hoses. I don't need to tell you they watered it more thoroughly than any storm or tempest would! But we had no leak at all.

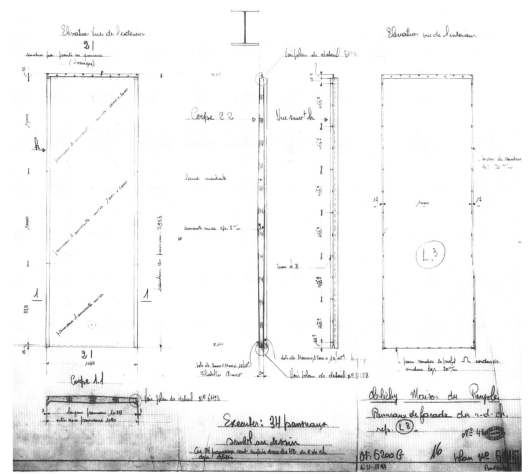

704,27

704,28

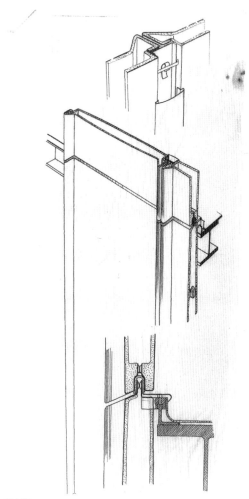

704,29

704,30

From this point of view it was very successful (see ill. 704,30)… You know, I saw the Maison du Peuple of Clichy recently and I'm absolutely astonished at the strength of the building after forty years; without maintenance, because the paint is worn down to the coat of anti-rust. And even the anti-rust is scaling rather! The building has never been repainted, which proves that the technique of folded sheet, which takes account of the threat of water infiltration both by atmospheric pressure and capillarity, is very effective… We took that into account at the time, at the same time as we dealt with heat insulation by means of a thermal gap… We hit upon the idea and I think we were the only ones building like that at this period… You can see the purity we achieved by using a sheet of metal. There was a real possibility of large-scale serial industrial production, components that would have made possible the construction of very varied buildings… The two men who installed the panels put up forty panels a day, that was 160m², since each panel was 4 m². Two men managed to close in a facade and seal the joint. Quite a little record for the time. There's a prototype panel made, photographed in the workshop (ill. 704,33). For hanging the panel, you see, it was simple: a little winch with a pulley, then a triangle that took the two panel hooks, which moved it up the facade. You hung it on and that was it. That's a small detail of the window stop. **The windows** opened outwards. We decided to make outward opening windows and we obviously had to stop them blowing in the wind, so there was a complicated system of springs and handles. By this time we were designing in a highly mechanical spirit and these pieces were bronze. I think at Clichy they removed some of these sheet windows and replaced them with aluminium windows. It's horrible, because they have enormous aluminium placards that are not at all in the spirit of the building…".
Before deciding to use outward-opening windows, the J. Prouvé Workshops studied several variants: casement windows opening outwards or inwards, pivoting windows, sliding windows. Plan 6940: the windows actually used with a window opening outwards (ill. 704,34); plan 6941: ground floor facade panels (ill. 704,35).

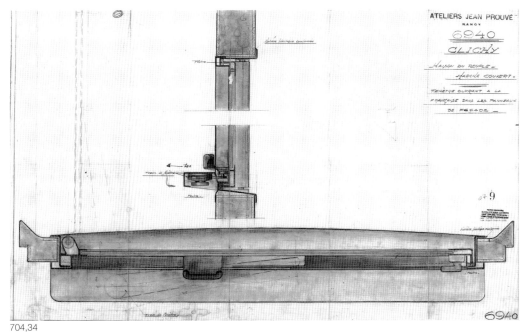

704,34

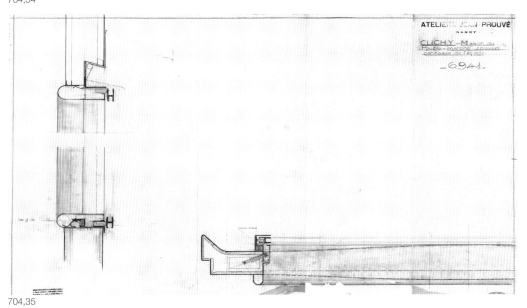

704,35

704,33

The J. Prouvé Workshops drew many studies for **the awnings.** Undated and unnumbered study: proposal with braces (ill. 704,36). Jean Boutemain told us during a conversation: "Bodiansky made the calculations… The brackets were made at Baccarat – we couldn't fold 5 mm sheet at our place…"; sketch by Jean Prouvé showing the development of the idea actually carried out: folded sheet bracket that reduced perforation of the curtain wall to the minimum (ill. 704,37); photograph of the brackets at

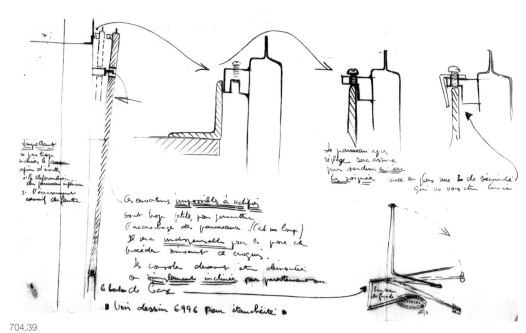

704,39

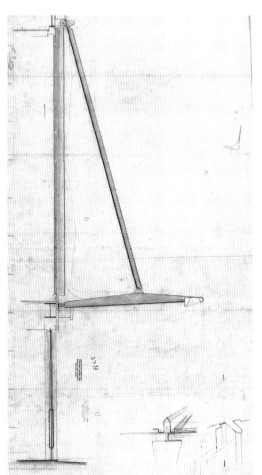

704,36

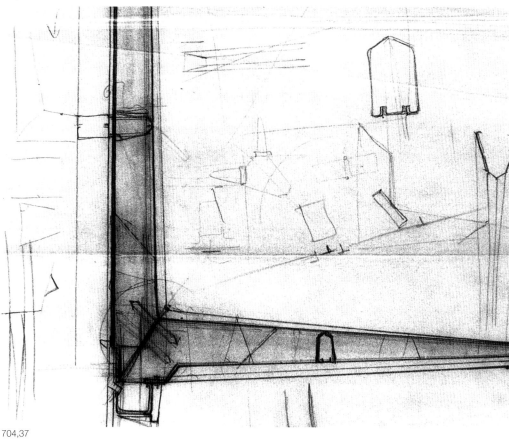

704,37

the corner of the curtain wall, with the lower mounting to the posts, penetration of the string course and upper mounting, photograph taken in 1998, after the restoration (ill. 704,38); sketch by Jean Prouvé with recommendations for the site workers (ill. 704,39). It seems that the installation of the panels to the brackets was not easy. The brackets of the glazed facade of the auditorium are different: they contain the down water-pipe. Plan 7068: section of the string-courses of the awning (ill. 704,40).

704,38

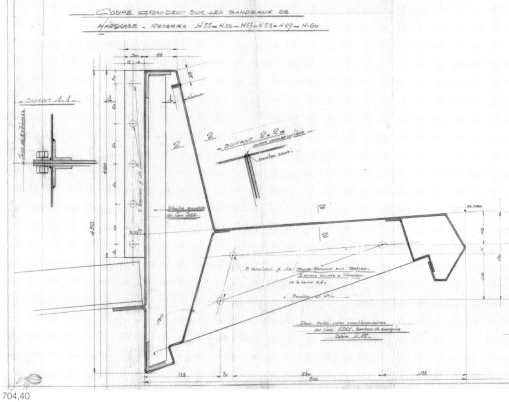

704,40

Facings and glazed doors. The metal structure frame made by Schwartz-Haumont being in drawn sections, the J. Prouvé Workshops "faced" it with folded sheet components. In the J. Prouvé Collection there are a large number of plans showing these components: facing of the posts and upper beam of the main entrance, facing of the breaks in the wall, of the facade courses, the beams above the doors, the terrace courses, etc. The glazed doors were important components of the covered market, which opened on to three streets, and they were therefore carefully designed. Plan 5518: pivotinging bay (of the market), including two unoperable bays and two doors opening 180° (ill. 704,41); photograph of the entrance doors on the boulevard de Lorraine (704,42); plan 6433: doors on to the boulevard Lorraine and on the rue des Morillons sides (ill. 704,43); plan 6509: alterations to the profile of the doors in July 1937 (ill. 704,44); plan 6627: plan and elevation of doors on to the boulevard de Lorraine; plan 6814: handle attachment; plan 6469: upper and lower hinges; plan 7476: entrance doors of the offices. Unfortunately, all the glazed doors have been removed.

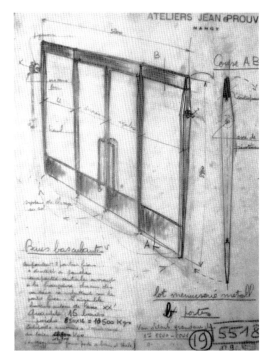

704,41

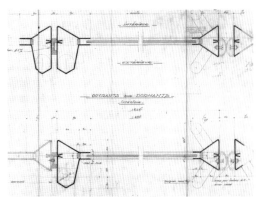

704,43

704,42

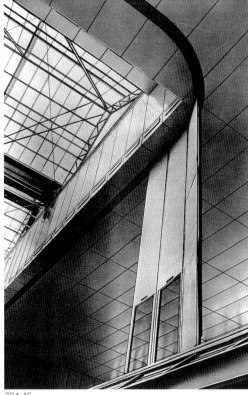

704,45

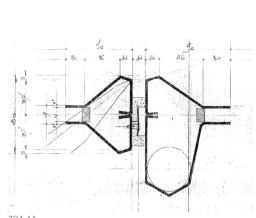

704,44

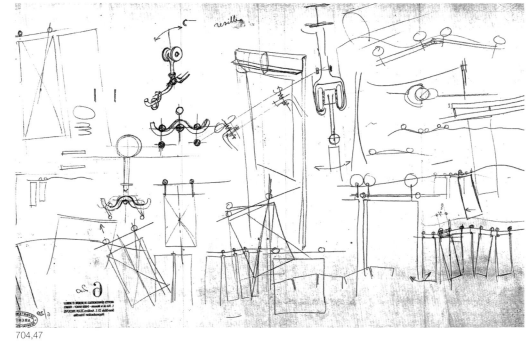

704,47

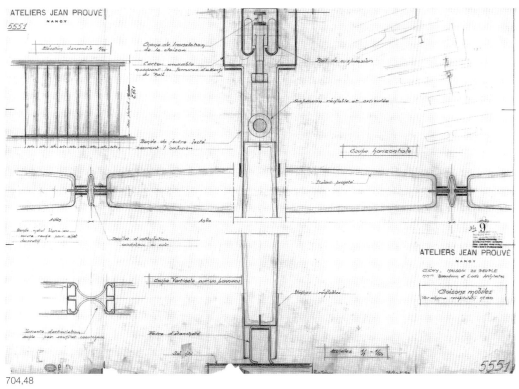

704,48

704,46

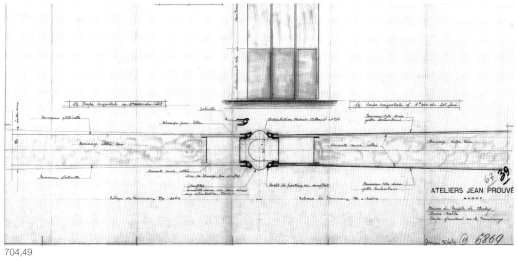

704,49

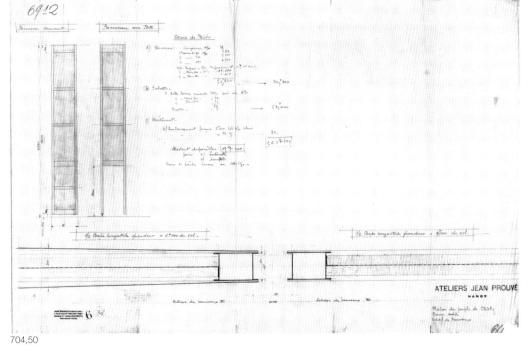

704,50

Jean Prouvé (during a conversation with Jean-Marie Helwig in 1982): "… These photographs show you the considerable size of the auditorium, which was above all conceived as a meeting hall. A mechanically controlled **operable partition** system (ill. 704,45 and 704,46) enables its volume to be decreased to make a room of, I think, 600 seats that can be used as a cinema or a dance hall, whatever. The partition consists of vertically hung panels that are stored in the space at the back of the building, and are operated by a button and close in the building. This partition is still in working order… It's a very fine articulated partition with flexible and articulated joints that run on a tubular track hanging in a groove." The J. Prouvé Workshops had already designed and made a operable partition for the town hall of Boulogne-Billancourt (see Complete Works, ill. 340,11 to 340,14). The design had been done by Jean-Marie Glatigny, who was also responsible for that of the Maison du Peuple from August 1936 to May 1938. The mechanism was designed and delivered by Fossier, Allard et Cie. Sketch by Jean Prouvé (ill. 704,47): plan 5551 of 28 August 1936 (ill. 704,48); plan 6869 of November 1937 with a new articulation design (ill. 704,49); plan 6837: details of the perforation, holes of 50 mm in the upper part, of 8 mm in the lower part, certainly the suggestion of the consultant engineer; unnumbered plan with the entry: "2 panels – prototype"; plan 6912 of 6 December 1937 with a perforated 5/10 sheet in the panel axis (ill. 704,50); plans 7058, 7060 and 7475: floor-level sound-proofing.

The operable floor made necessary a **retractable balustrade** that was designed and made by the J. Prouvé Workshops. Three variants of August 1936: plan 5531 (ill. 704,51), detail of plan 5544 with metal netting and springs (ill. 704,52) and detail of plan 5545 (ill. 704,53); plan 6608 of July 1937, on a different principle, with tilting folded sheet spindles with a counterweight (ill. 704,54). At the time of the restoration retractable balustrades with counterweights were discovered. The J. Prouvé Workshops also made fixed balustrades, the balustrades on the components of the operable floor and the balcony railing. Photograph of the sliding doors on to the boulevard de Lorraine, taken in 1984 (ill. 704,55); plan 6903: sliding windows on the balcony (ill. 704,56).

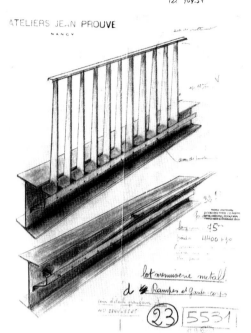

704,51

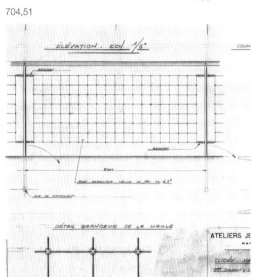

704,52

704,55

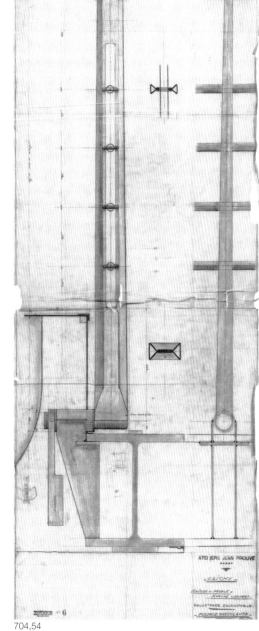

704,54

704,53

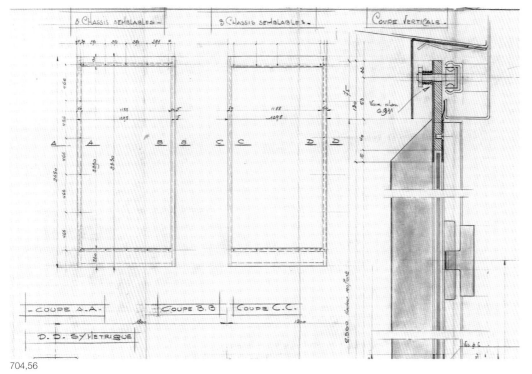

704,56

Jean Prouvé (during a conversation with Jean-Marie Helwig in 1982): "... All **the ceilings** were in sheet. Initially the building was heated by radiation from the ceiling. There was a network of pipes that heated to a high temperature. The steam heated the ceiling, which radiated a moderate temperature that was comfortable for the occupants. This system, instead of being repaired and maintained, was simply cut off at its source and replaced by wretched radiators placed all round the building, installed any-old-how, without any respect for anything... That is the framework of the ceiling. There was insulation under the steel roof, of course, a quite thick layer of compressed glass wool, then, below that, stiffeners on which the ceiling components were placed, simply held on by springs. At the end, in order to make an inspection, with an architect friend we took down the ceiling components, and it was all working properly. We took the ceiling down and put it up again quite easily. There were also warm-air nozzles to supplement the spatial heating." Plan 6592: installation of mounting brackets for the beams of the under-terrace heated ceiling (704,57); sketch by Jean Prouvé showing the heated ceiling (ill. 704,58).

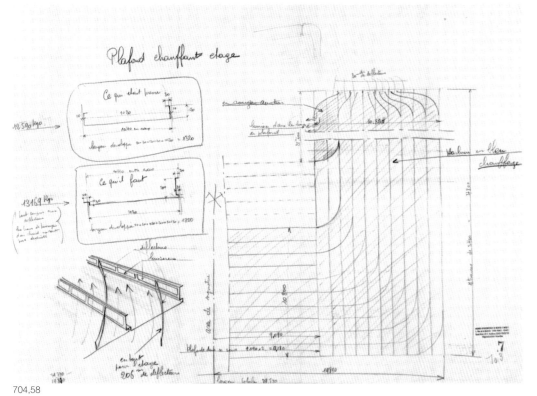

704,58

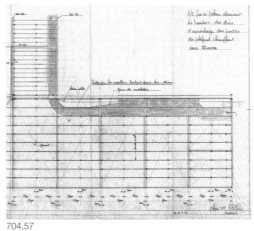

704,57

704,60

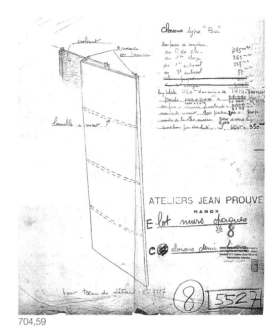

704,59

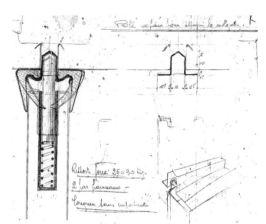

704,61

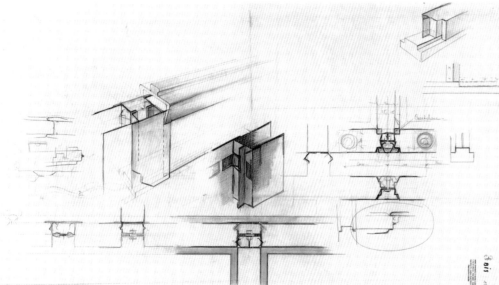

704,62

For the office section of the Maison du Peuple Jean Prouvé developed a new system of **movable metal partitions** very different from the system patented in 1931 (see no. 190). On plan 5527 of August 1936, the bid plan, we still see the "Buc-type partition" (ill. 704,59); but in Jean Prouvé's sketches we can see a "single-piece" partition with rubber sections coming into being (ill. 704,60, 704,61 and 704,62); plan 7609 of September 1938 showing the final solution (ill. 704,63); plan 7406: glazed door; photograph of a glazed component taken in 1984 (ill. 704,64). The geometry of the joint was taken up later by many partition systems. For the toilets, the J. Prouvé Workshops proposed and made "single-piece" metal cubicles. Photograph about 1939 (ill. 704,65).

704,64

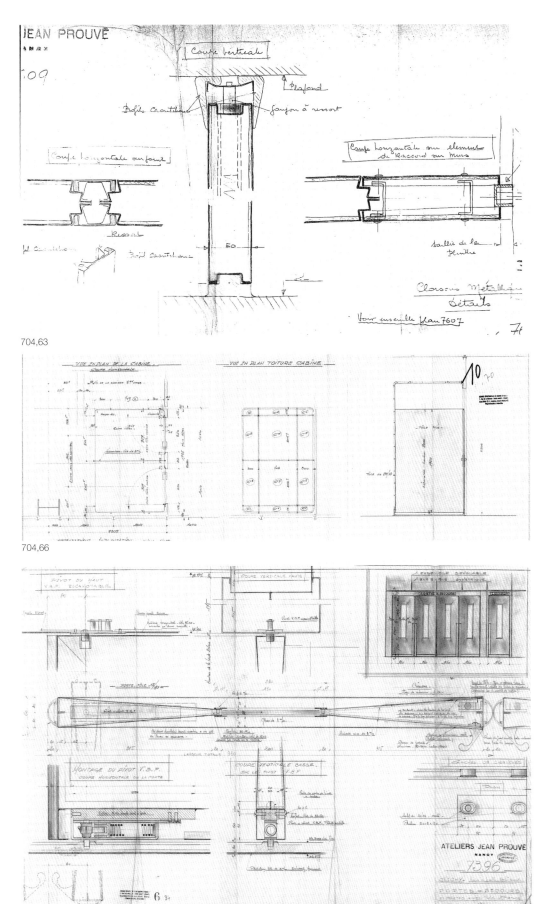

704,63

704,66

704,67

704,65

Jean Prouvé (during a conversation with Jean-Marie Helwig in 1982): "…As at Buc, we made the **toilet cubicles** in the workshop, and this photograph shows clearly enough the quality of the interior, though the toilet itself is not as attractive as you get today. However, I must say that there are some toilets today that have decorative pretensions and are unspeakable. At least these had a certain honesty. And the sheet work is impeccable…" They were simple sheet steel cubicles and, as he often did, Jean Prouvé avoided joints in the corners. Plan 7327 with the heading: "WC ensemble first and third floor offices" (Ill. 704,66); full-scale section of the WC, showing how the cubicles were connected to the partitions. In the J. Prouvé Collection there are documents about co-operation with the Forges de Strasbourg over the cubicles. Between the first floor auditorium, the escape stairs and the toilets, the J. Prouvé Workshops made two groups of doors in accordance with plan 7396 (ill. 704,67).

Jean Prouvé (during a conversation with Jean-Marie Helwig in 1982): "…To reach the auditorium from the street, there were two large **stairways** on the right and the left, which were very interesting from the construction point of view, because the two sides of the stairs, the two strings, created an 8 m span of beams. It was a folded sheet girder, delivered equipped with its hand-rail. Only the steps were installed on site, so as not to have too large a volume to transport…" Photograph of 1984 (ill. 704,68); plan 5810: entrance stairs (ill. 704,69); plan 5819: detail of the steps (ill. 704,70); plans 5864 and 5959: photograph of one of the escape stairs of the offices, taken in 1984 (ill. 704,71); plans 5584 and 7260: service stairs; plan 8128 of March 1939, one of the last plans (ill. 704,72).

Jean Prouvé (during a conversation with Jean-Marie Helwig in 1982): "…This building still exists, it's more than forty years old, and it has behaved wonderfully well when you consider that it has never been maintained. Rather than maintain it, the local council of Clichy preferred, for example, to remove the ground floor panels, which should have been repainted and maintained, because there was nothing wrong with them except the paint work. It preferred to remove them and replace them with brick, which means that the ground floor of this building is now in brick. There's nothing wrong with brick in itself, but I can't understand why it was done." There were other alterations to be regretted. In connection with the demolished balcony: " 'Improvements' were made by architects who had not designed the building and who have transformed the main facade into the frontage of a large Parisian hairdresser's; it's a shame, but you could, if you wanted, get rid of it. If the town of Clichy had made the necessary effort this building could have been restored; quite easily. For that you would need the agreement not only of the town of Clichy, but of the Ministry for Cultural Affairs. This building should be listed. (Author's note: Happily the building is now listed and restoration is under way. A great effort!) It can't be, because one of the architects, Eugène Beaudouin, is still alive. At that time Beaudouin and Lods were associates. Unfortunately Lods died a few years ago.

704,68

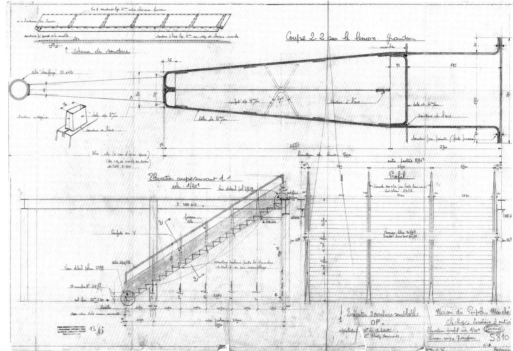

704,69

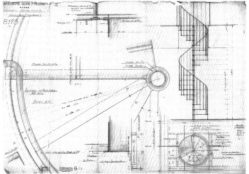

704,72

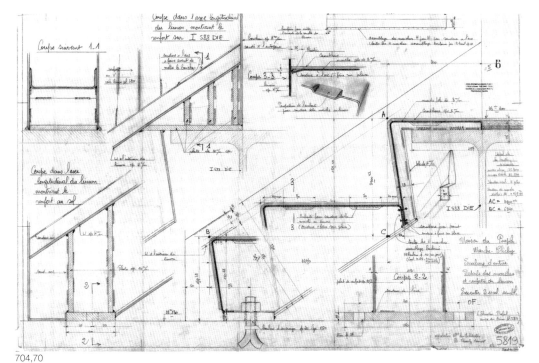

704,70

704,71

I wish Eugène Beaudouin a long life, but it's a pity we can't sort this problem out… Why all this decay and no watch kept on it? I'll never understand, because the building amazed the Americans at the time. I'll always remember a visit the architect Frank Lloyd Wright made to Clichy. You know what this architect had done, and he was staggered, absolutely astonished by the techniques and the innovation of the building. He said: "We haven't got as far as this in the United States!" And he was right that, in many things, we were ahead of the Americans: in mullions for the facades in between which plate glass could be installed, and in the panels which were for the first time called a curtain wall. (Author's note: The first similar curtain wall was made in 1951 in Pittsburgh for the Alcoa building, the architects of which were Harrison and Abromovitz. Its designer, Oscar Nitschke, certainly knew the Maison du Peuple.) …The building was finished between 1938 and 1939. There's no need to tell you that the war brought everything to a stop, and during the war the auditorium was turned into a clothes store, or a store for all sorts of things. The German occupation speeded up the damage, but there was no structural damage, no damage to the sheet metal…

I could never understand why Marcel Lods, who was still alive, who was the architect of the building, and who never ceased making claims for it and quoting it as an example, was able at the end of his life to let it deteriorate without making a stand. It's true that he had other things on his mind. At that time he was doing the Grande Mare and all those large metal buildings in the Orléans region, which I followed with great interest, but I noted that unfortunately he had withdrawn from what we had done. He suffered a very clear regression, because he began to build like the builders of the Eiffel period. He contributed nothing to industrialised building. Perhaps what I'm saying isn't very kind, but he did nothing in the way of industrialisation with the tendencies and aims of that of the Clichy market.

This proves that in work that is necessarily collaborative, architecture, you can't do it by yourself… At the present time there is a clear falling of standards in architectural design and construction. It's time to make a list of the exceptions. There are good things from time to time, but they're rare and they're not for the wider public. What is needed is collaborative work.

704,73

But collaborative work is only possible when a group of men share the same ideas. This doesn't mean there will be no arguments, differences, conflict. Nevertheless, they will have a certain line of action in mind, and I have to say that at the time I worked on Clichy there was in my workshop a spirit I have never come across elsewhere. The colleagues who built it and the designers who prepared things held nothing back. For them it was a competition. They were proud of what they were doing. The winner was the one who worked the fastest, the one who installed the fastest or manufactured the best.

It was absolutely true, and when I try to make the point now, people don't believe me. They take me for a bit of a dreamer. But I am sure of what I say, because I lived through it. And here's the proof, when you look at these things. If you look at a chair made forty years ago, you can see it's very well made. If the workman who made it had not had the taste to make it, it would not have been of this quality. And I believe that if you don't rediscover this in the world of building, you won't make anything…" Maison du Peuple after the restoration (ill. 704,73).

Important publications on the Maison du Peuple:
Charlotte Ellis, Prouvé's peoples' palace, *The Architectural Review* no. 1059, May 1985, pp. 41–47;
Bruno Reichlin, Maison du Peuple at Clichy – A masterpiece of "synthetic" functionalism, *Daidalos* no. 18, 1985, pp. 88–99;
Jean-Claude Bignon and Catherine Coley, *Jean Prouvé entre artisanat et industrie* 1923–1939, Ecole d'architecture of Nancy 1990.

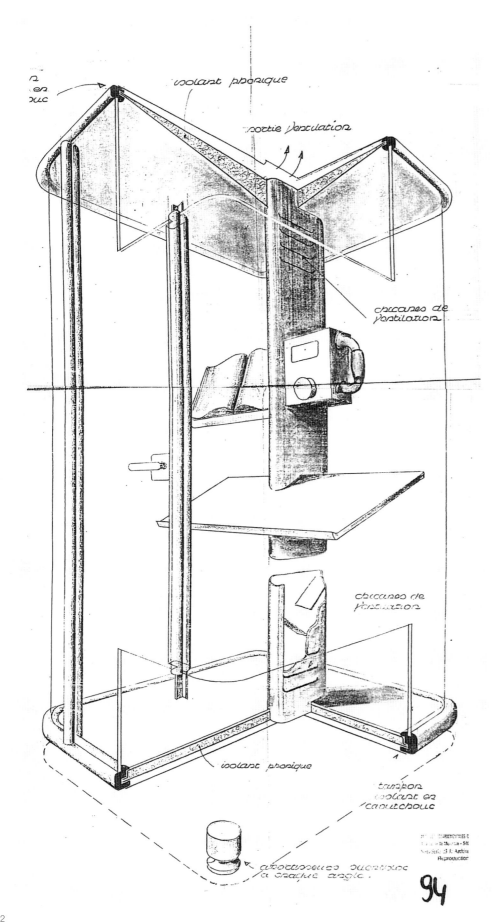

isolant phonique

sortie ventilation

chicanes de
ventilation

chicanes de
ventilation

isolant phonique

tampon
isolant en
caoutchouc

caoutchoucs amortisseurs
à chaque angle.

94

711,2

711. Design for a telephone box. 1937. In July 1937, R. F. drew a series of proposals for telephone boxes. In the plans inventory we find the entry: "telephone box – Le Mans – Gruzelle". Compared with the boxes of 1933 (see Complete Works, no. 350) and of 1936 (see Complete Works, nos. 607 to 609), these are revolutionary. Plan 6550: box with a central post, entirely glazed, with curved pane glass and rubber sections with integrated reinforcement; plan 6587: perspective section of the box of plan 6550 (ill. 711,2). For his lectures at the Conservatoire National des Arts et Métiers, Jean Prouvé drew a similar box: the post is aluminium tube, linking iron and cast aluminium pieces (ill. 711,4).

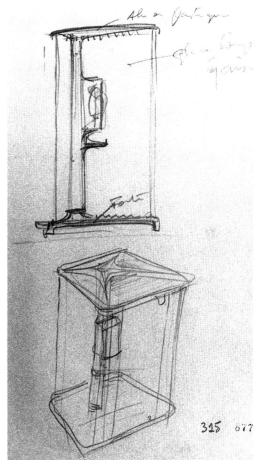

711,4

715. B.L.P.S. (Beaudouin, Lods, Prouvé, Strasbourg) demountable house in steel.

1937/38. Eugène Beaudouin and Marcel Lods, architects; the J. Prouvé Workshops and Forges de Strasbourg, constructors. The J. Prouvé Workshops made a prototype that was presented at the sixth Exposition de l'Habitation in the Salon des Arts Ménagers in January 1939. Marcel Lods personally demonstrated it. Despite a warm welcome from the public and the press, no order for it was ever given. There follows a description of this prototype, which has disappeared: "The external measurements of this small house are 3.3 x 3.3 m. It consists of a room 3.3 x 2.25 m, amply lit, with two articulated divan beds, a drop-leaf table hiding crockery shelving and two hinged cupboards, a kitchen and a toilet. Made entirely of sheet steel, it weighs 1,420 kg, to which must be added 300 to 500 kg of various accessories with which it is equipped. There is no doubt that after improvements have been made to this model (which is a prototype), the total weight will be lowered to approximately 1,500 kg, including accessories. The aim is to provide holiday accommodation that is comfortable enough to make for a pleasant stay even when there is continuous bad weather. Although it has not the immediate mobility of a tent, which can be carried about as a bag, it should, however, be light enough to be moved once or several times in a season. At the end of the season it should be quickly demountable for winter storage and be able to be re-erected anywhere at the start of the next season without any advance preparation. It should not take more than a few hours to erect (4 to 5 at the maximum); disassembly should take something like two hours. The reduced size, its lightness, ease of transport and the total absence of fixed fittings (water supply, drainage, WC) aim to solve the problem associated with camping, but on the other hand the house will provide what is practically impossible in normal camping installations: a heated room, lit so as to allow reading and work, a

715,1

ARCHITECTES : E. BEAUDOUIN ET M. LODS
CONSTRUCTEURS : ATELIERS JEAN PROUVÉ ET FORGES DE STRASBOURG

PRIX : 25.000 Frs.

Volume	30 m³		*Année de construction*	1939
Surface construite	11 m²		*Durée de montage*	5 heures
Surface habitable	8 m²		*Durée de démontage*	environ 2 heures

INTÉRIEURS :   *LA NUIT*   *LE JOUR*   *DÉTAIL DE LA CUISINE*

715,2

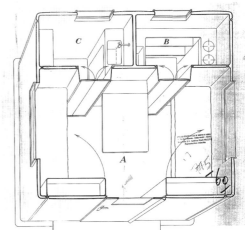

715,3

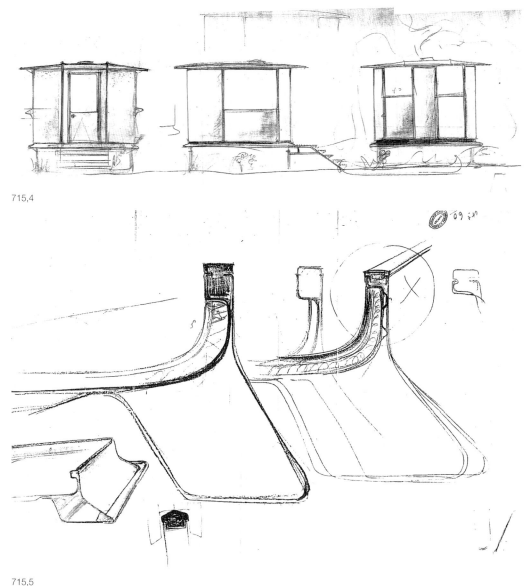

715,4

715,5

kitchen in which hot food can be produced, and toilet and shower". Contemporary photographs showing the exterior (ill. 715,1) and the interior (ill. 715,2); publication drawing: A – living-room, B – kitchen, C – toilet, shower (ill. 715,3). The documents in the J. Prouvé Collection enable us to reconstruct the co-operation between the architect and the J. Prouvé Workshops: in July 1937 Jean-Marie Glatigny made the first drawings, plans 6510 and 6511, showing the holiday house as a whole; in September Jean Prouvé's design office drew plans 6690 to 6701, which more or less define the house; plans of the Beaudouin and Lods office drawn between 11 October 1937 and 7 January 1938, relating mainly to drainage, furnishing, the shower niche, the principle of the central core, and a proposal not carried out for division into panels "of 9 similar components)". This leads one to believe there was intense collaboration between the architects and the J. Prouvé Workshops. In the J. Prouvé Collection there are approximately fifty undated and unnumbered sketches, including several by Jean Prouvé and his brother, Henri. Elevations (ill. 715,4); details of the floor (ill. 715,5); details of the assembling of the external panels with the roof (ill. 715,6); rubber sections, draft by Jean Prouvé: "always the most advanced technology" (ill. 715,7). In a conversation with me, Jean Prouvé explained: "…B.L.P.S. was entirely made at my place… an enormous number of innovations… like the system of assembling the panels…

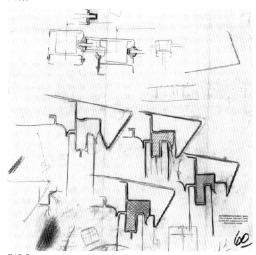

715,6

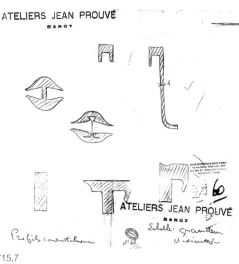

715,7

It's equipped like a boat... I remember all the details. Les Forges de Strasbourg paid very little... (The prototype was) made in the rue des Jardiniers at the time of Buc and Clichy... We didn't waste time, it took a week... My brother (Henri Prouvé), who was quite young, did some drawing... some sketches by me..." In the plans inventory and in the J. Prouvé Collection there are fifty-three numbered plans, mostly drawn by Henri Prouvé and Jean-Marie Glatigny. Plan 6691: roof in perspective (ill. 715,8); plan 6701: floor in perspective (ill. 715,9); plan 6692: joints between the panels (ill. 715,10);

715,8

715,9

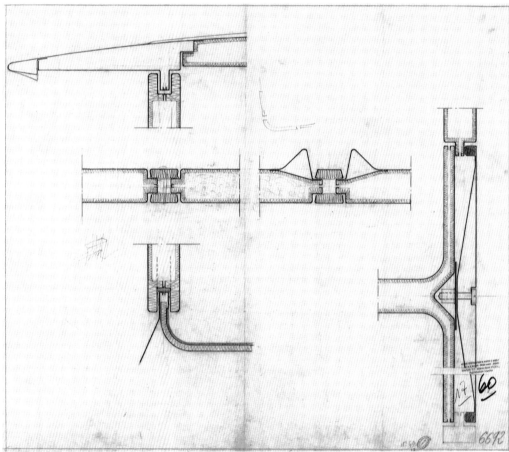

715,10

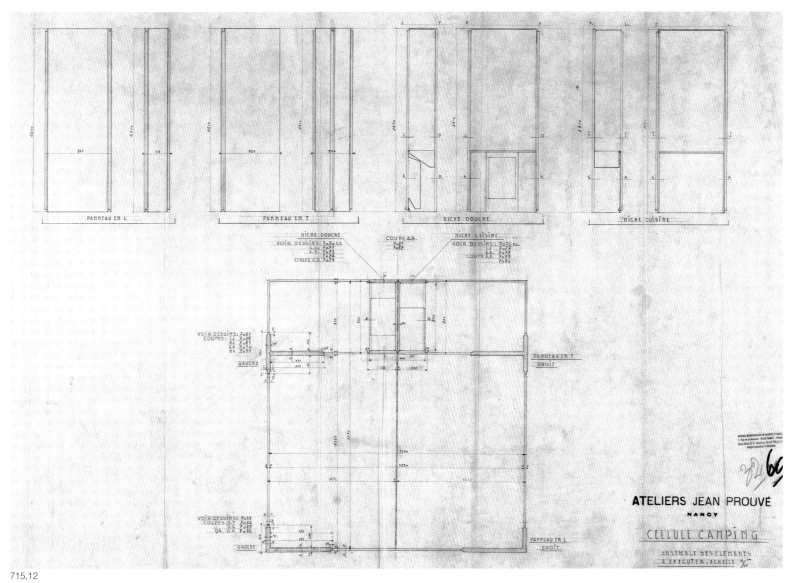

715,12

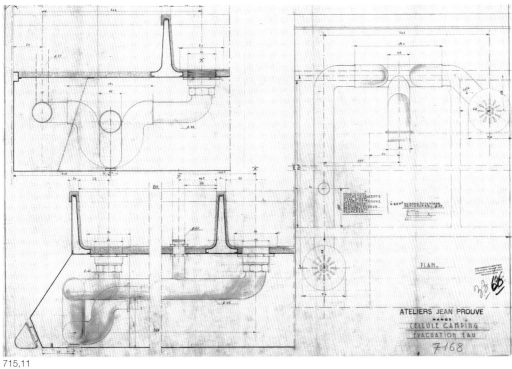

715,11

plan 7168: water drainage (ill. 715,11); plan 7092: ensemble of components to be made (ill. 715,12). There are also approximately forty unnumbered sketches. After the B.L.P.S. house, Jean Prouvé took up the idea of the "weekend house" again in March 1939 (see no. 804).

716. Works carried out for the French Legation building in Ottawa, Canada. 1936–1938. Eugène Beaudouin, architect; A. Mouette and M. Parizeau, inspecting architects. According to the plans inventory of the design office, more than four hundred plans relating to this project were drawn between April 1936 and October 1938, and this does not take into account unnumbered plans. The first studies were for folded sheet metal building fittings. This large order was carried out in extruded bronze. The sections were extruded by Maier et Cie of Lausanne. Four bow-windows: contemporary photograph (ill. 716,1); construction plan 6254: horizontal section of the bow-window with the numbers of the extruded sections, showing the double-glazing and the thermal separations (ill. 716,4); running casement windows mounted on a tube hinge, similar to those of plan 6254. Doors and glazed bays: plan 5854: six bays for the drawing room, 6.22 m high, the upper part in fixed triple glazing and the lower doors mounted on tube hinging (ill. 716,5); internal doors; bay of the hall, 6.94 x 10.35 m; drawing room bay; entrance portico, internal and external doors in bronze; French windows in bronze for the library; living room bay; doors for the anteroom and the boudoir; bays and doors in bronze for the gym room. Other works carried out: stairway similar to that of the U.A.M. pavilion (see 654,1 to 654,3); skylights, chimney stacks and hoods; design for a garage door; sketch and proposals by Jean Prouvé for railings and balustrades; lamp stands for the great drawing room, blueprint of a sketch by the architect (ill. 716,7) and by Jean Prouvé (ill. 716,8); sketch by Jean Prouvé explaining the installation of the caravel in the garden pond for the Jacques Cartier monument.

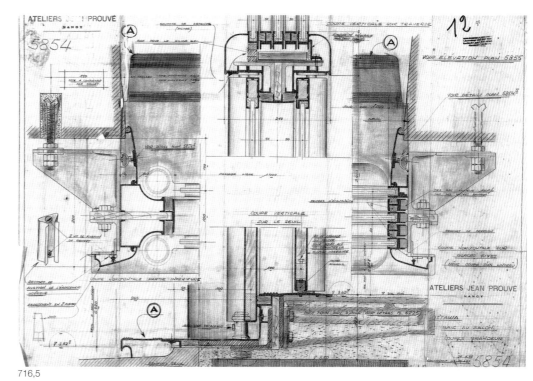

716,5

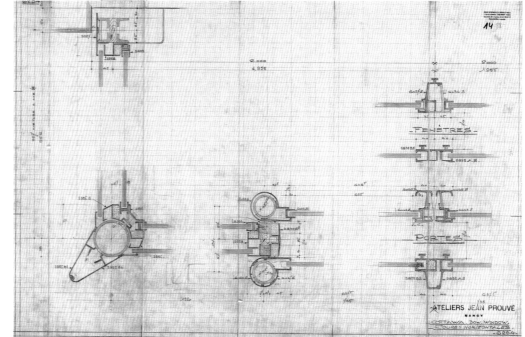

716,4

716,1

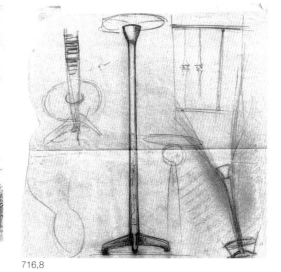

716,7   716,8

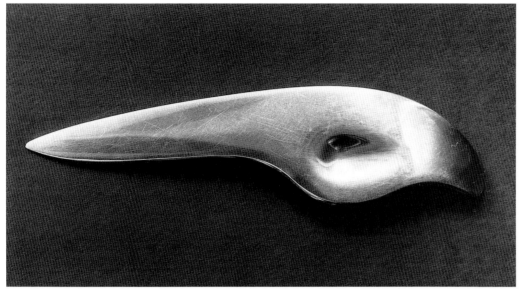

731,4

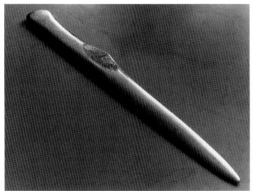

731,5

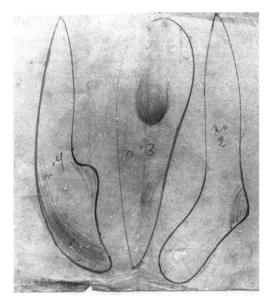

731,2

731. Stainless steel paper-knife. About 1938. There are three variants of these paper-knives, presents for architects and made by Pierre Missey. Sketches by Jean Prouvé numbered 1 to 4 (ill. 731,2); cardboard models made by Pierre Missey so as not to damage the sketches; photograph of the paper-knife shown in sketch no. 4 (ill. 731,4) and of a model for which there is no sketch (ill. 731,5).

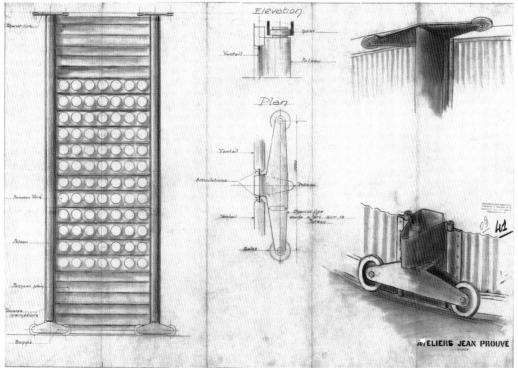

739,3

739. Design for an articulated rolling door for a circular aircraft hangar. 1938. Door approximately 12 m high. Unnumbered plans, drawn by Jean-Marie Glatigny: overall plan; details of the post and the bogie, with reductor mechanism and articulation; detail of bogies and variant door with portholes (ill. 739,3). On the plans we find the entry: "R = 60 m". This was probably a proposal by the J. Prouvé Workshops for the design for an aircraft hangar by the engineer Eugène Mopin in collaboration with the architects Eugène Beaudouin and Marcel Lods, published by Jean-Claude Bignon and Catherine Coley (1990, p. 56).

786. Design for a demountable barrack unit for the Ministry of Aviation. 1938. This competition, launched in August/September 1938, was for barracks to accommodate married non-commissioned officers, unmarried non-commissioned officers, and the ranks. This building with a 40 x 8 m metal framework had a ceiling height of 3.5 m. The J. Prouvé Workshops study includes thirty drawings relating to two variants: one with a structure of central portal frames (see no. 786.a and no. 786.b); the other with an external structure frame (see 786.c). These two principles were taken up later by Jean Prouvé in numerous designs and works carried out.

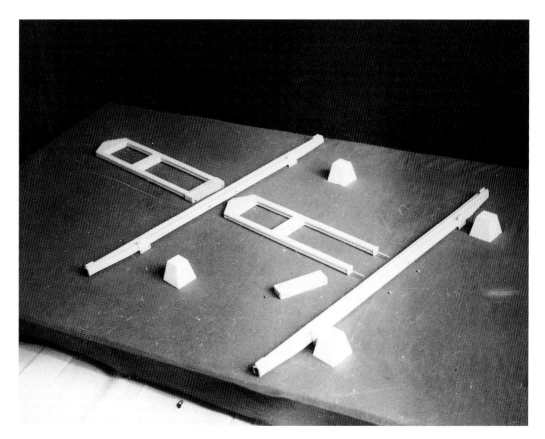

786.a,1

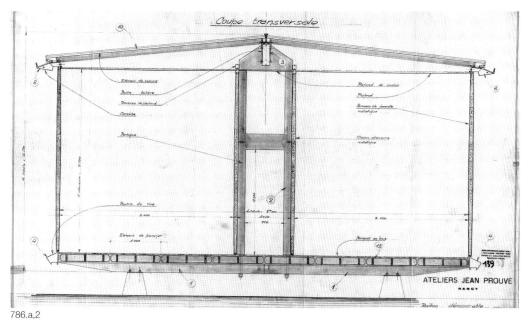

786.a,2

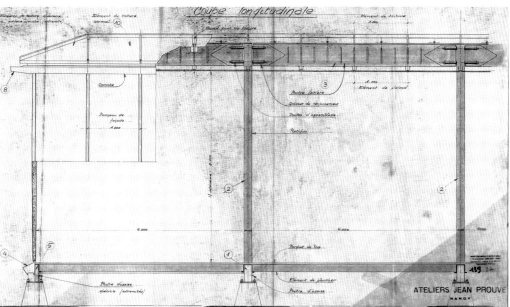

786.a,3

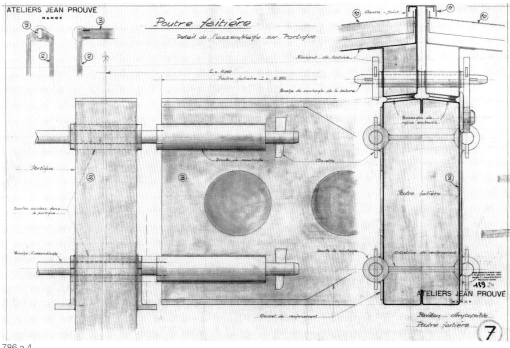

786.a,4

786.a. Design for demountable barrack unit with central portal frames. For the competition Jean Prouvé presented plans numbered 1 to 26 and a model. There is a series of photographs of this model showing the assembly sequence (ill. 786.a,1). The twenty-six plans were drawn between November and December 1938 by Jean-Marie Glatigny and Jean Boutemain.
Plan 7731 (no. 1); plan 7733 (no. 3): cross section (ill. 786.a,2); plan 7734 (no. 4); longitudinal section (ill. 786.a,3); plan 7737 (no. 7): ridge beam, detail of assembly on girder (ill. 786.a,4);

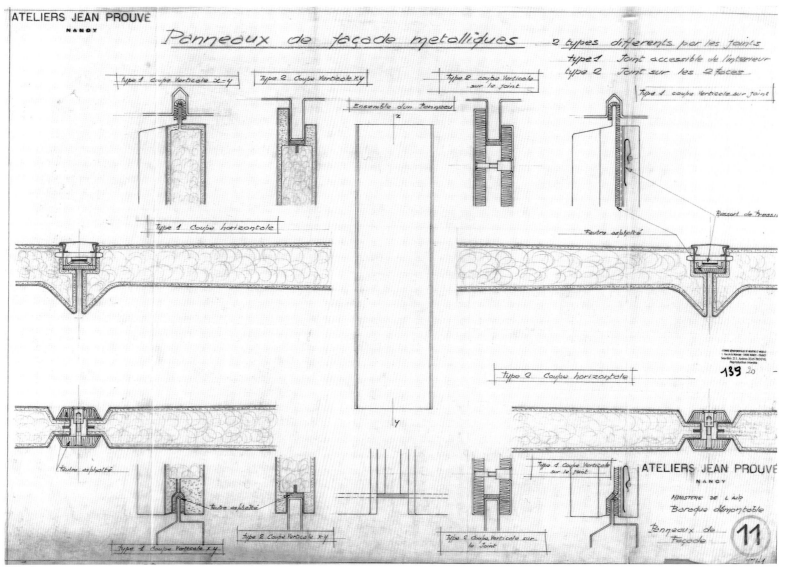

786.a,5

plan 7741 (no. 11): metal facade panels (ill. 786.a,5), with two different types of joint, one of which had already been used for the Maison du Peuple (see no. 704) and the other for the B.L.P.S. demountable house (see no. 715); plan 7900 (no. 26). Probably at the request of the client, there is also a bid for masonry facades and partitions, and a bid for cladding in prefabricated wood and fibrociment sections. For this project there exist strength calculations for the structures (wind, snow, overload, heat, expansion …). According to Jean Prouvé's curriculum vitae, it was this competition that "led to the creation of the portal frame structure", but unfortunately in the J. Prouvé Collection there is no sketch by Jean Prouvé relating to this important project.

786.b. Patent no. 849.762, "Demountable metal frame structure". Entered on 2 February 1939, published on 1 December 1939.

786.c. Design for demountable barrack unit, variant with external structure frame. Plan 7753: perspective section showing the external frames linked by drop and spandrel panels forming a windbracing beam (ill. 786.c). This principle was used with modifications for the open-air centre of Onville (see no. 828) and the military barrack units (see no. 850).

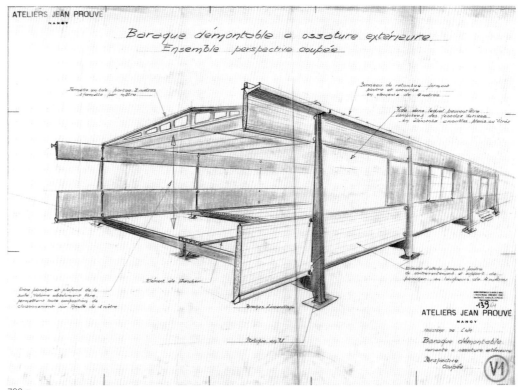

786.c

790,3

790,5

790,6

790. Design for a prefabricated metal house.
1938–1944. Eugène Beaudouin and Marcel Lods, architects. In the J. Prouvé Collection there are blueprints of architects' plans of October 1938 relating to the construction of this house in wood. Study with sketch by Jean Prouvé, unfortunately undated (ill. 790,3); another study for this "BL" house dated December 1938, based on the portal frame system (see no. 786); plan 7834: metal framework for a building with stressed skin; seven plans of the BL house with estimate of costs: plans 7834.1 to 7834.7 (one of the variants has wooden cladding). Between November 1943 and April 1944 Jean Boutemain drew the construction plans of the domestic house with prefabricated components and a quarter of the house was made as a proto-type in the workshop of the rue des Jardiniers. The folded sheet frame stands on the ground on four posts. The floor and ceiling beams are perforated folded sheet with brackets for the balcony and the entrance. The folded sheet facade panels are double-skinned. In the "model village" of the Expo-sition de la Reconstruction in Paris in December 1945, the Lods/Prouvé team exhibited a 1/10th scale prototype, probably made by the J. Prouvé Workshops (ill. 790,5 and 790,6). Annotations by Jean Prouvé in the margin of an article that appea-red in *Reconstruire* in December 1945: "entirely de-signed by J. P. During the war, a quarter of the house having been made full scale in the work-shops of the rue des Jardiniers, all these works ha-ving been two-thirds paid for by Lods. Lersy, archi-tect, collaborated in these designs. Two portal frames are still in existence at Maxéville (unloading bridge made with these two pieces). It is right to remember in connection with this house the crea-tion of the company that Lods thought up with Christian Monder (Neuflize bank), an impetuous operation typical of Lods that caused my total break with him." (A single share was intended for J.P.!)

791. Furniture for a holiday camp at Saint-Brévin-l'ocean. 1939. Jacques and Michel André, architects. Caisse Départmentale des Associations Sociales, client.

791.6. Holiday camp at Saint-Brévin, refectory table. Table with legs in electroplated metal and six tube serviette-holders, top in fibrociment "granipoli", fixed by six special brass screws. Plan 7941, drawn by Jean Boutemain on 9 January 1939, annotated with questions about the details (ill. 791.6,1); photograph taken at the Galerie Jousse-Seguin, Paris (ill. 791.6,2).

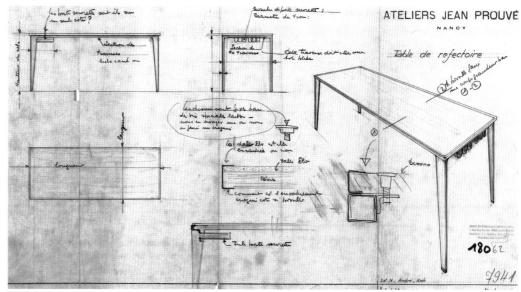

791.6,1

791.6,2

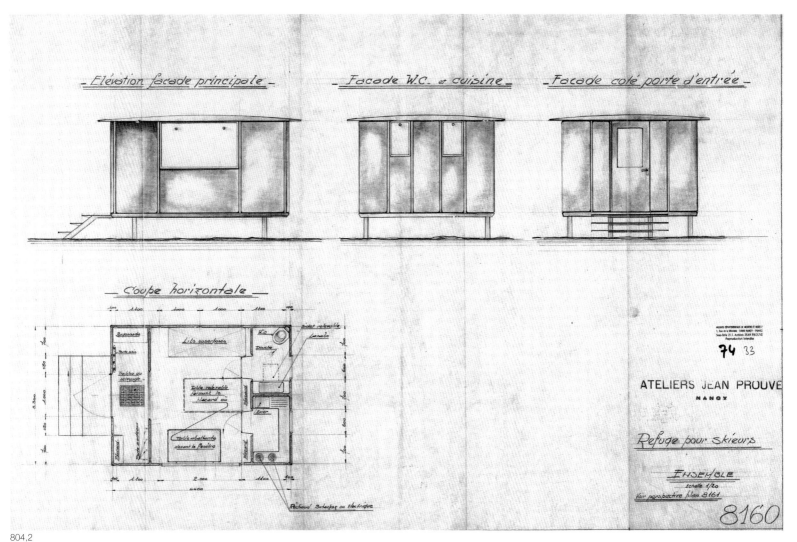

Élévation façade principale   _Façade W.C. et cuisine_   _Façade côté porte d'entrée_

Coupe horizontale

ATELIERS JEAN PROUVE
NANCY

Refuge pour skieurs

ENSEMBLE
échelle 1/20
Voir perspective plan 8161

8160

804,2

804,3

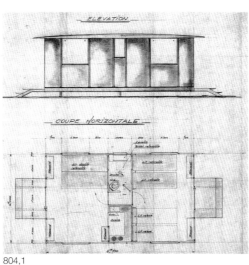

804,1

804. Studies for a holiday house/weekend house/ski refuge. 1939. The studies for weekend houses were continued in February 1939 with plans 8066 to 8068, drawn by Robert Feck, headed B.L.P.S. (see no. 715). The design of plan 8095, drawn by Jean-Marie Glatigny, is similar to the B.L.P.S. house. Plans 8096: section of a panel and 8098: perspective section, drawn by Jean Prouvé, have not yet been located in the J. Prouvé Collection. Louis drew plans 8144: holiday house in two sections (ill. 804,1) and 8166: holiday house in three sections, after a sketch by Jean Prouvé, and plan 8160: ski refuge (ill. 804,2). In a sketch Jean Prouvé placed it on piles and drew a variant with pine-log cladding; detail of this plan 8161 with an "entirely metal" solution (ill. 804,3).

149

It was perhaps in this context that Jean Boutemain drew plan 8123: asbestos cement constituents for a metal-framed house (detail, ill. 804,4). On 17 May 1939 Jean Prouvé drew plan 8257: holiday house on piles (ill. 804,5), which is incorrectly dated as 1930 in many publications. On the same day he drew plan 8258 (ill. 804,6), a perspective of the same house without piles. In May Robert Feck drew plans 8277 to 8280, showing a weekend house that once again is very similar to the B.L.P.S. house.

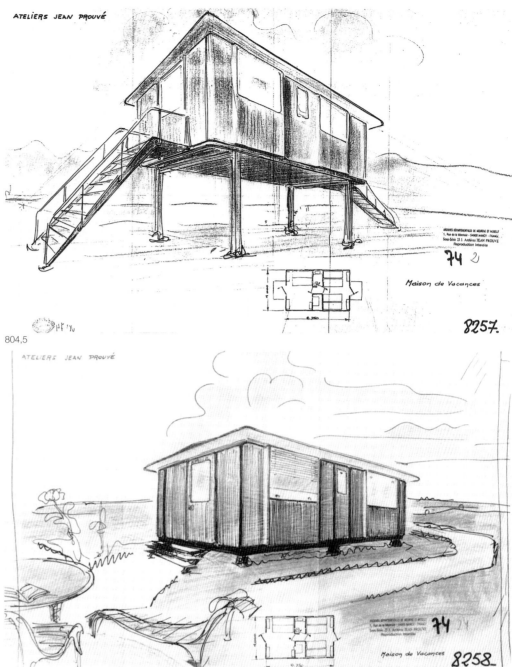

804,5

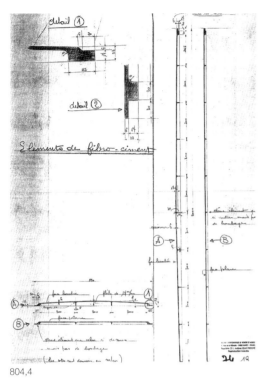

804,4

804,6

815. Table on casters. 1939. Special order. Extending wooden top, welded sheet steel legs in a shape typical of Jean Prouvé, directional casters (ill. 815).

822. Patent no. 853.226, "Sash window the frames of which open by pivoting on vertical axes". Entered 19 April 1939, granted 13 March 1940. Jean Prouvé entered the patent only a few weeks after Jean-Marie Glatigny had designed the sash window (plan 8150 of 22 March, plan 8165 of 27 March 1939) for the Institut d'Astrophysique (see Complete Works, no. 821).

815

828,3

828. Holiday camp of Onville. 1939. Jacques and Michel André, architects. The J. Prouvé Workshops designed and carried out the 6 x 8 m demountable refectory and twenty tent frames. Studies were made simultaneously by the architects, who in May 1939 designed a caravan to act as the kitchen, the washbasins and showers, and plans for the refectory. In their first designs, plans 8203 and 8206, the J. Prouvé Workshops proposed a frame with two posts and a ridge beam. In May Jean Prouvé returned to the principle of an external frame, already proposed in 1939 for the Ministry of Aviation competition (see no. 786.c), and drew the perspectives of plans 8255 and 8256 (ill. 828,3), as well as other sketches. Between 20 June to 19 July Jean Boutemain drew the construction plans, for example plan 8393: portal frames (ill. 828,4). Photograph of the refectory re-installed in the Robert Antoine shop in La Bresse after restoration by the J. Prouvé Workshops (ill. 828,7); plan 8402: "frame – external – metal for tent".

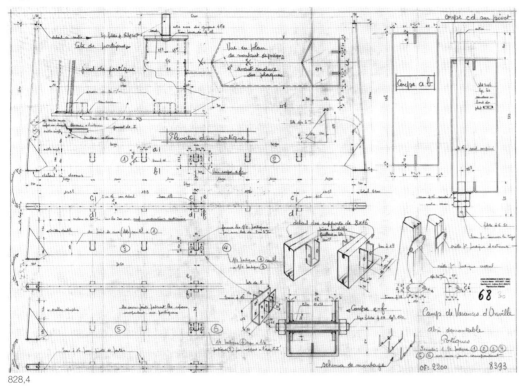

828,4

828,7

850. Demountable barrack units for the Engineers Corps. 1939. In a conversation with the author, Jean Prouvé related the unusual history of this project: "I was in Carnac, in Brittany, seeing my family, when I received a telegram calling me back to Nancy; 'General Dumontier of the Engineers Corps of the 5th Army wants to see you'. I met the general. He asked me if I was able to make combat units for twelve men…, that could be assembled in a few hours… I spent the night making all the drawings with all the details. A prototype (made in a week) was shown to General Dumontier (who was director of the Ecole Polytechnique before the war)". Of the hundred and twenty workshop staff, about thirty were left, because many of them had been called up in September 1939. Clearly Jean Prouvé was able to develop the design in a very short time because he had already made a building on the principle of a similar external frame, the building of the holiday camp of Onville (see no. 828 and the design no. 786.c). Jean Prouvé drew about thirty sketches, including one with several principles, such as a lower beam and a post that could be folded for transport. It was in making another sketch that Jean Prouvé must have found the answer to the problem of the detail of the lower beam and the post that rotates around an upper bolt. A sketch of a wooden panel carries the words: "panels to be bellied by lathe". Jean Prouvé drew several plans on 19 November 1939: plan 8515 (ill. 850,4), plans 8516 to 8518 and plan 8519. In November also Jean Prouvé drew a series of sketches for a 7.50 x 20 m demountable barrack unit. The plans for this project were probably drawn by Robert Feck: plan 8520: sections; plan 8521: perspective; plan 8522: gable; plan 8523; standard facade; plan 8524: overall plan. Plans 8525 to 8527 are construction plans for wooden panels, types A to C. There are six sketches by Jean Prouvé for the prototype: one of the beams, with the entry "make 2 similar beams, see detail drawing", the others respectively of the four posts, two main beams, four main beams, the sixteen panels, and of the division of the panels. The prototype was made in eight days by Pierre Prouvé, of whom his brother Jean used to say: "He's a very good engineer". Photographs of the prototype in the workshop (ill. 850,7 and 850,8). According to Jean-Claude Bignon and Catherine Coley (1992, p. 11), the general ordered twenty examples on the spot, to be delivered in less than a month. They also give a price list for the units: 8,000 francs for the 4 x 4 m; 11,050 francs for the 4 x 6 m; 19,205 francs for the 4 x 12 m. The presentation of the first of these units to the General Staff of the Engineers Corps, assembled in three hours at Birkenwald in Alsace, led to an immediate firm order for two hundred and seventy-five examples… to be delivered during the following month.

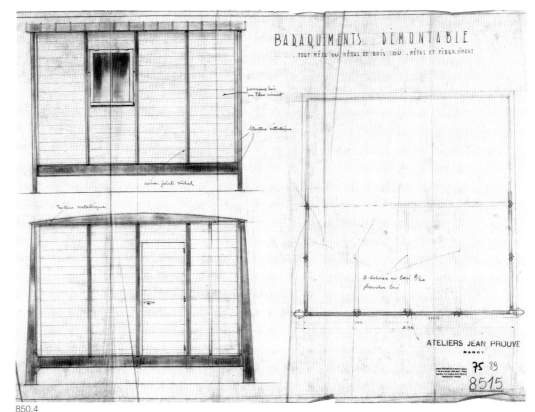

850,4

850,7

850,8

850,9

850,10

850,11

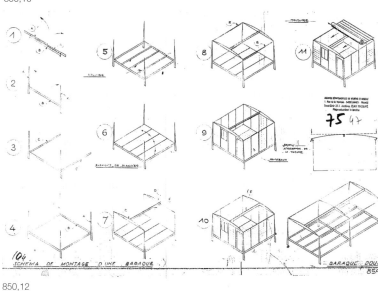

850,12

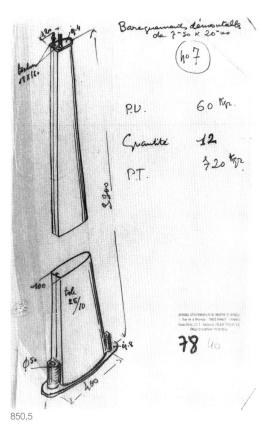

850,5

Photographs of the assembly of the prototype (ill. 850,9 and 850,10). Serial production was organised in a hired workshop. A photograph of a stock of posts for about seventy-five units has been published by Jean-Claude Bignon and Catherine Coley (1992, p. 10). Photograph of the 4 x 12 m barrack units (ill. 850,11). New plans were drawn on 5 December 1939: plans 8528 and 8529: 4 x 6 m barrack unit in metal and wood or asbestos cement; plan 8535: full-scale details; plan 8536: interior lay-out of a 4 x 4 m unit for 10 men; plan 8537: interior lay-out for a 4 x 6 m unit for fourteen men; plan 8538: interior lay-out for two 4 x 4 m units placed side-by-side for fourteen to sixteen men; plans 8540 to 8542: interior lay-out; plan 8544: floor, roof and panels in wood; plan 8593: assembly diagram (ill. 850,12). The exact number of barrack units made is not known, and the often-published figure of eight hundred has not been verified. This subject has been carefully researched in the book by Jean-Claude Bignon and Catherine Coley (1992). The development of the barrack units continued. Plans 8543 and 8548: concrete hut for the company Chambert in Toulouse; plan 8558: assembly and levelling diagram; plan 8591: setting up of a lumber/WC hut. A colonial variant was also designed: sketch by Jean Prouvé about 1940 (ill. 850,13); plans 8545 and 8546 of January 1940; demountable colonial build-

ing. Among the other documents: plan 8594: information on screws and bolts; plans 8636 to 8638: wooden panels; plan 8663: installation of tarpaper; plan 8738: roof component. Jean Prouvé had one of these units put on the top of his garage for the children. "Military style" huts were delivered to the site of the Société Centrale des Alliages Légers (S.C.A.L.) at Issoire in 1940 (see Complete Works, no. 854.k). In November 1940 the design office drew a version with a wooden framework (see Complete Works, no. 852) and in 1944/45 an entrance lodge for the Ferembal factory in Nancy (see no. 943) was based on the frame of the military huts.

851. Patent no. 865.235, "Demountable barrack unit". Entered 16 January 1940, published 16 May 1941.

153

854,1

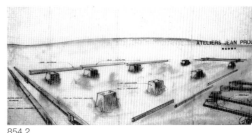

854,2

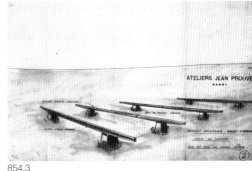

854,3

854. Works carried out for the Société Centrale des Alliages Légers (S.C.A.L.) at Issoire.

1939/40. Pierre Jeanneret, architect. Georges Blanchon, general agent of the J. Prouvé Workshops, who was later to become the director of the Bureau Central de Construction (B.C.C.), general contractor. These were the first buildings to be made with central portal frames (see nos. 786.a and 786.b), and it was the start of the fruitful collaboration between Jean Prouvé and Pierre Jeanneret, a former partner of Le Corbusier. In a conversation with the author, Jean Prouvé, speaking about this work for a large aluminium factory (a building by the architect Auguste Perret) in which there were neither offices nor accommodation, expressed his admiration for Pierre Jeanneret: "Le Corbusier, thinker, initiator; Pierre Jeanneret, his cousin at the drawing board… He drew everything in detail. Pierre Jeanneret was very interested in what I built… He designed buildings with the components, such as portal frames, that I had invented. He was very exact, very Swiss… a refugee in Grenoble… during the war. I used to go regularly across the border (the zone not occupied by the Germans) by bicycle… With Pierre Jeanneret there was no need to explain things much…"

For the Issoire site the J. Prouvé Workshops made metal components and the Bureau Central de Construction (B.C.C.), the general contractor, provided the wooden components and was responsible for installation and delivery of the finished buildings. It is clear that the collaboration with team made up of Pierre Jeanneret, Charlotte Perriand (until her departure for Japan in June 1940) and Georges Blanchon was important for Jean Prouvé.

Photograph of one of the Issoire sites (ill. 854,1). The first batch included the drawing office, the club building, the engineers' accommodation, and military style barrack units. For the Issoire project Jean Prouvé drew two series of perspectives headed "installation instructions", which we publish here in chronological order (ill. 854,2 to 854,16): 1. preparation of the ground; 2. positioning of foundation girders; 3. installation of the lower edges (with the entry: "after installation of these components, proceed straightway to adjustment by surface planing and exact squaring…"); 4. positioning of A-frames secured by the ridge beams; 5. putting in place of

joists and floor components; 6. installation of external ridge beams and gables (by use of the special device described in no. 7); 7. detail of the device for supporting gables and the installation of felt in panels (on this plan are indicated the heights of the various buildings for the Société Centrale des Alliages Légers); 7. (variant) putting in place of upper edges supported by some panels; 9. putting in place of a first roof span (0.50 m components); 8. (variant) putting in place of ceiling ribs and fixing clamps; 8. (variant) general arrangement of roofing; 9. (variant) installation of roofing and ceiling components; 10. details; 11. installation of panels; 12. internal partitions.

Some of the buildings have been displaced and were still existing in 2001.

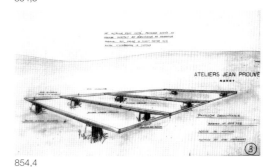

854,4

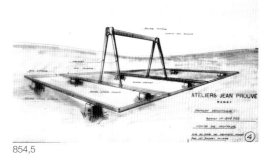

854,5

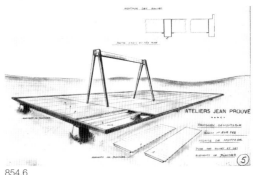

854,6

854,7

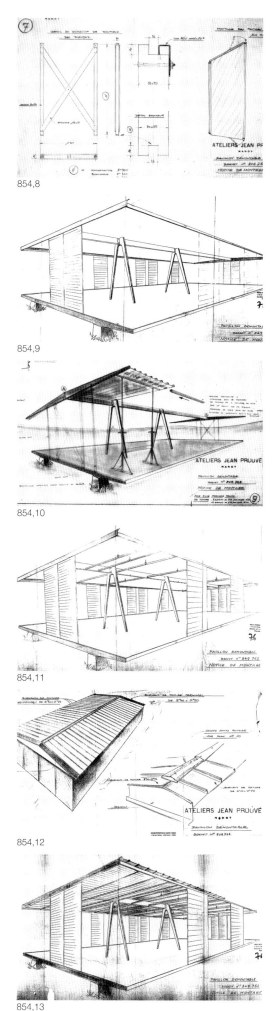

854,8

854,9

854,10

854,11

854,12

854,13

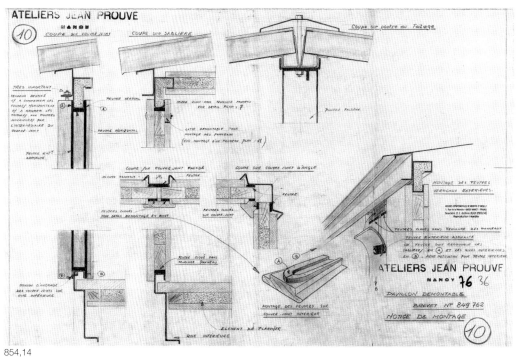

854,14

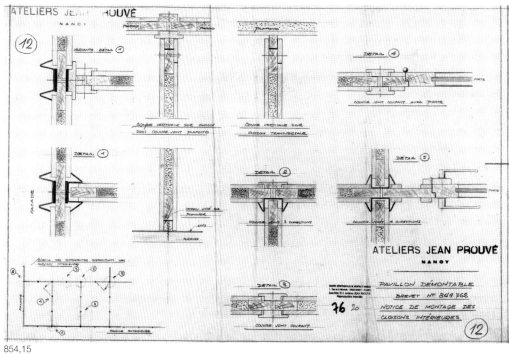

854,15

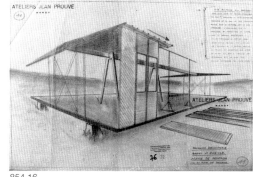

854,16

854.a,1

854.a. S.C.A.L. at Issoire, design building.
1939/40. An 8 x 8 m building, double height with
gallery with one portal frame. Architect's drawing
of 13 December 1939 (ill. 854.a,1); architect's plan
3590: horizontal section of facade panels; plan of
the portal frame, 4.816 m high, 100 mm diameter
tube (ill. 854.a,4); plan of two 15/10 folded sheet
ridge beams (ill. 854.a,5); photograph taken about
1940 (ill. 854.a,6).

854.b. S.C.A.L. at Issoire, club building. 1939/40.
Blueprint of an architect's drawing of 6 December
1939, showing a building with an internal portal
frame similar to that of no. 853, with a sketch by
Jean Prouvé; an 8 x 20 m building with four portal
frames, photograph taken about 1940; plan 8612:
detail of portal frames. Tube was used because of
the shortage of sheet metal.

**854.c. S.C.A.L. at Issoire, two accommodation
buildings.** 1940. Architect's plan no. 3600 of 31
January 1940: twenty four bedrooms; photograph
taken in 1940; plan 8566 of February 1940: twelve
folded sheet portal frames; plan 8599: design identical to that of plan 8566, but with portal frame in
tube.

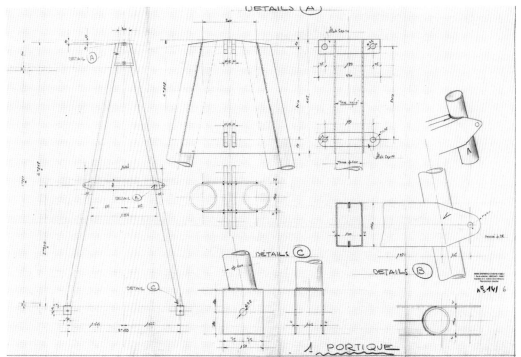

854.a,4

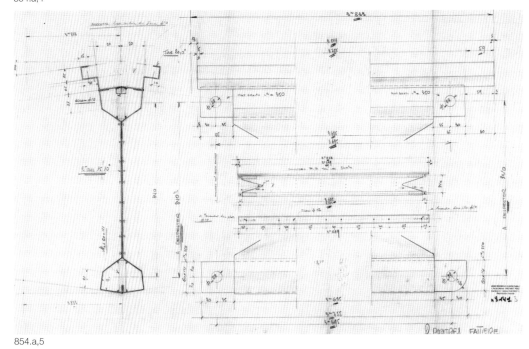

854.a,5

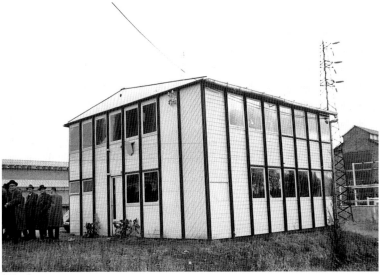

854.a,6

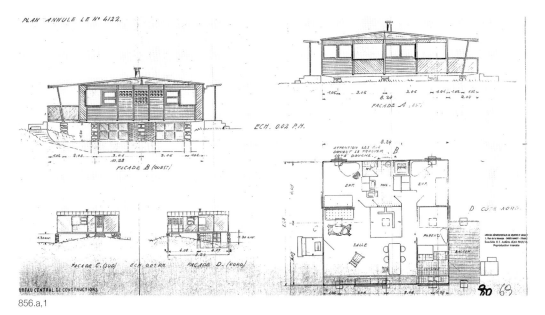

856.a,1

856.a,5

855. Demountable building F 8 x 8 m B.C.C.
1941/42. Pierre Jeanneret, architect. The study was carried out by the Bureau Central de Construction (B.C.C.) and Pierre Jeanneret in Grenoble and by the J. Prouvé Workshops in Nancy, more or less in parallel and in touch with each other (there are many blueprints of B.C.C. plans in the J. Prouvé Collection, such as plan no. 4214 with the note: "plan not final Prouvé"). The B.C.C. plans dated January to July 1941 show a building with a wood frame; those of the J. Prouvé Workshops, a building with a folded sheet frame and a wood and metal frame. Some examples: plan 8868 of January 1941: cross-section; plan 8872: details of the central chimney; plan 8961 of January 1942: portal frame in sheet and ridge beam in wood; plan 8962: portal frame and ridge beam in wood; plans 8963 to 8968: fittings for frame in wood; plans 8997 to 9001 of February 1942: joint covers, edges in folded sheet. The last plans, headed: "B.C.C. F 8 x 8" are of August 1943. A study by Jean Prouvé of aluminium roofing (plan 8836 of November 1940, variants A to E) should probably be placed in the context of the collaboration with the B.C.C. Charlotte Perriand, 1998, p. 221: "During the Occupation, the shortage of materials and the difficulties of communication with the Jean Prouvé Workshops forced Pierre, from the start of 1942, to design prefabricated works in wood, which he did not mind doing, without breaking in any way with the Prouvé approach".

856. Works carried out for Alais, Froges et Camarques (A.F.C.) in Saint-Auban. 1941/42. Pierre Jeanneret, architect; Bureau Central de Construction (B.C.C.), general contractor; J. Prouvé workshops system. The Bureau Central de Construction constructed several buildings in Saint-Auban.

856.a. Building F 8 x 8 m. B.C.C. plan no. 4170 (ill. 856.a,1); B.C.C. plan no. 4214 of November 1941: framework F 8 x 8; interior view (ill. 856.a,5). The houses were fully equipped, furniture included.

856.b. Demountable buildings. On land near the Route National there were, until 1984, an 8 x 32 m building of four apartments (corresponding to B.C.C. plan no. 4180), an 8 x 24 m building and two 8 x 8 m buildings.

870. "Pyrobal" stove for poorly combustible fuel. 1941/42. Made in collaboration with the mining engineer Victor Balazuc, in accordance with his patent no. 817.128, "improvement of hearths", granted on 26 August 1937. In the J. Prouvé Collection there are twenty-five plans drawn by Robert Feck or Jean-Marie Glatigny relating to this stove, which was made with mediocre quality sheet and lined inside with fireproof brick. According to Jean-Claude Bignon and Catherine Coley (1992, p. 11), production increased regularly: 73,000 francs in October, 205,800 francs in November (1941). Photograph taken at the Centre Georges Pompidou during the *Jean Prouvé, constructeur* exhibition in 1990 (ill. 870).

871. Bicycle frame. 1941/42. During a conversation with the author, Pierre Missey recounted that he had made a dozen of these frames in sheet metal, which was difficult to weld. These cycles were intended primarily for the employees of the J. Prouvé Workshops, especially Pierre Missey who was then able to get around to supervise the installation of the charcoal furnaces (Jean-Claude Bignon and Catherine Coley 1992, p. 11). Photograph of the frame made by the N. J. Cugnot Technical Lycée of Toul for the *Jean Prouvé, constructeur* exhibition at the Centre Georges Pompidou in 1990 (ill. 871,1). The first drawings by Jean Boutemain, plans 8905 and 8906, date from September 1941; construction plan 9049 from march 1942 (ill. 871,2); plan 9050. The frames of mopeds are today manufactured in accordance with this "single-beam" principle. With Jean Prouvé this application remained at the sketch stage.

870

871,1

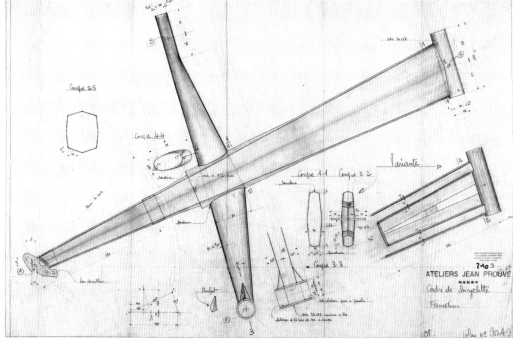

871,2

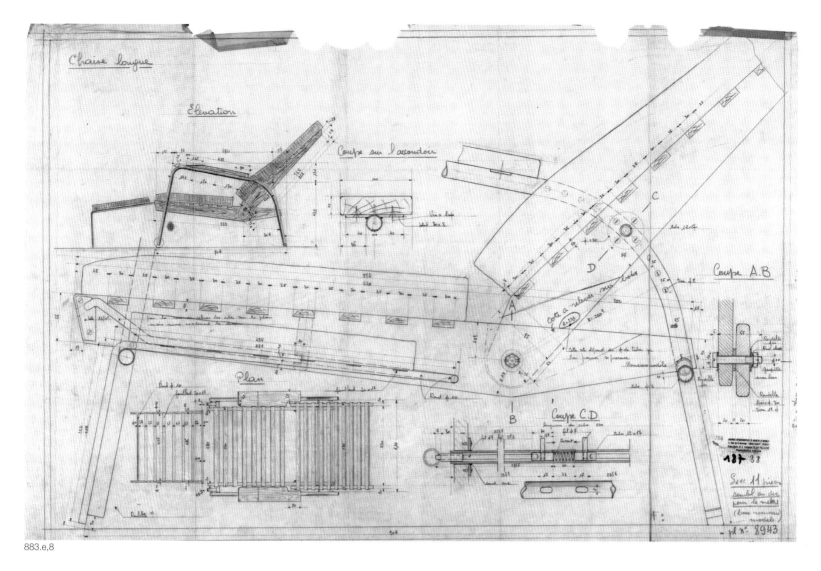

Chaise longue
Elevation
Coupe sur l'accoudoir
Coupe A.B
Coupe C.D
Plan

883.e,8

883. Designs and works carried out for the Etablissements Solvay in Dombasle. 1941/42.

During the years 1941/42 the J. Prouvé Workshops designed or made many projects for the Etablissements Solvay. The furniture designs that led to models that went into serial production, the three-legged table, or the "easy chair" are examples that show Jean Prouvé knew how to adapt his ideas and production to the possibilities of each new period (I have dealt with this subject in my contribution to the Centre Georges Pompidou monograph on Jean Prouvé, Peter Sulzer 1990, p. 127).

883.a. Works carried out for the Solvay recreation park in Maxéville.
M. Parisot, architect. Plan 8916: sketch by Jean Prouvé; plan 8918: four folded sheet frames and two end half-frames, four folded sheet swing-boats with breaking mechanism; plan 8912: variant for a four-place swing; plan 8942: 6 m diameter roundabout with six folded sheet arms, linked by two rings in tube; design for a giant's stride.

883.b. The Solvay Association in Maxéville.
There was a Solvay quarry in Maxéville with a ferry to Dombasle. Plans 8926 and 8926A: folded sheet entrance vestibule.

883.c. Etablissements Solvay, factory furniture.
1941. Plan 8917: "foremen, 4-seater desk – assistant head of production, 1 table with 3 drawers" (with folded sheet legs); plan 8918: "head of production, 1 drawing board" (with folded sheet legs);

plan 8969: "Ets. Solvay, factory furniture – foremen, one 4-seater desk – 1 meal table with heated section – assistant head of production, 1 table, 1 meal table with heated section – head of production, 1 B.S. desk ("standard desk", probably one of the first examples of this model) – head of production, 1 drawing board"; sketch by Jean Prouvé for the frame of a table with six legs, with notes; "Marchal… make this, please, single piece of 12 to 15/10 sheet + Dulox… weight 21 kilos, 17K 350 4 legs". An example that shows Jean Prouvé passed the sketches directly on to the workshops.

883.d. Etablissements Solvay, cloakroom lockers.
1941. Plan 8927: "2 groups of 10 single cloakroom lockers; plan 8928: "1 group 5 double cloakroom lockers, 1 double locker, 1 group of 4 single cloakroom lockers".

883.e. Furniture for the Solvay hospital. 1941/42.
Jacques and Michel André, architects. In June 1941 Jean Boutemain drew a plan and a perspective of the communal room (plans 8929 and 8930), and other plans relating to: a large table with eight chairs, three tables with two chairs, a bookcase and three easy armchairs. Plan 8931, drawn by Jean Boutemain and showing a large table, bears the entry: "make a table similar to the drawing". As far as we know, this is the first plan for this model with four wooden legs held by a tubular metal crosspiece (for entirely metal legs see Complete Works, no. 825). Unnumbered plan: "Solvay Hospital – communal room – three-legged table",

with four-legged variants, carries the entry: "not to be presented". Unnumbered plan of November 1941: three-legged table; plan 8935: bookshelf. On 26 July 1941 Jean Boutemain drew plan 8963 which carries the entry: "easy armchair – make 5 armchairs similar to drawing". As far as we know, this is the first plan for this armchair which was to be so successful under the name "visitor's chair" (see no. 912). Plan 8923: hospital table casters with the entry: "make 8 tables similar to the drawing" (for a similar table see Complete Works, no. 534.7). Plan 7730: night table carries the entry "Solvay Hospital – make 6 examples similar to drawing"; a similar had been drawn in November 1938 for the hospital of Lons-le-Saunier (see Complete Works, no. 782). Plan 8933: caster axle; unnumbered plan: "Solvay Hospital – chaise longue", with wooden legs. Plan 8934 of June 1941, similar to construction plan 8943, drawn by Jean Boutemain and carrying the entry: "make 11 examples similar to the metal drawing (wood new model)". The back of this chaise longue can be adjusted by means of a spring mechanism (see section C – D [ill. 883.e,8]). Plan 8936: design for a wardrobe entirely in wood; plan 8937: design for a Dutch table entirely in wood; plan 8941: sideboard with the entry: "make 1". This piece of furniture, which has two sheet metal brackets fixed to the wall and two sliding doors in plywood and wood stiffener/handles, is not yet the "Prouvé sideboard".

159

883.f. Etablissements Solvay, various pieces of furniture. 1941/42. Plan 8950: linen trolley with sheet metal top and wooden compartment, three wheels; plan 8960: sideboard for a ping-pong room; construction plan 8973: sliding doors with stiffener/handles. Plan 9006, drawn by Jean Boutemain, showing a stool with four wooden legs and a metal crosspiece, is in the Solvay file. The J. Prouvé Workshops made a similar stool with three legs.

883.g. Design for furniture for the Solvay Casino. 1942. Plan 9011, drawn in February 1942 by Jean Boutemain and headed: "Solvay Casino – dining-room – tables", shows two variants: the left-hand table – similar to the table for the Milan Triennale of 1952 – has sheet metal legs and an mahogany top; the right-hand table is a variant for the lycée of Metz (see no. 534.6), but with legs at 45°. Plan 9017: perspective of these tables; plan 9016: sideboard in wood with three metal drawers.

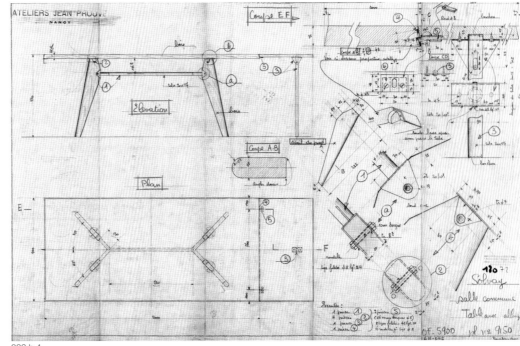

883.h,4

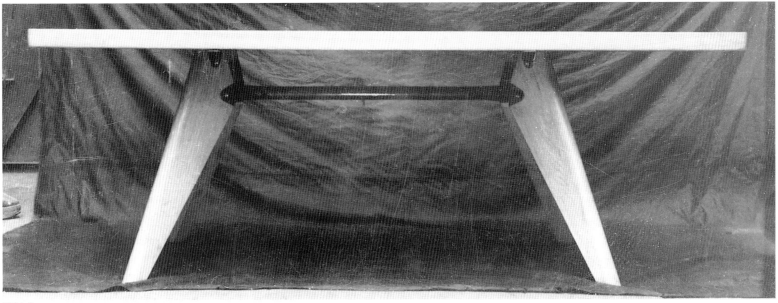

883.h,5

883.h. Etablissements Solvay, family and housekeeping centre: (design for) movable equipment for a family house. 1942. In collaboration with the Bureau Central de Construction (B.C.C.), Paris and Grenoble. This related to the fitting-out of a living room with kitchen in a worker's house, including all furniture. In the J. Prouvé Collection there are several blueprints of B.C.C. plans, with annotations, dated August 1941. J. Prouvé Workshops plan 9123 of July 1942: perspective of the communal room; plan 9122: perspective of the kitchen; detail of plan 9121, on which can be seen the rails (for the hanging furniture, see Complete Works, no. 891); plan 9124: wooden bench; construction plan 9150B: table with extension (ill. 883.h,4). The detail of the crosspiece/legs assembly is very different from that of the post-war models. Jean Prouvé in 1983: "There is a lot of wood in these models… and not much metal. That is because they were made during the war, and wood was easier to obtain… I developed this assembly system much further…" Photograph of a similar table, taken in

the J. Prouvé Workshops during the 40s (ill. 883.h,5): plan 9153: sideboard against stair partition, with the entry: "make 2 brackets…"; plan 9154: work table; plan 9155: coal store; plan 9156: draining board; construction plan 9151: shelving; plan 9152: sideboard under window, sliding doors in solid oak, brackets in 25/10 sheet metal.

883.i. Etablissements Solvay, housekeeping centre, (design for) first floor installation. 1941/42. Undated plan with furniture: a blackboard, a 60 x 60 cm table; eight 90 x 60 cm tables, a round table of 80 cm diameter, a hanging sideboard, a bed, a curved desk and a chair.

883.k. Etablissements Solvay, M. Calingaert's office. About 1941/42. Designs for a four-door cupboard and a filing cabinet with four shutters.

883.l. Etablissements Solvay, design for a filing cabinet. About 1941/42.

883.m. Etablissements Solvay, design for management cloakroom. About 1941/42. Coat stands and umbrella stands.

883.n. Etablissements Solvay, bicycle shed. 1941. Plan 8947: shed for eight bicycles in a semi-circle. According to Jean Boutemain, the J. Prouvé Workshops also made bicycle sheds for other factories.

883.o. Etablissements Solvay, design for fitting out the sports director's apartment. 1942. Study presented as "an up-to-date design, in harmony with the outlook of a sports director". Bureau Central de Construction (B.C.C.) plan and specification.

883.p. Etablissements Solvay, design for a 48-seat sheltered refectory. May 1942. Plan 9085: variant of the refectory building at Onville (see no. 828), but apparently with an external framework in wood and metal.

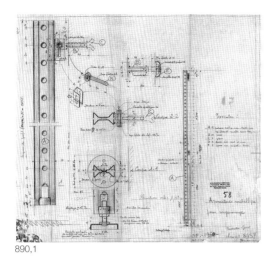

890,1

890,2

890. Works for the Poussardin shop in Epinal.
1941. Plans 8946, 8955, 8956: folded sheet frontage: plan 8957: metal framework for shelving in shaped folded sheet and spot-welded (ill. 890,1), probably the first application of this principle; photograph of a model of the rail (ill. 890,2); sketch by Jean Prouvé (ill. 890,3) showing the rail and the shelf supports that fit into the rail.

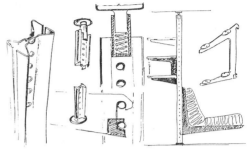

890,3

896. Typewriter table.
1941–43. It was during the war that the J. Prouvé Workshops designed and made, in parallel with the "standard desk" (see no. 897), a new model of the typewriter table using wood for the drawers. From the first desks and typewriter tables for the Compagnie Parisienne de Distribution d'Electricité in 1934/36 (see Complete Works, no. 396) and during the years 1937/38 (see Complete Works, nos. 665 and 681), the frames had parallel folded sheet legs. In June 1939 Jean-Marie Glatigny drew the first desk with " tapered legs" (see Complete Works, no. 838). Plan 8916 of May 1941: folded sheet frame, filing drawer in wood; unnumbered plan: modification of the typewriter table. In January 1942 Jean-Marie Glatigny drew presentation plan 8976 (ill. 896,1) with the entry: "typewriter table, metal tube frame, top and fittings in wood, smaller table model, top 1,000 x 500, standard model 1,200 x 600", fitted with a drawer and a drop-fronted paper compartment; construction plan 9273 of 1943; contemporary photograph taken in the J. Prouvé Workshops and corresponding to plan 8976; detail of a variant with three drawers. In these two photographs the handles are in folded sheet. Two contemporary photographs taken in the J. Prouvé Workshops (ill. 896,4) show a variant – perhaps a prototype – with a frame that differs in respect of the position of a front leg, a higher sheet metal file and handles in wood.

896,4

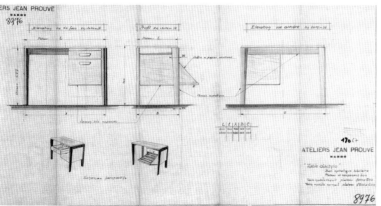

896,1

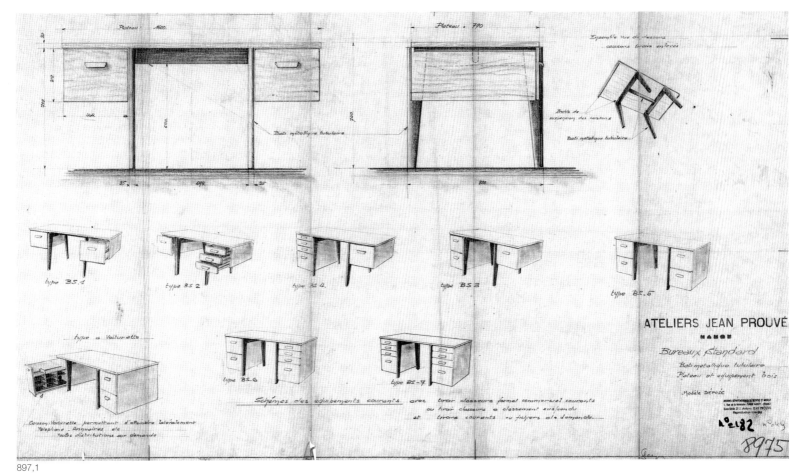

897,1

897. "Standard desk" (B.S.). 1942/43.

The "standard desk" was designed and made by the J. Prouvé Workshops in parallel with the typewriter table (see no. 896). The folded sheet frame has tapered legs that form two "portal frames", joined by a central cross-piece; it has an overhanging top. Plan 8975 (ill. 897,1), drawn in January 1942 by Jean-Marie Glatigny and headed: "diagrams of standard fittings with standard format commercial filing drawer or drawer for hanging files and standard drawers or special order files", with interchangeable fittings in wood and 790 x 160 mm top: plan 9007: "B.S. sliding drawer compartment"; plan 9162: "B.S., covers and drawers".

In the J. Prouvé Collection there are seventeen photographs of this desk with fittings and top in solid wood and wooden handles – perhaps a prototype, two examples of which are: examples of interchangeable fittings (ill. 897,3 and 897,4).

897,3

897,4

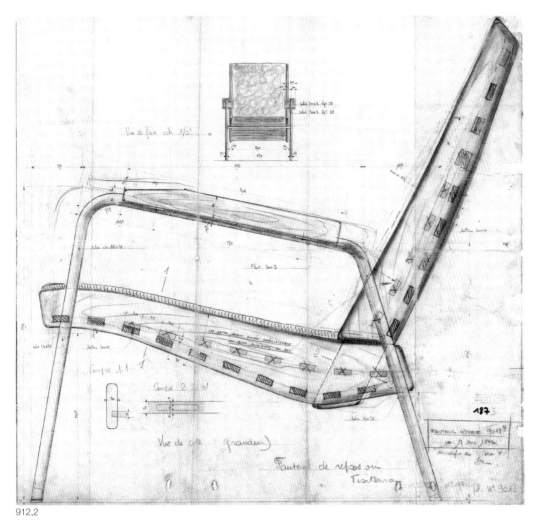

912,2

912. "Visitors armchair". 1942–44. In July 1941 Jean Boutemain had drawn for Solvay the "easy armchair" (see Complete Works, ill. no. 883.e,4). On 6 February 1942 Jean-Marie Glatigny drew presentation plan 9003 showing a similar armchair called "visitors armchair". Plan 9018: "easy or visitors armchair" (ill. 912,2), drawn on 19 February 1942 by Jean Boutemain, was altered in June 1943 and May 1944. It enables us to understand the early history of this model, which was made mainly in the 50s. The legs are in 15 x 21 mm tube; the seat, back and arms are in solid wood. The position of the 30 x 10 mm slats of the back and seat was altered. Plan 9448, drawn on 17 May 1944, carries the title "full-scale drawing of the wood frame of the "visitors armchair" 9018 modified"; the modifications relate to the position and number of slats, and the arms are rounded. Photograph (ill. 912,4) – taken at the Galerie Jousse-Seguin in April 1994 – of a similar armchair to that of 9448 – with a higher back; this piece of furniture corresponds to a model in a sketch of 18 May 1945 carrying the words: "back extended". All the "visitors armchairs" have wooden arms that are horizontal at the front so that things may be placed on them – a glass, for example. They must not be confused with the different models of the 50s.

913. "Visitors armchair" with adjustable back. About 1942. Photograph taken in Jean Prouvé's house (ill. 913,1). There are small wheels on the front legs.

912,4

913,1

914. Bracket light. About 1942. Jean Prouvé's bracket light is one of the results of the team work for the Société Centrale des Alliages Légers (S.C.A.L., see Complete Works, ill. 854.I,3). An earlier "support arm for a lamp" – very different from 854.I,3 – had been designed for the Prouvé family apartment in September 1942 (see Complete Works, no. 893.g). In an unnumbered plan (ill. 914), with the entry "make 1 arm type A, 1 arm type B", the bracket is intended for installation on the rail for hanging furniture (see Complete Works, no. 891) and already has the hanging fitment (3 mm wire) of the bracket lights 1947 and the 50s.

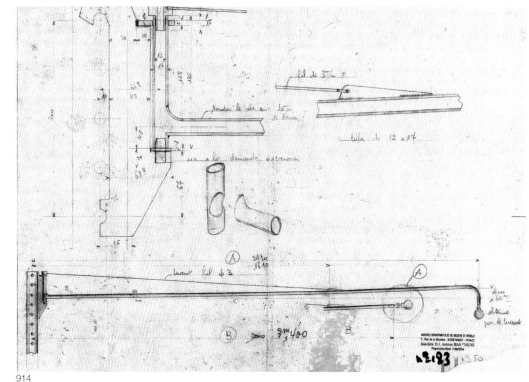

914

915. Chair entirely in wood. 1942. Earlier, in 1941, because of the shortage of steel, Jean Prouvé had begun to make studies for a chair in metal and wood with the Etablissements Vauconsant (see Complete Works, no. 879). In august 1942 Jean Boutemain drew plan 9140 (ill 915,1): wooden chair with visible tenons, seat and back in moulded plywood, but with a shape different from that of chair no. 4 (see no. 405); photograph of the chair (ill. 915,2); photograph of a variant with the tenons of the back legs not visible (ill. 915,4); variant with back legs of a different shape, perhaps a prototype (ill. 915,5). The chairs entirely in wood have a shape similar to that of the metal chairs, but they are not so strong. They were serially produced by Vauconsant. A demountable version was developed in 1948.

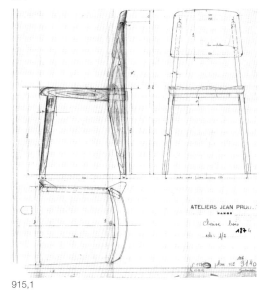

915,1

915,4

915,2

922,7

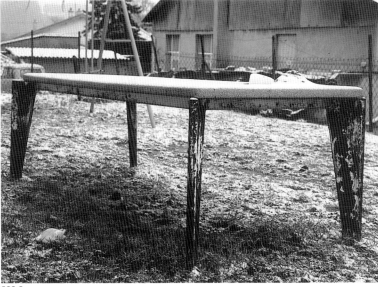

922,8

922. Furniture for the observation sanatorium of Flavigny. 1942–46. During our second visit, in October 1986, we saw and photographed many pieces of furniture by the J. Prouvé Workshops: two-seater classroom tables, tables, "standard desks" and "Flavigny beds". This furniture was later sold to a Parisian dealer. During a conversation, Jean-Marie Glatigny and Jean Boutemain remembered that they had taken furniture to Flavigny in the spring of 1945. The J. Prouvé Workshops plans for this project date from 1942 to 1944. Plan 9115: design for a table in solid oak, metal feet and a folded sheet central post of uniform strength, carrying the entry: "make with tube legs" and " with tubular legs in sheet"; unnumbered plan: eight 800 x 1,600 mm tables with slab top in comblanchien stone, legs and two central posts in folded sheet; plan 9116: sideboard, sheet brackets, with the entry: "Marchal 1 bracket 5 H. 1 drawer 2 H"; plan 9472 of August 1944: cupboards in wood and folded sheet; plan 9473, sawing of wood (thirty pieces); plan 9477 of May 1944 (in very bad condition): observation sanatorium of Flavigny; plan 9537 of December 1944: "Flavigny type" metal bed; plan 9539 of December 1945: thirty beds for dormitories. This bed was serially produced for several years. Description: "Metal frame in folded and welded sheet steel, stove-enamelled; head and foot panels of light polished oak; metal springing in slats and springs for a 1.90 x 0.80 m or 1.40 m mattress". Photograph (ill. 922,7). During the 50s there were several variants of the "Flavigny bed". The two tables we photographed, with a top in red artificial stone and folded sheet legs jointed by 20 x 40 mm tubes, had been placed outdoors (ill 922,8).

943,2

943. Works carried out for the Ferembal factory in Nancy. 1943/44. In June and July 1943 Robert Feck drew plans 9304, 9311 and 9313: drop-arm barrier; in November, plan 9328: bicycle rack; then in 1944 sections for chutes, stackable racks for lids and metal racks. The 4 x 4 m entrance lodge with an external folded sheet frame was based on the principle of the military barrack units (see no. 850), but with a different wood infill. Plan 9307: glazed panels; plan 9308: Bindschendler panel door. Happily, this building was taken down and saved. A photograph (ill. 943,2) shows it, with a temporary external facing, at the time it was exhibited at the Jean Prouvé exhibition of the Kunstverein Ludwigsburg (Germany) in 1998. The works for the Ferembal factory were extended by the order and making of factory offices with a portal frame structure in 1947.

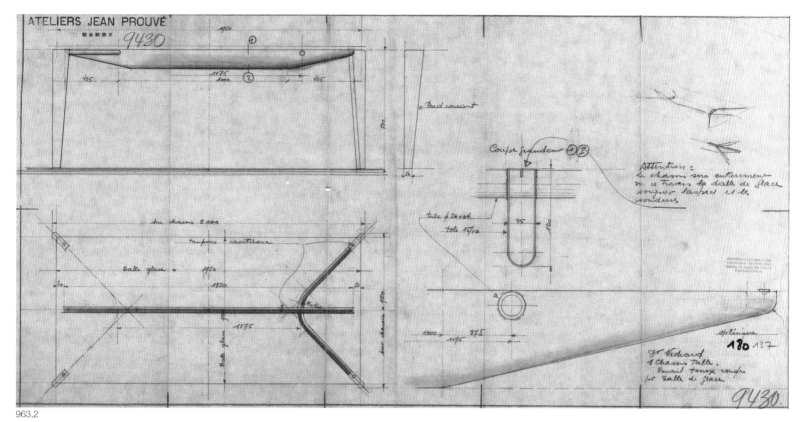

963,2

963. Frame for a table with a plate-glass top for Dr. Vichard in Vesoul. 1944. Unnumbered and undated plan with the same frame as table no. 825, with two beams that carry a 1,950 x 900 mm plate-glass slab, and the entry: "Dr. Vichard"; plan 9430 (ill. 963,2), with four standard legs, a central post of uniform strength, a 1,950 x 900 mm plate-glass top, with the entry: "enamel… red" and headed: "Dr. Vichard 1 table frame… for plate-glass slab"; photograph of the table with lighting from below, taken in the Galerie Cremniter-Laffanour, Paris (ill. 963,3). The slab top is not original – it was thicker.

963,3

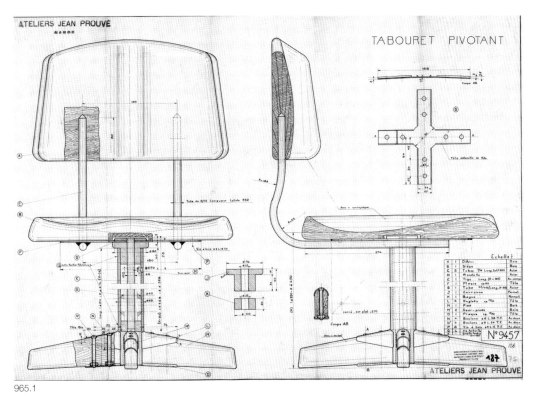

965.1

TABOURET PIVOTANT

965.1. Pivoting stool. 1944. In the J. Prouvé Collection there are four plans 9457 of July 1944 for this model with a maximum of wood and a minimum of metal. Construction plan with list of constituent parts (ill. 965.1).

965.2. Pivoting stool with sheet metal legs. About 1944. Similar model with folded sheet legs (ill. 965.2).

965.2

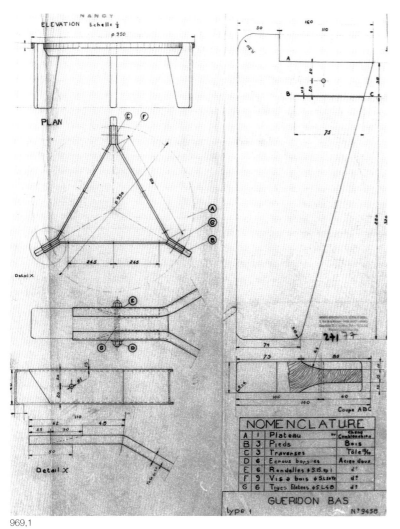

NOMENCLATURE

A	1	Plateau	ou Chêne Comblanchien
B	3	Pieds	Bois
C	3	Traverses	Tôle 15/10
D	6	Ecrous borgnes	Acier doux
E	6	Rondelles ⌀ 5.15 ép 1	d°
F	9	Vis à bois ⌀ 5.L 40	d°
G	6	Tiges filetées ⌀5.L 48	d°

GUERIDON BAS
type 1   N° 9458

969,1

969,3

969. Low round table. 1944. Furniture with demountable under-frame, typical of models developed during the war with a minimum of metal.
950 mm diameter top in solid oak or comblanchien stone, three wood legs, three 15/10 folded sheet steel cross-pieces, six acorn screws and three threaded rods joining legs and cross-pieces; the top is fixed with nine wood screws. Plan 9458 (ill. 969,1), we have not yet located an example corresponding to this plan; sketch by Jean Prouvé of 1965 (ill. 969,2); photograph of underframe (ill. 969,3). The first low round tables were probably delivered in 1942 (see Complete Works, no. 928). There were variants in 1949 (diameter 950 mm or 1,200 mm) and in 1952 (800 mm or 950 mm diameter).

1940-45

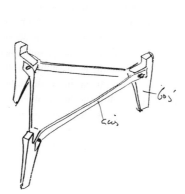

969,2

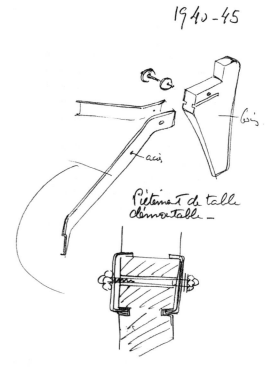

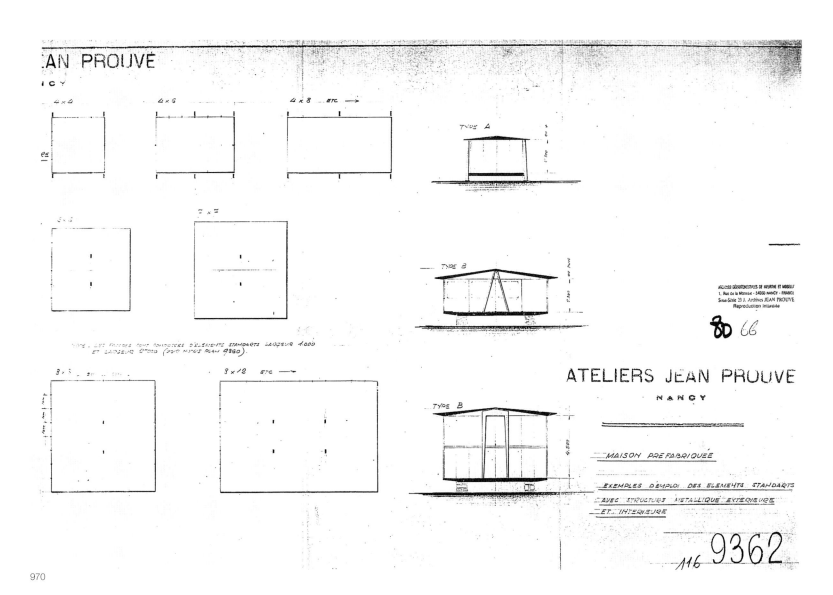

970. Specifications of different types of building.

970. Specifications of different types of building.
1944. After the designs and works carried out for
buildings with external frames (see Complete
Works, nos. 786.c, 828, 850, 852, 854.k, 883.p
and 943) and with internal portal frames (see
Complete Works, nos. 786.a, 786.b, 853, 854,
855, 856 and 858), Robert Feck in January 1944
drew plan 9360 headed: "dimensions of standard
panel components", and diagrammatic plan 9362
headed: "examples of the use of standard components with external or internal metal frames"
(ill. 970). Thus Jean Prouvé was preparing for post-
war reconstruction with the idea of making serially
produced prefabricated houses. Immediately after
the Liberation the J. Prouvé Workshops began to
design these buildings, and this was followed by
the serial construction of buildings for the war vict-
ims of Lorraine and the Vosges, orders placed by
the Minister of Reconstruction, Raoul Dautry.

Commentary

The reader should consult the Commentary of the Complete Works Volumes 1 and 2 for further information on such matters as the Jean Prouvé Collection reference numbers, the location of the works, and the names of the photographers.

Bibliographie

This bibliography does not pretend to be exhaustive; it contains publications used by the author and some general works. The reader could usefully refer to the bibliography published in *Jean Prouvé, constructeur,* Editions du Centre Georges Pompidou, Paris 1990.

Acier n° 1, 1937 (sur l'Exposition universelle de 1937).

Acier n° 1, 1938 (sur l'Exposition universelle de 1937).

Acier n° 1, 1944 (sur le stand Prouvé/Beaudouin et Lods à l'exposition de l'O.T.U.A., Office technique pour l'utilisation de l'acier, en février 1939).

Acier, 1945, p. 73–83, «La maison préfabriquée – Marcel Lods, architecte, Jean Prouvé, constructeur».

amc n° 33, mars 1974, p. 48–54, «L'architecture entre deux guerres – Conversation avec Marcel Lods».

Archieri, Jean-François et Levasseur, Jean-Pierre, *Prouvé, cours du CNAM (1957–70)*, Liège 1990.

L'Architecture d'Aujourd'hui n° 8, octobre/novembre 1934 (sur les cloisons mobiles de l'hôtel de ville de Boulogne-Billancourt).

L'Architecture d'Aujourd'hui n° 2, février 1939, p. 53–56 (sur la maison démontable en acier B.L.P.S.).

L'Architecture d'Aujourd'hui n° 7, juillet 1939 (sur la colonie de vacances à Saint-Brévin-l'Océan).

L'Architecture d'Aujourd'hui n° 2, juillet/août 1945, «Solutions d'urgence» (p. 54, baraques militaires, camp de vacances d'Onville; p. 55, Société centrale des alliages légers (S.C.A.L.) à Issoire; p. 57, pavillon de 6 x 6 m pour les sinistrés; p. 58, Société centrale des alliages légers (S.C.A.L.) à Issoire, mobilier d'urgence de Jean Prouvé).

L'Architecture d'Aujourd'hui n° 4, janvier 1946, «Préfabrication, industrialisation du bâtiment» (p. 11, Cité de la Muette à Drancy et marché couvert à Clichy; p. 12, aéro-club de Buc; p. 54/55, maison d'habitation à montage rapide Marcel Lods et Jean Prouvé; p. 56–59, maisons à portiques).

Baptiste, Hervé, «La Maison du Peuple à Clichy, Hauts-de-Seine» dans *Monumental* 1993, p. 69–77 (restauration du monument historique).

Barré-Despond, Arlette, *Union des Artistes Modernes*, Editions du Regard, Paris 1986.

Bignon, Jean-Claude et Coley, Catherine, *Jean Prouvé – Entre artisanat et industrie, 1923–1939*, A.M.A.L./Ecole d'architecture de Nancy, Nancy 1990.

Bignon, Jean-Claude et Coley, Catherine, *Jean Prouvé – Entre artisanat et industrie, 1939–1946*, Ecole d'architecture de Nancy, Nancy 1992.

Clayssen, Dominique, *Jean Prouvé, l'idée constructive*, Editions Dunoz/Bordas, Paris 1983.

Coley, Catherine, *Jean Prouvé en Lorraine*, A.M.A.L./P.U.M., Nancy 1990.

La construction moderne 50ème année n° 39, juin 1935, p. 838–857 (sur le sanatorium Geoffroy de Martel de Janville à Passy en Haute-Savoie; Pol Abraham et Jacques Henri le Même, architectes).

Courroy, Francis-Henri, *Histoire de la Chambre de Commerce et d'Industrie d'Epinal*, Editeur Gérard Louis, 1991.

Décor d'aujourd'hui n° 37, 1946, p. 18–29 (sur le mobilier des Ateliers J. Prouvé).

Dumont d'Ayot, Catherine et Graf, Franz dans *Faces* n° 42/43, automne-hiver 1997/98, p. 54–59 (sur la restauration de la Maison du Peuple à Clichy).

Ellis, Charlotte, «Prouvé's people's palace», dans *The Architectural Review* n° 1059, mai 1985 (sur la Maison du Peuple à Clichy).

Emery, P.-A., «L'architecture en Algérie, 1930–62» dans *Techniques et Architecture* n° 329, février/mars 1980.

Ernst, Almut et Rix, Tanja, Etude sur les baraques militaires (dessinée sur ordinateur), Université de Stuttgart 1991.

Goguel, Solange, *René Hebst*, Editions du Regard, Paris 1990.

Guidot, Raymond, «Matériaux», dans *UAM, les années 1929–58*, catalogue d'exposition, Musée des arts décoratifs, Paris 1988, p. 110–112.

H(ablützel), A., «Documents sur la fabrication industrielle des meubles chez Jean Prouvé» dans *Intérieur* n° 2, 1965.

Hammond, Bryan et O'Connor, Patrick, *Joséphine Baker*, Edition allemande, Munich 1992.

Helwig, Jean-Marie, «Grilles et portails de Prouvé» dans *Werk, Bauen + Wohnen* n° 1–2, janvier/février 1985.

«Hommage à Pierre Jeanneret», dans *Werk* n° 6, juin 1968, p. 377–396.

Huber, Benedikt et Steinegger, Jean-Claude, *Jean Prouvé, une architecture par l'industrie*, Les éditions d'architecture Artemis, Zürich 1971.

Illustration n° 4917, 29 mai 1937 (sur l'Exposition universelle de 1937).

L'internat du Lycée de Metz (plaquette de l'inauguration, publiée en 1935 ou 1936).

L'internat de l'Ecole nationale professionnelle de Metz (plaquette de l'inauguration, publiée vers 1936).

«Itinéraire Jean Prouvé» dans *Nancy découverte*, Editions de l'Est, Nancy 1991.

«Pierre Jeanneret», dans *Macmillan Encyclopedia of Architects* volume 2, London, p. 482/483.

Kistenmacher, Gustav, *Fertighäuser, Montagebauweisen, industriemässiges Bauen*, Ernst Wasmuth, Tübingen 1950 (sur les maisons préfabriquées, «Airoh-house», «Lustron-house»...).

Laprade, Albert, «L'école de plein air de Suresnes», revue d'architecture, 15 février 1936.

Levasseur, Jean-Pierre, *Jean Prouvé, cours du CNAM 1961–62*, J.-P. Levasseur/I.F.A., Paris 1984.

Lods, Marcel, *Le métier d'architecte*, entretiens avec Hervé Le Boterf, Editions France-Empire, Paris 1976.

Marcel Lods, 1891–1978, photographies d'architecte, catalogue d'exposition, Centre Georges Pompidou, Paris 1991.

Rob Mallet-Stevens, Editions archives d'architecture moderne, Bruxelles 1980.

Ossature métallique n° 1, 1937, «Le pavillon du club d'aviation Roland-Garros à Buc».

Perriand, Charlotte, *Une vie de création*, Editions Odile Jacob, Paris 1998.

Potié, Philippe, «Autour de la plieuse de Jean Prouvé» dans *Imaginaire technique*, p. 47–56.

«Jean Prouvé» dans *Architecture 54*, n°11/12, Bruxelles 1954 (numéro consacré à Jean Prouvé).

«Jean Prouvé» dans *Domus* n° 697, 1988 (réédition des meubles).

«Jean Prouvé» dans *Domus* n° 706, 1989 (réédition des meubles).

Jean Prouvé, catalogue d'exposition édité par la Galerie Jousse-Seguin et la Galerie Enrico Navarra, Paris 1998 (essentiellement consacré au mobilier).

Jean Prouvé, constructeur, catalogue d'exposition, Musée Boymans-van Beuningen, Rotterdam 1981.

Jean Prouvé, constructeur, collection Monographie, Editions du Centre Georges Pompidou, Paris 1990.

Jean Prouvé, meubles 1924–53, catalogue d'exposition, Abaques/Musée des arts décoratifs, Bordeaux 1989.

Jean Prouvé, rétrospective de l'œuvre, catalogue d'exposition, Centre de documentation d'architecture de l'Ecole technique supérieure de Genève 1977.

Prouvé, Madeleine, *Jean Prouvé, réalisations* (manuscrit de 45 pages, sans date).

Reconstruire n° 5, 1945 (sur la maison préfabriquée Marcel Lods/Jean Prouvé).

Richard-Monnet, Louis, «Les fêtes de la lumière et de l'eau», dans l'*Illustration* n° 4917, 29 mai 1937.

Schein, Ionel, «Jean Prouvé», dans *Bauen + Wohnen* n° 7, 1964.

Sers, Philippe (éd.), *Robert Mallet-Stevens, architecture, mobilier*, Paris 1986.

Siegel, Arthur (éd.), «Chicago's famous buildings», The University of Chicago Press, première édition 1965, 3ème édition 1974 (sur les façades non porteuses).

Simonet, Cyrille, «La peau et les os» dans *Faces* n° 42/43, p. 24–28 (sur la restauration des constructions en béton armé).
Sulzer, Peter, «Aspects de la méthode et de l'œuvre», dans *Jean Prouvé, constructeur*, collection Monographie, Editions du Centre Georges Pompidou, Paris 1990.

Sulzer, Peter (éd.), *Jean Prouvé, ein Seminarbericht*, (Schriftenreihe Baukonstruktion 25), Institut für Baukonstruktion, Universität Stuttgart 1990.

Sulzer, Peter, *Jean Prouvé, Œuvre complète/Complete Works, vol. 1 : 1917–1933*, première édition Ernst Wasmuth Verlag, Tübingen/Berlin 1995, deuxième édition Birkhäuser, Bâle, Boston, Berlin 1999.

Sulzer, Peter, *Jean Prouvé, Meister der Metallumformung*, arcus 15, Verlag R. Müller, Cologne 1991.

Techniques et architecture n° 9/10, septembre/octobre 1942, «Le bois II» (sur les maisons en bois à portique, Pierre Jeanneret, architecte).

Techniques et architecture n° 7–12, février 1946 (sur le projet de la maison de Marcel Lods et Jean Prouvé, présenté au concours de l'O.T.U.A., Office technique pour l'utilisation de l'acier).

Techniques et architecture n° 1, mars 1953, «Escalier» (sur l'escalier du Pavillon de l'U.A.M., Union des Artistes modernes, à l'Exposition universelle de 1937).

Techniques et architecture n° 6, 1955, «Maison du Peuple et marché couvert à Clichy, 1939», p. 80/81.

Techniques et architecture n° 5, mars 1957 (sur la maison de week-end B.L.P.S.).

Topos n°2, 1986, revue réalisée par le Conseil de l'architecture, de l'urbanisme et de l'environnement des Hauts-de-Seine (p. 20, réhabilitation de l'école de plein air de Suresnes).

UAM, les années 1929–58, catalogue d'exposition, Musée des arts décoratifs, Paris 1988.

Witteck, Karl, «Der Ostbau der Firma M. Steiff in Giengen (Württ.), 1903» dans *Der Architekt* n° 3/1991, p. 118 (sur le mur-rideau de 1903).

Zahar, Marcel, «Le cinéma dans l'immeuble rue Lord Byron», dans *Art vivant* n° 186, juillet 1937, p. 305/306.

Illustration credits

All recent photographs are made by Erika Sulzer-Kleinemeier.
All the other illustrations are taken from the Jean Prouvé Collection of the Departmental Archives of Meurthe-et-Moselle, Nancy.